The Flying Dutchman of Philadelphia
Ernest H. Buehl

The Flying Dutchman of Philadephia

Ernest H. Buehl

The International Story of the
Life and Times of a Pioneer Aviator

Mark Taylor

Published by QBMM Publishing · Billings, Montana · 2023

Contact Points

For permission to use any of the material contained in this book, please contact the author, Mark Taylor.

E: mark@buehlfield.info
T: 1-406-269-3110
W: www.buehlfield.info
FB: @erniebuehl

Availability

This book is available from
This House of Books
116 N. 29th Street, Ste B, Billings, Montana 59101
1-406-534-1133 www.thishouseofbooks.com
or from your favorite local indie bookstore

BISAC Subject Headinga

BIO 034000 BIOGRAPHY & AUTOBIOGRAPHY / Aviation & Nautica

TRA 002010 TRANSPORTATION / Aviation / History

ISBN 979-8-9876996-0-7

LCCN 2023901768

Cover and book design: Rosanna Buehl

for Sylvia

Sylvia B. Elliman, Buehl's daughter
PHOTO/AUTHOR

Contents at a Glance

Contents

Table of Figures

Acknowledgments

Thank you to everyone who encouraged me to write this book. This project started with a push from Ernest Buehl's daughter, Sylvia Elliman, and her son, Carlos Rodriguez Buehl. Throughout the writing, both were indispensable for their help with the background research. Also offering encouragement and insight was Sylvia's close friend, Shannon Jones. In addition, I gratefully note the acknowledgment of Sylvia's friend, Rep. Anna Eshoo, 18th Congressional District — California, who encouraged our efforts by including a tribute to Buehl in the *Congressional Record*, June 19, 2014.

Within the family, Michael Bauer, grandson of Buehl's brother, Karl, was exceptionally helpful for us to establish the German perspective on the story. Without him, we could not have told as much of the story of Buehl's early family.

Thanks to Wayne Klaw, who has generously allowed us to use numerous photos taken by his father, a professional photographer who specialized in aerial photography, under the business name SkyPhotos.

Thanks to Charles and Christina Anderson, son and granddaughter of C. Alfred Anderson, who was Buehl's student in the early 1930s. Through them, we also met Benny McRae, a well-respected expert on the subject of black history and close friend of C. Alfred Anderson. Monica Smith, a professional researcher, was another who provided some key information that otherwise would have been inaccessible to us. Our gratitude also to Roscoe Draper, one of the first trainers of the Tuskegee Airmen, who was kind enough to visit with us at length early in our research.

Also helpful was Chauncey Spencer, whose father was an important figure in opening aviation as a career for black pilots. The story of his father helped us put Buehl's contribution in perspective.

Thanks to Air Force historian Dr. Daniel Haulman, who provided archival material about Anderson that would have remained inaccessible to us without his help.

Among people who worked with Buehl professionally was a former student and employee at Buehl Field, Bill Lokes, who retired after a career as a captain for American Airlines. He has been enormously helpful, particularly with his insider perspective on aviation.

Finally, for their encouragement and the time they gave to this project, I especially thank Dr. Ernest Rockwell—former editor-in-chief of Air University Press, and Steven J. Drinnon, Lt. Col. USAF (ret.) —former chief editor of *Air and Space Power Journal* (ASPJ), the professional journal of the United States Air Force. Also, I am grateful to Dan Hargrove, Lt. Col. USAF (ret.)—former pilot of *Air Force Two*, Director of Aviation at Rocky Mountain College's aviation program, for graciously reviewing my manuscript.

Years ago, I helped start an independent bookstore in Billings, Montana, This House of Books. I am grateful to everyone I worked with there for giving me the opportunity to learn about the business of book publication.

ૐ

Foreword

As a little girl, I lived with my grandparents for a couple of years, and I lived within walking distance of their home until I was a teen. Naturally, being in their home, I saw a parade of people coming to visit, many of whom I have since learned were important in the field of aviation. There was a general who often came to visit. And, oh, that newspaper reporter is here again to talk about the early days. It did not mean much to me. At that time, I never stopped to think that this might not be the way things were in other homes around me.

Like the cigar smoke that swirled around his head when I was a kid, tales of Granddad's participation in the early days of aviation surrounded him. Of course, everyone could see that he'd owned and operated a series of airports for general aviation beginning in the late 1920s. The problem was that no one had the true story of his importance. They all had little tidbits of his history, but many unanswered questions remained. Often, I heard the stories his friends told, and other times I learned the stories from reading what the newspapers said about him.

Later, as a young woman, I had heard enough about him to know that Granddad had lived a remarkable life. The evidence was all around me. He had a trove of photos and news clippings related to adventures in which he had participated. Also, he had many admirers who told stories about him. He even had an antique, fabric-skinned biplane in his hangar at the airport!

I became more interested as he restored his old biplane at his ultimate airport, the one in my backyard when I was a teen. I hung around to lend a hand as he stripped it down to the spars and stringers, rebuilt the engine, and recovered the frame. As we worked side-by-side to recover the frame, I learned a little about sewing linen onto wings.

I started to be more interested in talking with him about his scrapbooks and memorabilia. I assumed that he and I would one day have a chance to look through all of it together. Of course, as it happened, everyone was busy. I was pulled away by my own life, and he was too distracted with airport business. By the time we might have had a chance to sit together, I had moved a couple thousand miles away to Montana.

Fortunately, I fell for and married a man with a curious mind. Whenever we got together with my family and talked about my grandfather, Mark took an interest. One day, boxes full of memorabilia, photographs, and newspaper clippings arrived from my Aunt Syl. She told Mark that it was now his task to go through them and assemble Granddad's story.

Over the years, Mark combed through the boxes and did additional research to pull together the story. There was quite a lot that we had not known about Granddad, but I can say that there is nothing in this book that really surprised me. The narrative presented here shows the man that I knew, admired, and loved.

—*Rosanna Buehl*
Billings, Montana, 2023

In my family, larger-than-life legends grew up around my grandfather, a pioneer aviator. Those stories were not only told within my family; my grandfather's name was known internationally and often appeared in newspapers, magazines, and books. Over time, those myths, legends, and personal folk tales became ever more shrouded by the mists of time and exaggeration.

I was sure there were stories about my grandfather that I did not know. I wanted to explore the myths surrounding him with the specific aim of discovering how much is true and how much is fiction. It is rare that a person gets the opportunity to deeply explore the life of an ancestor.

Mark Taylor, the husband of my cousin, took on the task. Over one and a half decades, he did impressive research. The picture that emerges is an unflinching story of one man, Ernest H. Buehl who, in the process of living his life, encounters and engages with some of the most important characters in aviation, allowing us to witness what it was like to participate in the birth of aviation in the United States. The story told here is clear, accurate, and well-documented. This is the book I wanted.

I suffer from an unadulterated, sincere, life-long, all-consuming interest in anything aviation-related, regardless of how esoteric or obscure. I was pleased to help with the research of this book, and to share my memories of my grandfather.

My grandfather existed in legends in our family, but now we have a sense of the actual man himself. Words fail to describe the thanks and sincere appreciation for Mark's incredible dedication to the truth. It is truly a credit to his character. Enjoy this journey. He traced a good one for you.

—*Carlos F Rodriguez Buehl*
Miami, Florida 2023

Author's Foreword

Aviation has been described as a "defining technology" of the twentieth century. It changed our relation to one another, our relation to other nations, our relation to distance, our relation to time.

This book, *The Flying Dutchman*, is the close-up and personal story of the life of one man who entered the field early, took aviation seriously, and worked to make it part of our lives. This man is Ernie Buehl. Even during his lifetime, many stories related to Ernie's life and work took on a life of their own, acquiring the status of fabulous legends.

The Flying Dutchman is written for the nontechnical reader who wants a book that combines history of aviation with a human-interest story. It also has a good amount of detail that should appeal to serious aviation buffs, as well as an unusual perspective that derives from the fact that it does not rehash the familiar stories of already famous people and events.

Covering a timespan from the late 1890s to 1990, the backdrop of *The Flying Dutchman* picks up the story of aviation from nearly its beginning. The book presents a remarkable, international story that begins for us over one hundred years ago in Germany and concludes in the United States.

Ernie's personal story is colorful and engaging. Ernie came to the United States from Germany in 1920. At that time, shortly after World War I, Germany was much more aviation-minded than the United States. Germany had developed some of the world's most advanced aviation technology and training, while in the United States aviation still was regarded as a novelty. When Ernie came to the United States, he brought with him a vision of aviation as a vital industry.

Before coming to the United States, Ernie had worked on the first airplane in the world to fly high enough to leave a vapor trail, and in 1919 he had helped Anthony Fokker get his start in civilian aviation in Holland following World War I.

Almost immediately upon arriving in the United States in 1920, Ernie flew the first airmail delivery across the entire continent. The following year he helped to open an air route to newly discovered Canadian oil fields near the Arctic Circle. In 1923, he participated in some of the pioneering work to use airplanes in the vital task of topographic mapping. From 1928 on, through his ownership of airports and the training he provided, he brought aviation to large numbers of people.

In the 1930s, Ernie turned out to be the only qualified trainer in the United States who would work with a black student. He trained C. Alfred Anderson and forcefully insisted that Anderson be fairly examined for the commercial pilot's license. Because Ernie acted as he did, Anderson is now widely regarded as the "Father of Black Aviation." It even can be argued that training Anderson planted the seed of the civil rights movement for black America.

A work of narrative nonfiction, the factual basis of *The Flying Dutchman* is well documented from Ernie's scrapbooks, writings, recordings, family interviews, and archival research. It is well-illustrated with photos from Ernie's personal collection.

—Mark Taylor
Billings, Montana, 2023

INTRODUCTION

The Tapestry

This book started as a simple biography. It would describe the life and times of Ernest Herman Buehl, a pioneer aviator whose first direct contact with airplanes came in 1910, only seven years after the Wright Brothers' first flight. Retiring in 1969, the same year men landed on the moon, Buehl's career in aviation, from apprenticeship to retirement, spanned 58 years. Beyond that, his involvement with aviation spanned nearly his whole life.

As the material of his biography came together over the years, I began to see Buehl's life as the warp threads that tie together the fabric of a broader topic. The events he witnessed make up the weft and pattern of a tapestry depicting the invention of civilian aviation.

I began to imagine a very large tapestry hanging on a wall in a museum. The history of flight is woven into the tapestry in full detail, from the first manned balloon ascension in 1783 by the Montgolfiers, to NASA sending the first men to the Moon in 1969. Follow the threads of the tapestry, and they lead to various aspects of aviation history. In writing the biography of Buehl, I discovered that the threads related to Ernest Buehl led to the story of the birth of civilian aviation.

CHAPTER 1

The Story Begins

In November 1984, I married Buehl's granddaughter. In April 1985, when I was just getting to know her family, Rosanna and I traveled from our home in Montana to Philadelphia on the occasion of Buehl's 88th birthday. I did not know much about the old man, but this was the point at which the story began for me.

When Rosanna was growing up, she learned many amazing stories about her grandfather. She filled me in on what she knew about him. Skimming the highlights, she told me:

- Buehl was from Bavaria, and he had flown for the German military during World War I.
- He was an expert mechanic and had helped Anthony Fokker, the original Flying Dutchman, get his airplanes to fly.
- He was brought to the United States after World War I to demonstrate German Junkers aircraft to the US military.
- Buehl's pilot's license was #824 and was signed by none other than Orville Wright.
- He had been an airmail pilot and flew the first airmail across the North American continent.
- He opened air routes into the Canadian arctic.
- He flew to the North Pole with Roald Amundsen.

I was skeptical of much of this. I had to keep an open mind, but

(above) The towers of Frauenkirche from the ground.

(below) Looking across the gap between the towers
PHOTOS/AUTHOR

these stories reminded me of the things I knew about a fellow who lived just down the street from me when I was growing up. This individual told lots of stories about himself, aided with various props. For example, he literally kept a live eagle in his house, he had what he said was a fragment of the Dead Sea Scrolls, given to him by David Ben Gurion (the first prime minister of Israel), and even though we were in Billings, Montana, he kept a Chinese sailboat (a "junk") in his front yard. The local newspapers repeated whatever he said, persuaded that he was an important world explorer. Later, his stories nearly all unraveled. I was just about sure it would be the same with Buehl.

As an example of an unlikely story about Buehl, many people in the family believed he had flown an airplane between the towers at Frauenkirche Cathedral in Munich. According to the story, in consequence for endangering one of Germany's most beloved architectural landmarks, he was required to pay a heavy fine.

Being skeptical, I looked at pictures to see what this stunt would involve. The space between the towers is very narrow. I had to ask myself, would it even be possible to fly an airplane between these towers? Could you get through there even if you put the airplane on its side and flew knife-edge? I went to Munich, climbed one of the towers, and looked across the gap. The answer was yes; an airplane could be flown between the towers even with wings level! The space between the towers is 13 meters, and the wingspan of a Fokker D.VII is a bit less than nine meters.

One remaining factor that makes the story unlikely (though not impossible) is that at that time, Buehl was an inexperienced, self-taught flier. Certainly, it could have happened in a moment of youthful exuberance. One evening I was in Dayton, Ohio, in a room full of seasoned airmen and one of Buehl's grandsons told the story about Frauenkirche. The story brought approving chuckles from the old aviators present. They then shared stories of their own. Several distinguished aviators or descendants of some of the top fliers in history talked about one exuberant, cracked-brain adventure after another that they experienced in their youth. I admit it made for a fun and memorable evening.

I once heard Buehl tell a whopper at a family gathering at Buehl's home in Langhorne, Pennsylvania. The story was more important for what it told me about Buehl's sense of humor than about any particular event. A close friend of his daughter Sylvia was looking through scrapbooks with the old man. The friend, Shannon Jones, stumbled onto a photo of Buehl getting into an airplane clearly marked as belonging to General Charles deGaulle and United Free France (UFF).

I overheard as Shannon turned to Buehl and loudly exclaimed, "Ernie, I didn't know you knew deGaulle!"

"Oh, ja," Buehl replied with a twinkle in his watery blue eyes, "I was his pilot."

Everyone was stunned, but no one asked any follow-up questions. The thing was that everyone had heard a lot of amazing stories about Granddad, and this was just another of many, so they believed it. Out of all the stories about Granddad, as far as his family was concerned, this would not have ranked as the most amazing!

Naturally, it would have been very amusing if our government had assigned Buehl, a man with a heavy German accent, to fly deGaulle around the northeast. Many in the US government did not like

There had to be something to the story. After all, here is the picture of Buehl and "deGaulle's airplane." PHOTO/EBC

deGaulle, and they knew he had an abiding dislike of Germans. Did someone in our government deliberately set out to annoy this prickly French nationalist by assigning Buehl as his pilot?

It took a few years of research to conclusively disprove this story. In fact, within the family the story took on features of a conspiracy theory. It was true that deGaulle traveled to the US to raise money for the UFF, but while here it was reported that he only traveled in very large, multi-engine aircraft, accompanied by a large entourage. The *New York Times* and *Life Magazine* closely followed deGaulle on his visits, but the fact that none of these sources mentioned deGaulle taking little excursions in a single-engine Waco meant nothing. Maybe they just left out that part? Was deGaulle secretly loaded onto this little airplane and moved around while everyone believed that he was on bigger airplanes?

With some help from the National Waco Club and its president, Andy Heins, it was possible to track down the story of the Waco.* The UFF in this country originally owned this airplane and used it to fly its local leadership to fundraising missions. After the war, it was put on the market, and Buehl purchased it. He was always buying and selling

The author and his wife, Rosanna, ballooning at a family reunion in Colorado. PHOTO/AUTHOR

---

* Waco CUC NC14618

aircraft, and this was just another one of them.

Since I have had time to reflect on the story, I realize it was so risible that Buehl told it with the assumption that no one would believe it. This sort of humor was characteristic of Buehl.

The 88th birthday celebration was a big event, hosted at the Bavarian Club in Philadelphia. There were many people attending. The master of ceremonies was a Brigadier General who was also a founding member of AOPA (Aircraft Owners and Pilots Association). I was seated with the general's wife, herself a well-known balloonist who once held 15 world records for endurance in high-altitude ballooning. In this large group of intelligent, distinguished guests who had known Buehl for decades, no one doubted the stories he told that night. It was impressive, but it was not enough to crack my skepticism.

Several years later, in 2001, when descendants of Ernest Buehl were meeting for a family reunion, I heard the stories about him again, this time from Rosanna's cousins and her Aunt Sylvia. One cousin in particular, Carlos, was obsessed with anything to do with aviation, and he wanted to develop a *Wikipedia* page for "Granddad." To start, all we had were our recollections of stories told about him. We realized there was a lot we did not know. Once we put our information out there in *Wikipedia*, the reasoning went, maybe someone else would have more information, and we would be able to stitch together a more complete story.

I had long been interested in Amundsen, so the claim that Buehl was Amundsen's pilot in the arctic was interesting to me. After the reunion, I searched for any mention of Buehl among accounts of Amundsen's explorations. I found nothing. No history of Amundsen's arctic explorations mentions Buehl as part of his team. Worse, I easily confirmed that Amundsen never reached the North Pole in an airplane; he flew over it in a Zeppelin. Leads on the other stories also fizzled: Airmail? Nope. He is not listed among pilots who flew the early airmail. Canada? Nope. Canadian sources do not mention him. Fokker? Junkers? No, and no. He was never on the payroll at Fokker or Junkers. I could not confirm any of these claims made about Buehl.

Everyone in the family firmly believed the stories, though, so the idea of writing a *Wikipedia* entry still hung in the air for years. No one seemed willing to step up and take charge to make it happen, though. It was a good idea for which, evidently, no one had time. Of all the family, I was the only one who did much writing, but there were problems with assigning it to me. Most of my writing consisted of reporting the results of psychological evaluations, a widely reviled writing form not intended for public consumption. Also, I was frankly more skeptical than anyone else in the family. I suspect the fact that I kept asking for evidence finally triggered Aunt Sylvia in 2007 to send me a large box full of scrapbooks containing crumbling newspaper clippings and some photos, part of the collection of materials her father had saved.

Now that I had so many source documents, I looked through the collection several times for anything that would confirm any of the

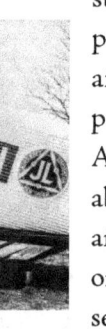

Buehl sitting on the wing of the Elizabeth, *Roald Amundson's aircraft.*
PHOTO/EBC

stories people told me. One day, I was looking at a picture of Buehl sitting on the wing of a Junkers airplane, and it hit me: the airplane had "Elizabeth" painted on the side. I recalled from somewhere that Amundsen once owned an airplane named the Elizabeth. Buehl was sitting on the wing of Amundsen's airplane! I started looking at other pictures near that one in the scrapbook and realized, finally, there were several pictures of Amundsen himself! At some level, the story of his connection with Amundsen was true! Now I was alert. What else was in these photos?

There was a lot in these scrapbooks. There was so much that I eventually realized that though people

Amundsen is second from the right. Others include Oscar Omdal (right) and John M. Larsen (middle). PHOTO/EBC

often mentioned Buehl's involvement with Amundsen, working with the famous explorer was among the less significant things Buehl did.

Many of the stories about Buehl were true, but some could not be verified, and some were, politely speaking, unlikely. When trying to verify these stories, there were two important things to keep in mind. First, Buehl was literally a legend in his own time, and many stories grew up around him. This meant there were a lot of instances in which we could not confirm accuracy. Also, of relevance throughout this book, it is important to understand something about the limits of human memory. The importance of this point will become evident many times in our account.

Sometimes it was hard to trace where these grandiose legends arose, but there were some common mechanisms. Buehl would share his stories with friends, and his friends would tell them to their friends. His friends would often mix up details or add embellishments without really noticing what they were doing. So, Buehl would tell his friends a story, and then his friends would repeat it as they remembered it. Their memory would not be as accurate as Buehl's, so it was common for people to add little embellishments. Churn some good stories for several decades, and eventually you might come to think that Buehl was something like the Davy Crockett of aviation.

Another thing that happens to stories and the way people remember them is that it is typical for people to unconsciously spackle over gaps in a story by just making up details that never happened. This is done so that the story seems to make sense to the person telling it. Also, it is human nature for people to want to put their friends in the action, and this could become an unconscious motivation for Buehl's friends to, in a sense, mentally "photoshop" Buehl into the image of the story they carry in their minds. Instead of telling their friends, "I knew a guy who knew some people who...", they could say, "My friend, Ernie Buehl, did this amazing thing." It makes a better story. It is important to emphasize that the person repeating the story is not lying; he just has a normally functioning memory, which in human beings is faulty.

When Buehl himself was telling the story, one has to keep in mind that he was more of a storyteller than a historian. The fact is that legends built up around Buehl, and frankly, he did not go out of his way to spoil a good yarn with a lot of picky details. As we will see, Buehl did not outright fabricate stories about himself, but he usually did not contradict some of the fabulous misimpressions people developed about him.

Buehl's goal was to tell a good story, and he did not mind if his listeners pictured him in the action. Buehl's listeners cooperated by hearing what they wanted to hear. Listeners might have had one or two questions but were not eager to pin him down on the facts. None of them wanted to spoil a good story, either.

The other thing is that even Buehl's memory would become contaminated over time. The cold fact is that eyewitness reports, unless they are recorded immediately, become more unreliable over time. When Buehl was telling stories 50 years or more after the events, his memories included his recollection of what happened, but also of what others had said about it over the years.

None of this is to say that Buehl was especially unreliable in telling his own story. In fact, the opposite is true. The point is that everyone is unreliable. For the purposes of this book, the stories Buehl told are taken as pointers to the story I tell here. As much as possible,

Sylvia believed this was Mrs. Roosevelt with her father. PHOTO/EBC

every story presented in this book is backed up by contemporaneous news stories and other sources that provide the context that surrounds what Buehl was saying and tests his story. In most cases, I find that Buehl's memories track well with verifiable history. If I could not confirm the story, I did not include it.

In 2009 Rosanna and I telephoned Sylvia, and in the course of visiting about the documents her father left, she told us one of the pictures she still had in San Francisco showed her father with Eleanor Roosevelt. Buehl had talked about carrying Mrs. Roosevelt as a passenger from time to time, so this seemed possible. Rosanna and I dropped everything and flew to San Francisco to look at the photo and examine the other materials. I do not believe the picture was of Mrs. Roosevelt—I have no idea who the woman was—but I took my Nikon and photographed the remainder of the collection.

Returning to Billings, I got more serious about unfolding the ancient, brittle newspaper clippings Sylvia had sent earlier. I had avoided many of these because they were so fragile. The simple act of unfolding them to read them also damaged them. Every time I looked at them, a shower of fine particles of decaying newsprint would cover my desk, and bits of the articles would flake off and get lost.

I consulted with a professional archivist at Tuskegee University, who explained that old newsprint not only deteriorates rapidly, even under archival storage conditions, it also contaminates everything it is near. It is not possible to preserve old newsprint. So, I started to unfold the clippings carefully. Then, even though I knew the heat would accelerate their decay, I ironed them flat and started scanning them. I started organizing, analyzing, and writing. As I cataloged the contents of the scrapbooks, the articles began to tell the stories that went with the mostly unlabeled pictures I had. Soon it became evident to me that the materials Buehl saved in his scrapbooks were not going to be enough to answer all of my questions. Buehl selected materials that told the story as he experienced it. Also, he tended to save the materials that told the story he liked. I wanted to fill in the story where Buehl left things out.

Finally, I had the bones of a story. Given what I had, and what I did not have, the story works best in chronological order. What I did not have were a lot of details about Buehl's personal thinking. I had a lot of articles that included Buehl, but he was rarely the subject of the article.

Further, he rarely talked with family about his thoughts and feelings. He talked about practical day-to-day matters, but not enough to reconstruct a story from his point of view. The lack of internal dialogue may disappoint some readers, but it really is not possible to confidently offer anything like that.

Over time I became aware that stripped of the varnish of fiction, the true story of Buehl's career is even better than the stories I was told. His career turned out to have been much more consequential than any of those widely circulated, hagiographic stories.

Because I started this project as a skeptic, I was motivated to get to some degree of verifiable truth about Buehl. Remove the hero worship and just deal with the man in a straightforward manner, and what emerges is an unconventional story that remains deeply interesting and compelling. His story is not only a testament to a unique and remarkable individual, but it is also an important story of his time.

Buehl Himself

Physically, in his prime, Buehl stood about five feet eight inches tall and weighed 150 pounds. The photos we have of Buehl show him to be quite good-looking, with medium brown hair and blue eyes.

Unlike some of Buehl's fellow aviators, there was never a serious hint of scandal in his family life. Although he would have had many opportunities, he was not a womanizer. There are no sour stories about improper relations with women before he was married. Once married, Buehl remained a devoted and faithful husband.

A combat veteran of World War I, Buehl worked in a dangerous profession all his life, often under exceptionally harsh conditions. He was tough and courageous and was not easily bullied. He accepted the risks associated with being an early aviator, but as compared to some of his contemporaries, he was not a thrill-seeker, and he did not take a lot of unnecessary risks.

Buehl circa 1930.
PHOTO/EBC

Buehl was patriotic and took seriously his duty to his country, both his native Germany when he lived there, and to the United States when he was a citizen here. Literally a flag-waving patriot, he always flew the stars and stripes at his home. In talking to people, he frequently expressed his gratitude for the life and opportunities he was given in the US. One might think that his loyalty to the US would have been tested when the US entered World War II against his native land, but Buehl was always clear about which side he was on. He deeply valued the ideal of equality under the law for all citizens that he found in the US, and he did all he could to defend that ideal.

Socially, he was gregarious, and he made friends easily. Buehl was the sort of person who felt energized from being around people. There was hardly anything he loved more than sitting down with someone over a beer and swapping stories.

One of the things that made him socially appealing was his gentle, often self-deprecating sense of humor. On the whole, he was a fun and interesting person to know. Even into the final years of his life, he remained lively and engaging. People liked Buehl.

In his stories, Buehl often placed himself with famous people and in the middle of the action driving important events. It is common when someone actually does a lot of significant things and is willing to talk about it that others might think he has an inflated view of himself. In these cases, the question comes up when we do not have enough information to put the individual's abilities and achievements into accurate perspective. Since, by definition, it is rare to meet someone who really is the best, a simple guess that the person is a self-aggrandizing blowhard is going to be correct in many cases.

Buehl (holding a cigar, above) loved swapping stories with his fellow aviators.

"I will match you glass for glass." (right)
PHOTOS/EBC

Buehl addressing the OX-5 Club in 1957. PHOTO/EBC

However, Buehl might be better described as a man who had a big personality. One writer of Philadelphia history, apparently intending it as a compliment, described him as a "charismatic, Damon Runyon-type character." He had a gift for telling engaging stories based on the things he did in his life, and he did a lot of things. He really did work with amazing people, he really participated in noteworthy historical events, and he really was recognized by his peers as being among the best of the best for his skills. His willingness to talk about things he did might make it easy to think Buehl was full of himself. Actually, Buehl had a realistic view of himself, but he was a born entertainer. Audiences loved to listen to him.

Buehl's grandchildren remember him as having been fun to be around. He was loving and playful. The grandsons who got to know him remember how he would include them as he did his work at the airport. Also, they remember his little jokes. For instance, he might cover one eye with a silver dollar and keep it there as though he were wearing a monocle. They would laugh at Buehl's spoof of a posh and pretentious man.

His granddaughter, Rosanna, my wife, remembers some of the silly things he would do to entertain her. She credits him with showing her how to play. Growing up as she did at an airport can be isolating for a child because there were no other children around, no peers with

Buehl, holding the tail, is playing the old joke: he is "helping to milk a cow" by pretending her tail is a pump handle, which he is operating to get the milk to flow. PHOTO/EBC

(above) Early evidence of Buehl's gentle sense of humor: young Ernest is up in a tree while everyone else is posing soberly on the ground. PHOTO/EBC

(left) Ernie cutting paper hats and snowflakes. This image, one of Rosanna's treasures, is inside a glass paperweight. PHOTO/R. BUEHL

whom to play. However, while the adults in the family were usually distracted by the details of operating the business, now and then the old man took some time with her, and together they would share some humor and lightness.

She lived with him in the early 1960s and remembers the way he would catch a ray of light with his watch crystal, causing a little circle of light to hit a dark wall—Buehl would tell her that it was a "Sputnik"—the name of the first artificial satellite ever launched into Earth orbit, in 1957. She also recalled how he would cut snowflakes out of typing paper and then put them on his head, expressing a gentle silliness that would please a little girl.

There were times when some people thought Buehl was having too much fun. There was one situation late in his life in which we found him outside, standing on a chair that he had put on top of a picnic table. He had shoved the table up near his flag pole and he was trying—well, actually no one can say what he was trying to do because people witnessing this were so alarmed to find him up there that they never caught the explanation. He was about 90 years old! There was a friend with him and they seemed to be having a great time, smoking cigarettes, sipping cocktails, and telling jokes. People might wonder about him taking unnecessary risks in this case, but evidently he did not see the situation as being as risky as others did. Furthermore, he saw whatever it was he was doing as being necessary.

There was another feature to Buehl's sense of humor that people would notice: he did not mind if people believed crazy things about him. An example of this sort of thing was already mentioned above. Buehl accidentally started a story about himself being deGaulle's pilot and then never denied it. He knew it was ridiculous. How could people believe it? Besides, sometimes things that are ridiculous are funny. Why not enjoy it?

In a final example of how Buehl handled many of these crazy stories, at his 88th birthday banquet, several speakers mentioned Buehl's exalted status as a German ace, and when Buehl himself got up to speak he did not deny the stories. He did not explicitly say, "No, I was never a pilot for Germany." Instead, he told everyone in a straightforward manner what he actually did during the War: he was stationed on Germany's eastern front, fighting in the trenches. He left out little bits of the story in order to avoid alienating his audience (after all, there was a risk that people would come to see him as the "Hun" with whom they exchanged fire), and he embroidered the story a bit to make it more colorful. His statement of the basic truth did not matter. Immediately after the banquet, if you asked most people who had been in attendance, they would have said that Buehl was a German ace! Even his own family persisted in the belief that he flew for Germany.

As a result of the way he handled them, many legends got out of control and Buehl did not mind. However, Buehl deserves respect for things he really did. In the field of aviation, he was respected mainly for three things: his skills as a mechanic, his dedication as a flying instructor, and for his dedication to an inclusive vision for aviation.

Buehl was an outstanding mechanic. During World War I, his skills at BMW were found to be indispensable. This finding was documented in his military record.[†] He quickly rose from test mechanic to BMW's chief mechanic, and he gained respect for being able to solve "impossible" problems. Later, he was recruited to come from Munich to New York in 1920 because of his skills as a mechanic, and then he was recruited to Philadelphia because of those skills. He became an excellent pilot, but he knew many pilots with better skills. He had little solo experience until a decade into his career, in the late 1920s. When he first applied for his Transport license in March 1928, he had only 75 solo hours. By the time he was evaluated, his skills were good but lacking in the precision one expects from an excellent pilot. In truth, all of Buehl's greatest adventures in flying involved him as the co-pilot, not the pilot. These were amazing, pioneering flights, and it was in his role as co-pilot/flight mechanic that Buehl helped to push back boundaries.

Beyond having excellent skills, to become recognized as a noteworthy pilot, you need to do things that seem to be impossible. He never approached anything like that standard. He certainly did not try to accomplish new or impossible things. His skills were not that good until, perhaps, 1930. After that, he did not engage in barnstorming

---

[†] As of 24 September 1917, his record shows that he was to be pulled from the fighting on the eastern front and returned to work at BMW. His skills were recognized to be indispensable and, therefore subject to an occupational deferment.

aerobatics because it would interfere with his vision for aviation. He was not a Waldo Pepper. He recognized aviation had an important place in civilian life, and his vision guided his actions for the rest of his career. Doing things that looked dangerous would send the wrong message.

His work as a flight instructor was noteworthy. In this role, Buehl became known and respected for giving many, many people the opportunity to fly. It was in this role that he most distinguished himself for his courage.

My research on this book started with my own questions implicating Buehl's credibility. Later in the book, we will see others who also questioned his credibility, so this is an important question. As I studied his life, I came to appreciate that, contrary to my skepticism, Buehl's peers, people who knew him from the old days and who also knew the people he talked about, found his stories basically credible. In fact, I observed this from practically the day I met Buehl at his 88th birthday celebration. At that event, Buehl faced a room full of people who themselves were distinguished, news-making aviators. No one present questioned any of the stories Buehl told that evening. Buehl was legendary, even to those in his circle who are now remembered in legends

Legendary pilot Bob Hoover with Buehl. They had considerable mutual respect. Buehl was honored to be photographed with Hoover, but Hoover also was honored to be photographed with this ancient dean of aviators, Ernest Buehl.
PHOTO/EBC

Selected Sources

Balloon Federation of America. "Constance C. Wolf Inducted into the U.S. Ballooning Hall of Fame on July 26, 2015," June 2017.

Bragg, Addison. "Sail-Ho! Billings to Bahamas." *The Billings Gazette*, August 5, 1973, sec. Sunday Magazine.

Bragg, Addison. "Visiting an Explorer." *The Billings Gazette*, November 2, 1969, Morning edition.

Department of Commerce. "Application for Pilot's Rating 1A Land." Department of Commerce, Aeronautics Branch, July 30, 1930.

Department of Commerce. "Pilot's Flight Test Report." Department of Commerce, Aeronautics Branch, June 7, 1928.

Hill, George Roy (director). *The Great Waldo Pepper*. Adventure, Drama, 1975.

Laskas, Jeanne Marie. *The Balloon Lady and Other People I Know*. 1st edition. Pittsburgh, Pa: Duquesne University Press, 1996.

Loftus, Elizabeth. "Our Changeable Memories: Legal and Practical Implications." *Nature Reviews. Neuroscience* 4, no. 3 (March 2003).

Merryman, Kathleen. "Explorer Survives Airplane Disaster in Desert near Nile." *The Billings Gazette*, November 1, 1979.

"Militär-Paß (Green Cover)," 1916 to 1919.

Silcox, Harry C. "Aviation Enthusiast Ernest Buehl and the Flying Dutchman Airport." In *Remembering Northeast Philadelphia. American Chronicles: A History Press Series*. Charleston, SC: History Press, 2009.

CHAPTER 2

The European Years

Family of Origin and Schooling

Young Buehl had his first direct contact with airplanes at an airshow in Freiburg, Germany, in 1910, only five years after the Wright brothers' first public demonstrations of controlled flight and only one year after their first demonstrations in Europe. Buehl's two older brothers wanted to attend the Freiburg show and let their 13-year-old brother, Ernie, tag along.

There were five brothers, including at least two who were interested very early in aviation: Fritz, Karl, George, Herman, and Gustav. Herman died during World War I. Fritz was the oldest. He became an

Freiburger Flugwache (Freiburg Air Show) in 1910. We believe that Ernie attended this event with his brothers Karl and Fritz.
PHOTO/MICHAEL BAUER, KARL'S GRANDSON

The four Buehl brothers reunite in Germany in 1956: Gustav, Ernest, Karl, and Fritz. PHOTO/EBC

aviation mechanic, starting his career at Rapp Motors in Munich. Karl was the second oldest. According to Karl's daughter, Anneliese, his first contact with aviation came when he was a boy. Karl often traveled the 76 miles to Friedrichshafen, where

Vital Statistics—Ernest Buehl
30 April 1897 to 25 May 1990
PARENTS: Gottlieb Wilhelm & Therese Bühl
US CITIZENSHIP: 26 September 1928
DEATH: 25 May 1990, at age 93

Count Ferdinand Adolf August Heinrich Graf von Zeppelin built his airships.

According to several sources, Buehl learned to fly in 1914, when he was 17 years of age. He never elaborated on the circumstances of how he learned to fly, other than to say that at that time, people basically taught themselves. He said, "In 1914, training was a hit-and-miss method. You learned through practical experience—or you didn't learn."

❧

Buehl's descendants all believed he was Bavarian. It surprised everyone when a dig through his papers showed that Buehl was born and raised in the state of Baden-Württemberg. For an American this was an easy mistake, since both are southern German states, they share a border, and they share many folkways. Later in life, too, Buehl was active in the Bavarian Club of Philadelphia, and in fact, that was the location of his 88th birthday party. In his family's defense, Buehl moved to Munich as a young adult, he served in the Bavarian army, and numerous newspaper accounts of Buehl's career stated that he was born in Bavaria. Everyone just believed what was printed in the newspapers.

His family lived in Neustadt im Schwartzwald, a charming community in the Black Forest, not on any major highway but located near a small, local resort. The closest city is Freiburg, about 20 miles to the west. Off the path for foreign tourists, there are no little shops selling souvenirs, and even the restaurants make no concessions to those who do not live by the idiosyncratic internal rhythms of the community. Public places are cared for with pride; for example, even places such as the platform at the railroad station or the islands in the median of the roadways are clean and decorated with cheerful, well-maintained potted geraniums.

In Germany, the family name is spelled Bühl. When going through customs several years ago, Rosanna did not even recognize her own name when the officer pronounced it in the German way. It is difficult for people in the United States because it contains a vowel sound that does not occur in standard American English. None of Buehl's descendants can pronounce it properly.

Buehl's 1919 certificate of nationality (passport) PHOTO/EBC

[Left to right, below]
Train station at Neustadt in 2007
PHOTO/R. BUEHL
1926 Postcard of Neustadt PHOTO/EBC
Neustadt Church, 2007
PHOTO/AUTHOR

*Buehl's mother,
Therese* PHOTO/EBC

*Young Buehl, in his
student days.* PHOTO/EBC

*This photo shows the Bühl family
home in Neustadt. It suggests
a prosperous, comfortable,
though not especially privileged
upbringing.* PHOTO/EBC

His mother was Therese Bühl. Buehl's baptismal certificate gives her maiden name as Theres Frey. Buehl's father was Gottlieb Wilhelm Bühl. We do not know for certain what elder Bühl did for a living, but it is believed he was an accountant. According to family lore, he made cuckoo clocks as a hobby.

As a young man, Buehl attended a vocational school in Konstanz, a small city near the border of Germany with Switzerland. Konstanz is about 53 miles from Neustadt. Today it takes a bit more than an hour to drive from Neustadt to Konstanz, or a train connects them in three hours and fifteen minutes. This last amount of time is likely to be what it would have taken Buehl to travel the distance.

At school, Buehl was a good student. In the academic year 1913-14, he received a commendation for his diligence in all subjects. He completed his work as a journeyman in his trade as a mechanic in July 1914, about one month after World War I started. He passed his written exam with honors in October 1914. When Buehl finished his training, Fritz guided Buehl to take a job at Rapp.

Rapp logo, 1916   BMW logo, 1920
scanned from letterheads PHOTOS/EBC

(above) Buehl appren-
ticed at Graf—one
of the best aviation
machine shops in
Germany. Given
Karl's connection
there, it may not be
a coincidence that
Buehl's apprentice-
ship was at Graf.
PHOTO/EBC

Fritz Bühl, on the left,
posing with a Rapp
engine. As the eldest
brother, Fritz may
have inspired Ernie
to become an aviation
mechanic. Fritz
started his career at
Rapp Motors. PHOTO/
EBC

BMW

Newspapers reported that Buehl's first job was at BMW, building aircraft engines. This was not technically true, as his first job was at *Rapp Motorenwerke*, a company founded in Munich in 1913 by Karl Rapp. Buehl started at Rapp in late November 1914. On 7 March 1916, the day Rapp Motors reorganized under new leadership as BMW, Buehl had already been working at the factory for a year and a half.

It is important to digress briefly to discuss the product that Buehl was building. It is not possible to understand Buehl's career without knowing a little about the engine BMW manufactured. The fact is, Buehl began his career at one of the world's most advanced high-tech companies, gaining experience that put him at the leading edge of aviation.

In 1915, Karl Rapp was building aircraft engines of his own design. These six-cylinder in-line engines were heavy and developed a vibration that could not be adequately controlled. Obviously, it is hard to sell aircraft engines that are marginally suitable for use in aircraft. As a result, Rapp Motors struggled.

Even so, the company was considered to be of strategic importance because of its production facilities and established workforce of 370. At the beginning of World War I, the German military ordered Rapp to stop production of his own design. Instead, he was to build engines designed by Paul Daimler and licensed from Austro-Daimler. These engines had twelve cylinders and required a supercharger in order to operate at high altitude.

A brilliant engineer named Max Friz was brought in from Daimler to help with the project. Before the factory tooled up for the new project, Friz showed the factory manager a proposal for an innovative carburetor that could operate at high altitude without a supercharger.

The Friz carburetor solved a key problem: at high altitudes, normal engines run out of oxygen and will stop operating. Even with ground-based engines in automobiles, not being able to get enough oxygen into the cylinders can be the factor that limits performance.[*] Adding a supercharger to force more air into an engine was one way to solve the problem. Superchargers added their own set of problems, though, so being able to build a normally aspirated engine that could operate at high altitude was a defining step forward for BMW. It was an opportunity to stay on an evolutionary path with better-established carburetor technology instead of committing to radical change by moving to the unproven technology of superchargers.[†]

After describing the new carburetor, and before a prototype had even been built, the German military decided to drop the order for the Austro-Daimler engine and instead order 600 units of a new engine designed by Friz, a relatively small, six-cylinder, inline engine

---

[*] In the days before computer-monitored, fuel-injected engines in automobiles, just driving Interstate-70 in Colorado, with its peak elevation of 11,160 feet, nearly choked many engines.

[†] There were patents for superchargers of one sort or another by the first years of the 20th century, but the problems of superchargers were only worked out by the 1930s.

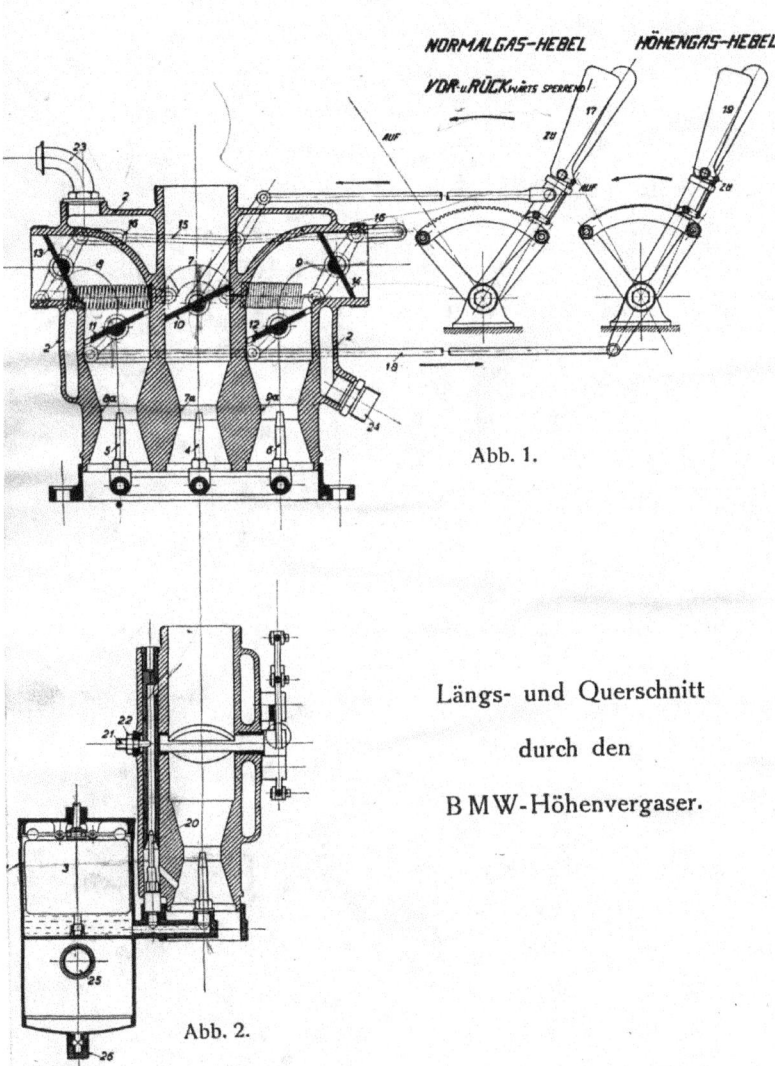

Tafel V.

Abb. 1.

Längs- und Querschnitt

durch den

BMW-Höhenvergaser.

Abb. 2.

Cut-away drawing of the BMW-IIIa *carburetor. Table 5 of the 1918* Beschreibung und Betriebsanleitung für den 185 PS Bayern-Flugmotor Type BMW-IIIa. [Description and operating instructions for the 185 hp Bayern aircraft engine Type BMW-IIIa]. PHOTO/ EBC, PUBLIC DOMAIN

Timeline: Wright Brothers

1903 Wright's first flight at Kitty Hawk

1904 Wilbur Wright makes the first controlled turn

1905 Wright's first public demonstrations of controlled flight

1906 Santos Dumont demonstrates the first heavier-than-air flight that is certified by the FAI

1909 Blériot crosses the English Channel.

1909 Wright demonstrates fully controlled flight, including the ability to remain in the air for as long as he wants, and the ability to change directions at will

1910 Buehl attends airshow at Freiburg

1914 Buehl begins to fly

that had some similarities to the Rapp engine—and some important differences. Cylinder volume was enlarged, and the compression ratio was increased. Better optimized design and materials made it significantly lighter than the original Rapp engine. The result was known as the BMW-III engine. Although the engine was given the number III, it was not the third product made by the BMW Company. The engine was calculated to have 185 horsepower in the German system. This would be about 138 kW, placing it in performance class III.

When the BMW-IIIa engine

A BMW-IIIa engine at the Smithsonian Air and Space Museum. PHOTO/AUTHOR

went into production in 1917, it set the benchmark in aviation technology. Not only was it powerful in relation to its size, it was economical, consuming fuel at about two-thirds the rate of other aircraft engines in its class. In fact, travel in a BMW-powered aircraft was sometimes more economical than driving in an automobile of the day. A BMW-powered airplane might cover a long distance between cities in a quarter of the time and use 20% less fuel than an automobile.

When the war ended in November 1918, as part of the demobilization of Germany, production at BMW was shut down. By that time, of the total 3,100 BMW-III engines that had been ordered, only 591 had actually been produced. According to the provisions of the Treaty of Versailles, the engines still at the BMW factory had to be rendered unusable, and Germany was prevented from further manufacturing aircraft engines.[‡] This put BMW in a precarious position, since the BMW-III had been the company's only product. Consequently, 90% of the 2,000 BMW employees in Germany were dismissed. Buehl was among the 10% who kept their positions.

Even in 1919, BMW continued to have interest in promoting its engine. During this time, in fact, BMW developed the prototype of a more powerful version of the BMW-III, and Buehl was involved in its development. Also, he was sent out as a consultant when

Buehl appears in this photo, sitting in front, second from the right. The Munich production shop is in the background. This photo was taken in 1918. Buehl was BMW's chief test mechanic. PHOTO/EBC

‡ Part V, Sections III and IV of the treaty generally deal with restrictions on aviation and the destruction of materials related to military aviation. Also, for six months following the implementation of the treaty the manufacture of aircraft engines was forbidden in German territory by Section III, Article 201.

other companies needed help adapting the BMW engine to use in their products.

Buehl left employment at BMW on 14 April 1920, just months before the company was sold to Knorr-Bremse, a company that manufactured railway equipment.

World War I

Buehl served in the German military between 1916 and 1919. For almost a year and a half, he fought in the trenches on the eastern front. He was then transferred back to Munich to work again at BMW.

There is more than one story about Buehl's participation in the German Army during World War I. Many articles that appeared even during his lifetime stated that he had been a pilot in the German air force. On 23 March 1921, the first story appeared in a US newspaper stating that Buehl flew for Germany during the War: "Ernest Buehl… served as an aviator with the German army during the recent war, being stationed for the most part on the eastern front. He came to this country about ten months ago."

In reality, Buehl was a German veteran who fought in the trenches. Like many men who have been in intense combat, Buehl did not talk much about his military experience except for a few stories that he would relate humorously. In fact, this pattern of behavior was very common among soldiers who survived World War I. They might tell a few amusing stories but say nothing more about their actual experiences.

However, from his behavior, members of his family could infer something more about Buehl's experience in combat. Buehl suffered nightmares, and sometimes after drinking too much in the evening, he would begin to "relive" the war. He would press his back to a wall and talk to long-gone comrades, warning everyone about the enemy pressing in on their position. He would imagine himself back in a trench, experiencing claustrophobic terror as the dirt overhead

rained down on him during a bombardment.§
Alarming and spectacularly bizarre when these
displays happened, they at least were rare.

When asked about flying for Germany,
Buehl did not directly deny it. Instead, he
would tell everyone that he had been assigned
as a cook on Germany's eastern front and that
he had been awarded the Iron Cross after he
was wounded while serving in that position.
How Buehl ended up being assigned to be
the cook for a unit that basically defended a
trench on the eastern front was a mystery to
him for his whole life, or so he said. When
he told this story, he embroidered it with
statements playing on the old joke about

*Soldiers posted in a trench
on the Eastern Front*
PHOTO/EBC

"military intelligence" being an oxymoron. The mystery he presented
in his story asked why the Army would assign an expert aviation
mechanic to the position of cook?

His statement about being assigned as a cook was only partially
true. Although he served as a cook, he omitted to say that his main
duties on the Front were to maintain the machine guns. He was there
primarily as a mechanic. There was not enough work just oiling the
guns to keep him busy, though, so to fill his time he was assigned to
help out in the kitchen.

By the end of the War, Buehl was a seasoned combat veteran. His
military record begins on 4 April 1916. His rank was *Jäger* (rifleman,
what we would call a private) in the *Alpenkorps*. As a rifleman, he
was trained on the Gewehr 98, the standard rifle used at that time.
He was also trained on the *Maschinengewehr* 08 (MG 08), Germany's

---

§ One lifelong consequence of this experience was that Buehl was never as comfortable in
aircraft having an enclosed cabin as he was in an open cockpit.

Buehl's unit is posing with a couple of MG *08s on sledge mounts. The gun was water-cooled and could fire 400 rounds per minute. Its practical range was two kilometers. Buehl appears in this group photo in the back, fourth from the right.* PHOTO/EBC

Timeline: Soldier

One can get a sense of where Buehl was serving from a summary of where the *Karpathenkorps* served.

AUGUST 1916 ✦ There was fighting in various places in the south of Poland, and by late August they had made their way down to Yablonitsky Pass.

SEPTEMBER 1916 ✦ The unit was fighting in the Carpathian Mountains.

1 OCTOBER 1916 TO 24 JULY 1917 ✦ The soldiers engaged in trench warfare in the western Carpathians.

25 JULY TO 10 AUGUST 1917 ✦ Their attention turned to, as they put it, the "liberation of Bukovina."

11 AUGUST UNTIL 16 SEPTEMBER 1917 ✦ The unit engaged in trench warfare on the eastern frontier of Bukovina.

24 SEPTEMBER 1917, Buehl received orders to return to Munich while the rest of the unit was sent to Italy.

standard heavy machine gun.☙

Besides his service record booklet, there are four military enrollment books (*Kriegsstammrollen*) that track something of Buehl's service. The southern states of Bavaria and Württemberg commanded their own combined army during the war, apart from the Prussian army. Therefore, Buehl's allegiance was sworn to King Ludwig III of Bavaria. In the earliest reference, Buehl was issued dog tag number 2243. Throughout his record, from his training and continuing through his combat experience, Buehl consistently earned the highest ratings for his behavior.

Early on, Buehl was a member of the 1. *Königlich Bayrisches JägerRegiment* (a part of the *Alpenkorps*). *Königlich Bayrisches* means "royal Bavarian." As a fighting unit, the *Alpenkorps* was evaluated after the war by US Intelligence as having been "an elite body, of a genuine combat value." Months after he was inducted, the *Alpenkorps* combined with others to form the *Karpathenkorps*.

This small portrait of Buehl is decorated with the badge of his unit, the Karpathenkorps. It consisted of a representation of deer antlers, with fir tree branches and sword. Unfortunately, Buehl's badge was broken in storage, so one antler was lost.
PHOTO/EBC

By late September 1917, as BMW was beginning to manufacture its new engine, the military realized that Buehl was more valuable in Munich, building airplane engines than he was in a trench on the eastern front maintaining machine guns or operating the field kitchen. Buehl was transferred back to Munich to work at BMW on 24 September 1917. He was discharged from active service in October 1917. His record shows that he was reassigned under an "Indispensable Exemption Regulation."

Over a period of years of discussion within the family, his descendants

---

☙ He is not listed among German pilots in a German source.

Buehl testing an engine.
PHOTO/EBC

One of Karl Bühl's many crashes as a test pilot. Karl is the man in bandages, second from the left.
PHOTO/MICHAEL BAUER, KARL'S GRANDSON

came to realize Buehl was not a combat pilot, but there was a reluctance to let go of the idea that he at least did some flying during the War. There was a story that Buehl flew when he was assigned to duty in Munich at the BMW plant. The idea of the argument is that when he was working on an engine, he needed to fly with it to be sure it operated properly. However, it would have made little sense for BMW to allow Buehl to test-fly an airplane. Mechanic and test pilot are separate positions, each requiring extensive training and specialized skills. One can compare Buehl's work at BMW to the wartime experience of his brother Karl, who actually worked as a test pilot. In Karl's case, his entire job was to demonstrate an airplane's flight worthiness. The only way was to fly it. But when Buehl would test an engine, he would send it to be mounted on a stationary stand, not in the nose of an airplane. He could fulfill his duty without leaving the ground.

Buehl's Iron Cross

One funny story that Buehl liked to tell was how he came to be awarded the Iron Cross. In the trenches one day, while he was affected by diarrhea and had his pants down around his ankles, Russian troops overran their position. Buehl was forced to flee, struggling to pull his pants up with one hand while with the other hand firing his rifle at the advancing troops behind him. Funny only in the retelling, Buehl would invite his audience to picture the ludicrous scenario: his rifle was the Gewehr 98, a bolt action Mauser with a five-round magazine. To operate it, he needed to hold the rifle with his left hand, then use his right hand to operate the bolt and pull the trigger. Each time a bullet was fired, the bolt had to be drawn back, the spent shell ejected, and a new cartridge pushed into the firing chamber. He had to do these things and run as fast as he could in full retreat while trying not to trip on his pants!

He was wounded, "shot in the schwanz [rear]," he remarked with appreciation for the irony, "while defending the front." For this, he was awarded the Iron Cross.**

Of course, one aspect of this story is that its humanity resonated even among those who faced the German Army as an enemy during the war. We all share some basic vulnerabilities of being human, among them the basic bodily needs we all prefer to take care of privately, in a calm manner, and with as little loss of dignity as we can manage. The conditions of extreme

Buehl's Iron Cross. It is missing its original ribbon PHOTO/EBC

** Given that Buehl's goal was generally to tell a good story, and given that he was known to embroider some stories to make them more engaging, it can be asked if this story is strictly true. After all, if he was shot in the rear rather than in, say, a leg, it is funnier. Here is what is known: Buehl had an excellent military record and was respected as a soldier. When he was fighting on the eastern front, he was shot and was awarded the Iron Cross which is now in the author's possession. None of his surviving relatives saw the scar from the wound, which suggests it was in an area generally covered by clothing. He did not suffer lasting orthopedic impairment from the wound, making it more likely the bullet went into muscle than bone or internal organ.

chaos and panic in which Buehl had to relieve himself, and that his fear and humiliation at that moment became widely known public information, and that he was even decorated for all this, was at once classically funny and deeply humanizing. It contrasts with the brutality one might hear in a story that says, "I helped operate the machine guns that turned a battlefield into a slaughterhouse." The story Buehl chose to tell reminded his hearers that he, too, was a vulnerable human being like themselves, rather than a bloodthirsty enemy.

Stratospheric Achievements

In 1919, for the first time in the history of the world, a pilot reached the stratosphere in a heavier-than-air craft. Franz Zeno Diemer achieved this breathless milestone on 7 June 1919 in an open-cockpit

Franz Zeno Diemer
PHOTO/BBC

biplane. Buehl was not only there to witness this seminal moment, but he was also the chief mechanic supporting the flight.

At this early stage of the history of flight, records such as this were achieved and then quickly broken. In fact, it was only a matter of months before fliers went higher than Diemer. The event triggered a big publicity push for BMW and Buehl saved several photos and a newspaper clipping related to the flight.

Beyond the issue of setting some briefly held record, some advances in aviation are especially significant because they represent a leap over major barriers. The first flight in a balloon got us into the air. The first powered flight in a heavier-than-air craft can be ranked as the next major achievement. Captain Chuck Yeager breaking the sound barrier is a major advance recognized by everyone, as are Major Yuri Gagarin's hop into outer space and Neil Armstrong's first step on the Moon. To this list, we should insert Diemer flying an airplane into the stratosphere.

Consider, even though people soon were orbiting Earth, Gagarin's

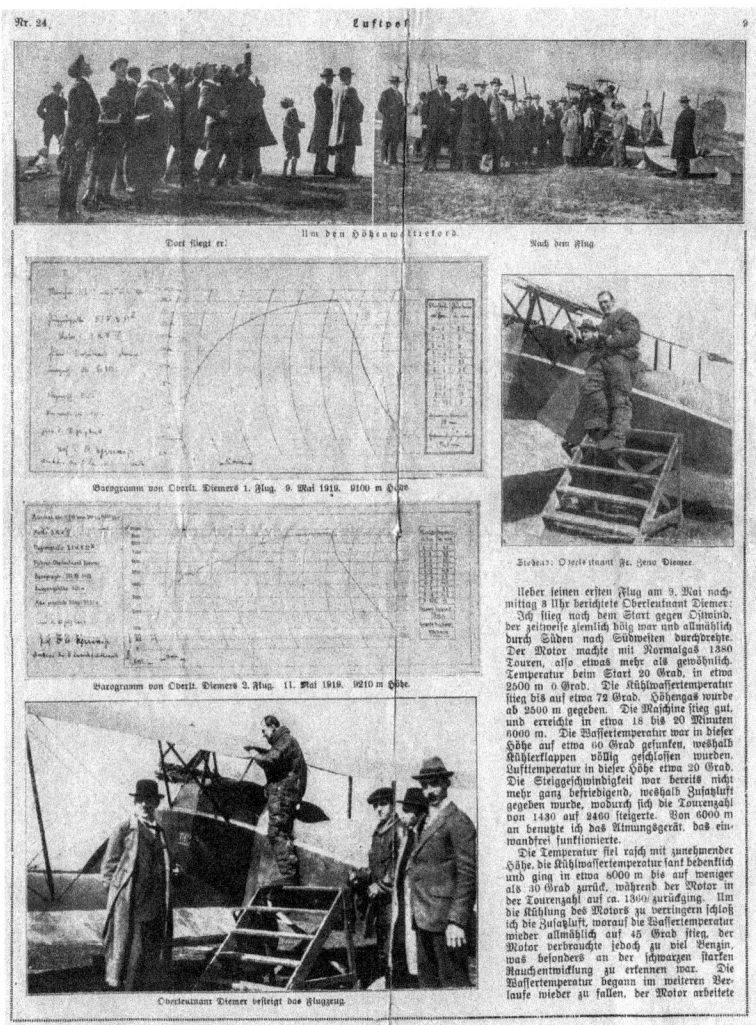

Luftpost article, one page of a two-page spread PHOTO/EBC

Diemer climbing into the cockpit for his record-breaking flight. Buehl is standing just behind the stairs, with Fritz Bühl nearby. This is the photograph that appeared in the Lüftpost. PHOTO/EBC

short flight will always be important because it represents the first time anyone flew beyond Earth's atmosphere and even beyond Earth's gravity. Similarly, when we eventually set foot on more distant worlds, the landing on the Moon in 1969 will always be important because it represents the first time any creature in the multi-billion-year span of life on Earth stepped onto a planetary body that was not Earth. The numbers set in record books for achievement will always advance, but achieving the first step sets a record that will always be memorable.

Diemer's Flight

Taking off from Oberwiesenfeld, the airfield associated with the Munich BMW plant, Diemer flew a Deutsche Flugzeugwerke F37/III to an altitude of a little over 32,000 feet or 6 miles, about the cruising altitude of contemporary passenger aircraft in the 21st Century. He did this only fifteen and a half years after the Wright Brothers' first little 284-yard hop of a flight at Kitty Hawk, North Carolina.

The stratosphere is generally thought of as beginning at a little over 6.2 miles above Earth's surface. The distance from the Earth's surface to the bottom of the stratosphere varies locally, but for an airplane there actually is a bright line that separates the stratosphere from the troposphere (the layer of atmosphere we naturally inhabit). The bright line that appears in the sky is the vapor trail that begins to follow an airplane when it enters the stratosphere.

We know Diemer entered the stratosphere because the bright line of a vapor trail appeared in the sky behind his airplane. It was the

Timeline: Major Aviation Milestones

1783 Montgolfier brothers first
          manned balloon ascension

1903 Wright Brothers' first heavier-than-air flight,
          setting the stage for controlled, powered flight.

1919 Diemer enters the stratosphere.

1947 Yeager breaks the sound barrier.

1961 Gagarin enters outer space.

1969 Armstrong walks on the Moon.

first time anyone had seen a vapor trail. It was not expected. His little airplane was not visible to the naked eye, so people were puzzled about this phenomenon appearing in the region where they expected Diemer to be. What was it, and did it signal something terrible?

The engine Diemer used was the BMW-IV, a larger version of the BMW-III. Due to its size, the BMW-IV could develop more horsepower: over 240 hp (180 kW) versus 185 hp (138 kW for the BMW-III). It was the only engine used in the early race for record-breaking high-altitude flights that did not use a supercharger.

According to Diemer, even though the engine could have climbed higher, he had to begin his descent because he personally ran out of oxygen to breathe. He had to descend or risk passing out due to hypoxia.

Buehl did not talk much about what he did that day. He knew Diemer's flight was worth mentioning in certain contexts, but I suspect he did not talk much about it because most people showed little interest. People tended to be more interested in stories that featured Buehl in the cockpit rather than on the ground in his role as a mechanic. Also, I suspect most people could not put this event into perspective, and without perspective it does not make a good story to share with the boys over cigars and schnapps.

[left] Buehl and brother Fritz appear in this advertising photo used by BMW. Buehl is standing just behind the wing, while Fritz is standing at the rear, just in front of the tail.

[below] Diemer signing autographs for dignitaries in attendance. Fritz Bühl is second from the left. He is identified as "Foreman Bühl." PHOTOS/EBC

Ernie doing the final tuning of the engine for Diemer's flight. PHOTO/EBC

In the end, it would be characteristic of Buehl not to talk about something like this if he lacked any colorful stories about it. His role here was to tune the engine, the engine worked as expected, and the entire attempt came off without any difficulty. What would he talk about?

Why Isn't Diemer's Record Recognized?

The Fédération Aéronautique Internationale (FAI) is the official keeper of all records related to aviation. Although Germany was a founding member of the FAI, they were kicked out because of their role in World War I. As a result, *no* German accomplishments in aviation could be registered.

The *Guiness Book of World Records* has to follow the FAI, so it does not list Diemer's flight. Even BMW itself has to be careful in what they will say about this flight.

It is not that it did not happen or that what I am saying in this book is not true; the issue is that it cannot officially be recognized today because of the post-War political climate in 1919.

Fokker and the Beginning of Civilian Aviation

Anthony Herman Gerard Fokker's name may be best known today in the United States for his behind-the-scenes role in the Peanuts comic strip as the designer of the airplane flown by Snoopy's nemesis, the Red Baron. Snoopy, in costume as the World War I pilot, takes to the air in his Sopwith Camel and then gets shot out of the sky by Germany's ace of aces, who flies a red, triple-winged Fokker.

Anthony Fokker in 1919
PHOTO/EBC

In real life, Anthony Fokker, the first man to make a million dollars in aviation, was an intuitive engineer and, it has been said, "arguably the most skilled pilot of his time." Among his accomplishments, Fokker became known as the first pilot in Germany to loop-the-loop.

Before continuing, it will become relevant to this story that Fokker had a difficult personality. He was said to be spoiled, whiney, egotistical, dominating, mercurial, and even emotionally unstable.[††]

Born in 1890, he first saw an airplane fly in 1906, well before Wilbur Wright demonstrated his Flier in Europe. Fokker built his first airplane in 1910, when he was twenty years old. Nicknamed the Spin (Dutch for "spider"), this was a small monoplane with so many bracing wires to hold up the wings and parts of the body that it looked like it was covered with a web.

The Flying Dutchman was an obvious nickname for Fokker, a famous aviator from the Netherlands. It is possible he was tagged with the nickname by Crown Prince Wilhelm of Germany. Later, the nickname also worked for Buehl, who was a flier and *Deutsch* (the word Germans use to name their own nationality). For both of them, the name, touching on old folktales as well as Richard Wagner's 1843 opera, had a familiar ring to it that made it easy to remember.[‡‡]

Buehl made a small but noteworthy contribution to putting Fokker in the air as a major player in the murky civilian market of

---

[††]   This characterization is controversial.

[‡‡]   Stretching the association of Dutch/Deutch works in English because in English they are nearly homophones. In German it does not work. The actual name of Wagner's opera is Der Fliegende Holländer, which would translate literally from the German as "the flying person from Holland." For the origin of the nickname as applied to Buehl, see Chapter 4.

post-War civilian aviation.

After the War, the question for Fokker was simple, but the answer was not obvious. There were many war surplus aircraft dumped onto the market after the War, so it was necessary to ask, what good are airplanes? People could think of uses, to be sure, but until then airplanes had only been used as either military machines or for sport flying and were not suitable for civilian purposes.

By summer 1919, it was becoming evident that aviation would be important in civilian life. John Alcock and Arthur Brown completed the first nonstop crossing of the Atlantic on 15 June 1919. They took off in a modified Vickers bomber from Newfoundland, Canada, and landed in Ireland. About six weeks later, on 3 August, Alcock appeared at a major airshow in Holland and was received with the adulation of a modern rock star. It was reported that tens of thousands of people turned out to greet him.

Poster from ELTA—*Eerste Luchtvaart Tentoonstelling Amsterdam* PHOTO/PUBLIC DOMAIN

The airshow was ELTA [*Eerste Luchtvaart Tentoonstelling Amsterdam*; English: First Aviation Exhibition Amsterdam]. This was the first major opportunity following the end of World War I to promote the idea of peacetime aviation, and it became one of the most important aviation shows in history. During its run from 1 August to 12 September 1919, the number of people who attended is unknown, but estimates range as high as one million.

The First Aviation Exhibition Amsterdam—ELTA—facilitated the success of two major aerospace players: the airline

KLM [*Koninklijke Luchtvaart Maatschappi*; English: Royal Aviation Company] and N.V. Fokker [*Nederlandsche Vliegtuigenfabriek Fokker*; English: Dutch Aircraft Factory Fokker]. The airshow also made Holland a major hub of commercial air routes. Because of ELTA, to this day anyone who has booked a flight to Europe is likely to become familiar with Schiphol Airport in Amsterdam. After ELTA, in 1920, Fokker introduced his F.11 model, an airplane designed to carry civilian passengers in some comfort. It had an enclosed cabin that could seat as many as four people. It was this airplane he marketed to KLM.

Buehl traveled to Amsterdam in August 1919 to work with Fokker, so this placed him in Holland at the time of the ELTA Air Show. Because Germany was officially excluded from participation, having Fokker invite Buehl to work there was a good thing for Germany. There is an entry in Buehl's military service record booklet that orders him to Holland from 1 August 1919 to 1 November 1919.

The relevance of his work with Fokker to the German military related to the conditions imposed on Germany by the

Cover of Buehl's Militar-Paß booklet PHOTO/EBC

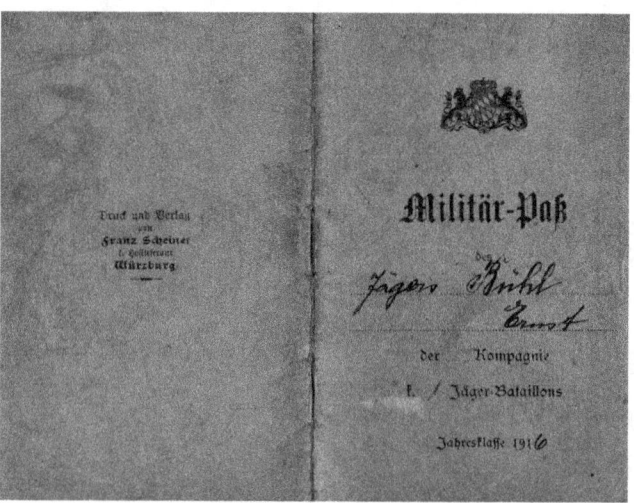

Treaty of Versailles. As a condition of the Treaty, Germany was not allowed to own submarines, tanks, airplanes, and so on. Also it was forbidden from maintaining its aircraft industry within its own borders. Sending Buehl and other mechanics abroad for this kind of work kept the country from losing technical knowledge related to creating and maintaining weapons systems.

Fokker and Buehl

Though he had been manufacturing his aircraft in Schwerin, Germany, rather than in the Netherlands, as the war came to an end, in order to escape the deteriorating social conditions in post-war Germany, Fokker moved parts and engines for hundreds of planes to the Netherlands, where he was able to resume manufacturing.[§§]

Anthony Fokker had used the BMW-III engine in his most capable fighter of World War I, and he wanted to continue to use that engine after the war. However, even though the engines worked beautifully in Germany, in Holland the engines were vibrating so hard and running so hot that they were burning up. According to the story Buehl told about their meeting, none of Fokker's mechanics could adjust the engines to run properly.[℀]

The problem was the Dutch fuel, which was of higher quality than the German fuel at that time. Germany had little access to oilfields and had to create a synthetic gasoline out of the coal that was available within its own borders. The fact that the BMW engine had trouble running on the Dutch fuel foreshadows the difficulty experienced in 1920 when the BMW-III was brought to the United States.

[§§]   Although there is a story that he smuggled the parts out of Germany, he made this move early, before export sanctions were imposed.

[℀]   There are video recordings of Buehl telling this story on two occasions: one at the Bavarian Club in Philadelphia on the occasion of his 88th birthday, and another time at a meeting of the Experimental Aircraft Association. A basic implication here is that Buehl is now internationally recognized as a world-class aviation mechanic.

Frustrated, Fokker demanded BMW "send your best man" to come and make the engines work. In response, BMW sent their chief test mechanic, Buehl, but when Buehl showed up, Fokker began giving him a hard time. Nearly shouting in his high-pitched voice as he glared at Buehl, Fokker complained that BMW had sent *"ein kind!"* [a child]. When they met, Fokker was not much older than Buehl (they were both in their twenties), and Fokker had taken quite a bit of guff from the German military because of his young age.

According to one story, when Fokker first demonstrated his air-craft-mounted synchronized machine gun, Crown Prince Wilhelm, who was observing, declared that he doubted that little Tony could have invented it, saying more-or-less: "Did you invent this yourself, Herr Fokker, or was it your father?" The treatment he received may have suggested to Fokker a way of dealing with this other boy-genius who showed up when he called for a mechanic.

Buehl was young, but he was hard to intimidate. He replied, "Give me an hour. If I cannot fix it in that time, I will just leave." When Buehl was able to fix the problem, Fokker was so relieved that he broke down, crying. After all, he had a large order of airplanes that had to be fitted with this engine, so there was a lot at stake.

In the end, Fokker did not acknowledge Buehl with even so much as a simple thank you letter.

Therefore, when Buehl finished his work in Holland, he was given a routine certificate*** on Fokker letterhead saying only that his work had been satisfactory. The certificate is not signed by Fokker himself, and it is doubtful that they ever had contact again after the day of their

---

***   The text reads:
Certification
We hereby certify to the fitter Ernst Bühl that he was active here from August 6 to September 22, 1919[1] on behalf of the Bavarian Motor Works.
His task was to adjust the B.M.W. engines for the fuels used in Holland, and he completed this task to our satisfaction.

initial meeting. The blubbering response Buehl got when he informed Fokker that he had solved the problem of making the engines run on Dutch fuel was just a passing gust of emotion, nothing deeper.

ॐ

N.V. NEDERLANDSCHE VLIEGTUIGENFABRIEK „FOKKER"
BUREAU ROKIN 84 · TELEFOON CENTRUM 3004

AMSTERDAM, 24. September 19 19.

B e s c h e i n i g u n g .
= = = = = = = = = = = = = = =

Wir bestätigen hierdurch dem Monteur Ernst B u h l ,dass er vom 6. August bis 22. September 1919 im Auftrage der Bayrischen Motorenwerke hier tätig gewesen ist.

Seine Aufgabe war das Einregulieren der B.M.W. Motoren für den in Holland zur Verwendung gelangenden Brennstoffe, und hat er diese Aufgabe zu unserer Zufriedenheit gelöst.

N.V. Nederlandsche
Vliegtuigenfabriek „FOKKER"

Fokker letter. PHOTO/EBC

Selected Sources

Associated Press. "Yuri Gagarin Killed As Test Plane Falls." *New York Times*, March 28, 1968, sec. Obituaries.

BMWDrives. "BMW History in Detail." www.bmwdrives.com/ (corporate website)

Buck, Olga. "Eddington's Buehl Airfield Home to Oldtime Flying Dutchman." *Bucks County Sunday Press*. Dec. 13, 1953.

Decker, Horst. "List of 817 German pilots before the outbreak of war in 1914." autoveteranen.de.

Department of Commerce. "Application for Mechanic's License." Department of Commerce, Aeronautics Branch, February 26, 1927.

Dierikx, Marc. *Anthony Fokker: The Flying Dutchman Who Shaped American Aviation*. Smithsonian Books, 2018.

Duryea, James Frank. Engine and carburetor. United States US605815A. Springfield, Massachusetts, filed June 14, 1897, and issued June 14, 1898.

G-2 United States Army. American Expeditionary Forces. General Staff. *Histories of Two Hundred and Fifty-One Divisions of the German Army Which Participated in the War (1914-1918)*. Washington : G.P.O., 1920.

"Gewerbe Berein Konstanz," October 31, 1914. (certificate affirming completion of apprenticeship and advancement to journeyman.)

Glines, C. V. "Fokker." *Aviation History* 9, no. 1 (September 1998): 38.

Graf, Adolf. "Zeugnis-Graf," November 21, 1914.

Grand Forks Herald. "Aviators Guests of Club; Served in War in Opposing Armies." March 23, 1921.

Gregg, Spencer. "Aircraft to Order." *Popular Aviation*, May 1940. Flying Magazine.

Jacobs, A. J. *The New Domestic Automakers in the United States and Canada: History, Impacts, and Prospects*. Lexington Books, 2015.

"Karpathenkorps." In *Wikipedia*, September 6, 2014. http://de.wikipedia.org/w/index.php?title=Karpathenkorps&oldid=122730599. Buehl's presence in Bukovina is noted in his personal military documents, but other places he may have been stationed are not listed. The question arises, where else was Buehl fighting when he was a soldier. It has been impossible to find American sources that track movements of the Bavarians in Eastern Europe, leaving this reference in the German Wikipedia, as the only available source. This is not a key question in Buehl's story, but its answer fills what would be a gap in the story.

Kriegstammrollen 1914-1918, 11804, n.d. http://www.gda.bayern.de/.

Kriegstammrollen, 1914-1918, 12266, n.d. http://www.gda.bayern.de/.

Lewin, Tony. *The BMW Century: The Ultimate Performance Machines*. Motorbooks, 2016.

Lonergan, Aidan. "Alcock and Brown: Seven Facts about the World's First Transatlantic Flight That Landed in Galway in 1919." *The Irish Post*. June 16, 2019.

Maksel, Rebecca. "Who Holds the Altitude Record for an Airplane?" *Smithsonian Magazine*, May 28, 2009.

"*Militär-Paß* (Green Cover)," 1916 to 1919.

"*Militär-Paß* (White Cover)," 1916.

Mulder, Rob J.M. *E.L.T.A.: The First*

Aviation Exhibition Amsterdam-1919. Spikkestad: European Airlines Rob Mulder, 2009.

National Aviation Hall of Fame. "Fokker, Anthony Innovator/Industrialist," 1980.

Rapp Motorenwerke. "Zeugnis-Rapp," March 24, 1916.

The Globe and Rutgers Fire Insurance Company against John M. Larsen. Vol. 5929. Supreme Court of New York, Appellate Division-First Department, 1924.

Weezepoel, Paul van. "Fokker Scourge: In Which It Is Shown How Fokker Invented the Synchronized Machine Gun." Dutch Aviation. (web page)

Weyl, A. R. *Fokker: The Creative Years.* Reprint edition. London: Putnam, 1987.

Wilford, John Noble. "Neil Armstrong, First Man on Moon, Dies at 82." *The New York Times,* August 25, 2012, sec. Space & Cosmos.

Young, James. "Mach Buster | General Chuck Yeager." General Chuck Yeager | the Official Website.

Zino, Ken. "Milestones: 90th Anniversary of a BMW Powered Flight That Set an Unofficial Altitude Record: Flying at 32,000 Feet Is Quite an Achievement for 1919. Still Is." *The Detroit Bureau,* June 29, 2009.

CHAPTER 3

The Larsen Years

Coming to the United States

Buehl was brought to the United States by John M. Larsen, a man who was a significant player in US aviation from 1920 until 1922. For the next few years, Buehl's story intertwines tightly with Larsen's. To tell Buehl's biography, it is necessary to talk about Larsen.

The other person important here is Hugo Junkers. Although there was no direct relationship of Buehl with Junkers, it is important to set the work of Junkers into perspective in order to understand the importance of what Buehl was doing in the United States.

John M. Larsen

John Miller Larsen, born in Denmark, moved to the US in 1893. From modest beginnings, he opened a creamery business in Wisconsin. The demands for refrigeration began to occupy his interest, so he moved into manufacturing. Although not formally trained, his engineering skills were very good and he was soon selling his refrigeration equipment internationally. Over time, he also developed

Buehl and Larsen, smiling as they stand in front of a shiny new JL-6, the enterprise full of promise and just getting underway. PHOTO/EBC

patents for preserving food. He made a lot of money.

On the side, he developed an interest in automobiles, and then airplanes. In May 1919, Larsen was working with Curtiss, selling airplanes in Europe. While demonstrating a Curtiss "flying boat," Larsen had his first look at a new airplane made by Junkers, the F-13. As soon as he saw the F-13 he lost all interest in Curtiss.

Larsen quickly traveled to Dessau to meet with Hugo Junkers to discuss selling the F-13 in North America.

Hugo Junkers

Highly intelligent, deeply creative, and formally trained, Junkers was capable and visionary. Unlike many informally trained aircraft designers of the day, such as Fokker, Junkers did not have to depend on seat-of-the-pants knowledge as he worked at the leading edge of technology.

Hugo Junkers developed the concepts behind the F-13 during the War with the awareness that no matter who won, military orders would drop to nothing after the end of the conflict. The major obstacle to staying in business was that there was no civilian market for airplanes. Junkers set about to remedy that fact.

From the start, his vision for the F-13 was to create a civilian airliner. Actual production of the F-13 did not begin until after the War. As a civilian aircraft, it was not covered under the Treaty of Versailles.

Because the future of aviation was so clearly embodied in the design of the F-13, many people were interested in this advanced aircraft, but as much as Junkers wanted to sell his airplane globally, he struggled to find people who had sufficient capital to be seriously considered as dealers. Larsen actually had the financial strength to be taken seriously. He signed a sales agreement with Junkers in 1919 in which he agreed to import unassembled F-13 airplanes from Germany, put them together in the US, and then sell them throughout North America,

The JL-6: The Reason Buehl Came to the United States

The story of the JL-6 is central to the story of Buehl. To this day, it remains a controversial aircraft, though, so it is necessary to discuss it at some length.

When first looking for information about the JL-6, the comments found were universally negative. Visiting the Postal Museum in Washington DC, for example, no display featured the JL-6, only a terse comment in a display of DeHavilland aircraft stating that the early choice to use the JL-6 to carry air mail had been "a big mistake."*

Before launching this discussion, it is important to understand that the F-13 and JL-6 are so similar that people often use the names interchangeably when talking about the aircraft. One might find photographs in which the airplane in the US or Canada is labeled an F-13, but Junkers did not directly sell F-13s on this continent. These planes were brought to the market in North America by Larsen as JL-6 aircraft. In this book, the name F-13 is used when the discussion focuses on Europe and Junkers, but in American contexts this book refers to the airplane as a JL-6.

The Distinctive JL-6

Junkers' inspiration behind the F-13/JL-6 is easily understood. He imagined a future in which many civilian transportation needs would routinely be served by air. Of course, from the moment people first saw airplanes in flight, they could imagine the benefits of rapid, continent-hopping travel, but it was obvious to everyone that the airplanes they saw were nothing like what would be needed. The first planes were designed only for the hardiest and most adventurous travelers,

---

* Beyond the generally low opinion of the JL-6, there is a practical reason why there is no example of a JL-6 on display in Washington, DC. The problem is that the aluminum alloy used to manufacture the airplane slowly deteriorated simply with exposure to air.

and they were dangerous.

Junkers understood before anyone else realized it that passengers would not be willing to endure the discomforts of flying in an open cockpit aircraft designed for military use. Civilians would want to be out of the wind and cold and isolated from the noise of flying. They would demand a comfortable enclosed cabin, and they would need reliable, sturdy, and safe vehicles. Finally, the aircraft would have to be economical to operate and have good range before commercial services could flourish. With these things in mind, the Junkers F-13 was the first airplane designed from the start as a passenger airliner.

Three major features immediately struck people about the JL-6:

+ At a time when most airplanes could only seat the pilot and one or two passengers, the JL-6 could accommodate a crew of two, plus four passengers, as well as their luggage. It was described as "mammoth" in size.
+ It was a monoplane but did not rely on a web of wires and cables to brace the wings.
+ It was made entirely of metal, which was unheard of in any other production aircraft at the time.

Among the most striking features were the wings. The low-positioned wings of the JL-6 were powerfully cantilevered from the body and were entirely made of metal. Given this design, they were effectively one unit that spread itself on either side of the body. The wing was so strong, it was said, that 85 men at once could stand on it without causing any damage.

A key feature that Junkers designed into the aircraft was that it was comfortable and well-appointed. The interior was remarkably comfortable, according to passengers who rode in it. The upholstery and furnishings in the cabin were uniformly compared to those found in the most deluxe limousine automobiles of the 1920s. None of these appointments had been available to airplane passengers before.

In the tradition of the original limousine automobile, in which the chauffeur sat outside the covered passenger compartment, the area occupied by the crew was not as protected as that for the passengers. The crew shimmied in and out of the JL-6 through the open cockpit while the passengers used the door to the cabin. There was nothing to cover the cockpit opening during flight, so the crew was exposed to the cold, the wind, the precipitation, and whatever the engine might be spitting out while they were flying.

One of the most distinctive features of the F-13/JL-6 was its corrugated metal skin made of an aluminum alloy. Junkers first used aluminum in 1916, well before anyone else understood how to use aluminum in production aircraft. Aluminum was still considered in those days to be a new material for any purpose. Although it is the third most common element on Earth, it was exceptionally difficult to extract from its main ore, bauxite, and only became available in commercial quantities after 1886. By 1916, aluminum was a high-tech material, requiring significant expertise to use.

Replacing the wood and fabric of a conventional airplane with all-metal construction meant that the JL-6 was not only strong but, it was thought, "fireproof." Eddie Rickenbacker, America's top ace during World War One, endorsed the JL-6 for its safety, mentioning this exact reason. He is quoted in the *Salt Lake City Tribune* as saying: "This monoplane is about what the people have been waiting for. The dangers attendant on riding on a plane of any kind have kept people away from it. They are waiting for something safe. This machine is fireproof and seems to be proof against most everything."

Anti-German Attitudes and the Reception of the JL-6 in the US

For the enterprise to be successful, Larsen had to sell the machines in a hostile market. The issue of anti-German prejudice was significant in the US even before World War I. Following the War, there were many hard feelings against Germans. It would take decades for these feelings to subside, but Larsen wanted to bring German aircraft and personnel to the US only a little more than 400 days after the end of the War.

Larsen needed a way to make the airplane he wanted to sell seem less German. This became an issue when he was selecting team members who could demonstrate the capabilities of the JL-6. On the one hand, he needed a team of top experts, but on the other hand, he needed to consider their links to Germany. The pilot who demonstrated what the airplane could do would be the team member who was most visible to the public. In the end, for Larsen's lead pilot, being German created impossible problems.

To identify the experts he needed, Larsen turned to Junkers for recommendations. In 1919, when Larsen went to Dessau to negotiate with Junkers about selling the F-13 in the United States, he would need an experienced pilot but would have to balance skills and politics.

Larsen considered two pilots. His first choice was Hugo G. Schafer, a German pilot with an English-sounding name who spoke fluent English. The second was Emil Monz. There were many problems with Monz, but tragically, Schafer died in a crash on 3 February 1920.

Larsen hired Monz, but knowing the harsh prejudice Monz would face as a German, Larsen insisted that he must never indicate that he was a pilot. Instead, he should present himself as an engineer. He was to say that his role was to be a manufacturing consultant, and he was to declare that he intended to become an American citizen.

Larsen tried to prepare Monz, even giving him detailed guidance on how to avoid negative attention, but it seemed Monz was incapable of taking Larsen's advice. Adding to the many problems, Monz blabbed to passengers on the ship that brought him to New York on 4 March 1920 that he had participated in the bombing of London during the War. By the time Monz arrived at the pier in New York he was already notorious.

In addition to Monz, Larsen's choices for the technical team included Charles Kirkham as his chief engineer. Kirkham was very well-known as an engine designer. He is known to this day as the lead designer of the popular ox-5 engine.[†] Also, he had no German ties, so he was a safe choice. Buehl, as the chief mechanic, worked out of the spotlight, so his na-

Emil Monz, standing by the door of a JL-6. Buehl is in the cockpit. PHOTO/EBC

tionality was little problem. Even so, Larsen took steps to conceal Buehl's origin. In early stories in the press, Buehl's name was released as "Wallie Bugh."

First Test Flight in the US

The result of the first test flight in the US set up the reason why Larsen hired Buehl. The first F-13 from Junkers was shipped to Larsen on 29 December 1919. It arrived in February 1920. Fitted with a 160-horsepower Mercedes engine, the airplane was received by Americans with a mixture of admiration and open resentment. *The New York Tribune*, 27 March 1920, presents the front page headline, "First German Plane Flown Here Crashes: new commercial machine driven by enemy pilot smashed in fall as Allied mechanics refuse help."

The "enemy pilot" was Emil Monz. Because he was German, his presence stimulated undisguised hostility among the mechanics who

---

† In 2023, there is an active ox-5 club that was established in 1955. It is dedicated to preserving the legacy of aviation pioneers. Buehl was member number 17. Buehl's granddaughter, Rosanna, is member number 23130.

worked at Roosevelt Field, near Mineola on Long Island. The fact that a large packing case with "Germany" stenciled on the side had arrived at Roosevelt Field about a week earlier did nothing to help the Americans at the field to relax.

On the day of the test flight, only 23 days after Monz arrived in the United States, he rolled the F-13 out of the hanger and, using the plane's self-starter, started the engine himself. He took off, quickly got up to 1,000 feet, and circled the field at 110 miles per hour, which was considered to be "a remarkable achievement for so low-powered an engine." It was observed that he had a little engine trouble during the flight. He landed perfectly but got stuck in some mud. The mechanics at the field refused to help him. He got himself out of the mud and took off again. This time, he only got up to about 100 feet when the engine failed. He crashed, damaging the aircraft, but was himself uninjured. Neither Monz nor Kirkham, Larsen's chief engineer, could work out the problems with the engine used for this first flight.

Recruiting Buehl

When Larsen communicated to Junkers the trouble he had experienced in the first US test flight, Junkers arranged for a German mechanic who would work with Larsen. Recalling the way BMW recommended Buehl to Fokker when he was having trouble with his German engines, Junkers contacted BMW, which agreed to send Buehl.

Buehl's part in Larsen's business was to do the mechanical work to make the engines operate in the United States. It was obvious that the German engines would require some modification and expert tuning to operate on US fuel. Just as Buehl had helped Fokker make his engines run on Dutch fuel, he would do something similar for Larsen in the US. Buehl never actually piloted airplanes for Larsen.

In April 1920, Larsen, Kirkham, and Monz traveled to Junkers headquarters in Dessau, Germany, to meet with Buehl. Everything was worked out before Larsen traveled to Germany. Even Buehl's salary was negotiated in advance by a telegram from Larsen to BMW. Also part of the deal, when the arrangements were settled with Larsen, Buehl terminated his employment with BMW as of 14 April 1920. Though they met at the Junkers factory in Dessau in early April 1920, Buehl was never an employee of Junkers.

Larsen and Kirkham returned to the US separately, but Monz and Buehl sailed together from Germany to New York, entering the US on 13 May 1920. When he boarded the ship in Germany, Buehl officially declared that he planned to stay in the United States for only about six months, he was not going to be meeting any friends or family, and he did not intend to become a US citizen.

When Buehl arrived in the US, he stepped into a world of anti-German prejudice. He was hired because he could make the German-made engines that powered the aircraft work, but for the enterprise to be successful, they had to sell the machines in a hostile market. Larsen needed to demonstrate the JL-6, so he needed a team to make the airplane itself to work. Larsen also needed to rebrand the JL-6, to make it seem less German.

Need for Good Publicity

While manufacturing plans were being made, good publicity was paramount. By June, Larsen had involved American ace pilot, Eddie Rickenbacker. His approval was a good way to make the product seem more acceptable to Americans. In 1920, Rickenbacker was America's most famous aviator and one of the two great American heroes to emerge from the War (the other being Sergeant Alvin York).

Larsen then quickly launched a series of demonstrations. To dilute the prejudice against Monz, Larsen hired American Bert Acosta, one of the best pilots of his time. A rivalry immediately emerged between these two outstanding pilots. Beginning in May 1920, they were making record-setting flights, for speed, economy, and performance at high altitude.

On 31 May 1920, a little more than two weeks after he arrived in the United States, Buehl was whisked off to Washington D.C. to help show the JL-6 to the US Army Air Service, the US Navy, and the US Post Office. The price per plane (new) was about $30,000 each. Buehl did not pilot any of these demonstrations. His major role, as usual, was working behind the scenes to make sure the engines worked.

Buehl spinning the prop on a JL-6. The JL-6 had a starter, but this procedure was necessary to draw fuel into the cylinders. PHOTO/EBC

Total Sales of JL-6s

In all, Larsen made no more than 23 sales of JL-6 aircraft: eight to the US Air Mail Service; four to the US Navy; three to the US Army Air Service; two to Mercury Aviation; two to Imperial Oil in Canada; two to the Mexican government; two to Roald Amundsen (actually, these were not sold but donated to Amundsen, and in any case were used aircraft); and one Larsen received was converted to the armored JL-12 attack plane, which did not sell.

Airmail

During his lifetime, people often would say that Buehl had been an early airmail pilot. It was not exactly true, but an early airmail flight was the first of Buehl's great adventures. This was not just another airmail flight; it was the first one to cross the continent.

Although he had learned to fly five or six years earlier, he had little experience as a pilot. The airmail flight was the first time Buehl spent significant amounts of time in the cockpit. Sitting in the co-pilot's chair, he informally learned a lot about cross-country flying from Bert Acosta.

The Purpose

Creating airmail delivery meant solving any number of problems, only some of which had to do with selecting what airplane to fly. How, for instance, could one find one's way from point to point over long, poorly-mapped distances and under all kinds of conditions? Where

FLIERS OFF TO PACIFIC COAST—Carrying eighteen persons, three Larsen all-metal monoplanes left Central Park, Long Island, yesterday for San Francisco. The planes carry one hundred pieces of mail for the Post Office Department and will make seven stops. In the group are: John M. Larsen, designer; Gould Dietz, Omaha, Neb.; E. E. Allyne, Cleveland; Major L. B. Lent, superintendent Air Mail Service; William B. Stout, Detroit; Captain Eddie Rickenbacker, Lieutenant Charles R. Colt, John Bookhorst, Ernest Bull and pilots Captain H. E. Hartney, Emil Mons and Bert Acosta. (© International.)

Individuals participating in the airmail flight, just before take-off from New York. Buehl is standing in front, on the left. PHOTO/EBC

could one land? How could an airplane be protected while on the ground? How could an airmail plane be serviced? In large areas of the country in 1920, when Buehl flew the first transcontinental airmail delivery, none of these questions had been answered.

Although a bag of mail from New York was delivered to San Francisco at the end of Buehl's flight, this was not an official airmail delivery run. Official transcontinental airmail service was not scheduled to begin until 7 September 1920. The mission of this flight was primarily to survey the route as a whole. As Major L. B. Lent, who flew along as the US General Superintendent of the Aerial Mail Service, explained:

> This is a reconnaissance trip to make a general survey of the transcontinental air mail route. [...] The present trip is to make final arrangements for the preparation of the airdromes, selection of intermediate landing fields, and emergency stations with their emergency "gas" and oil equipment; and to gather all permanent data which may enable the mail to be flown safely and expeditiously over this route. The trip will be made in JL-6 all-metal monoplanes, which will be later used in considerable numbers in the transcontinental mail service.[...] We are taking mapping and 'movie' cameras to get real pictures of landing fields, difficult mountain passes, and all other information which may assist in the expeditious transmission of mail. Recording barographs and other instruments also are being taken with the idea of getting all available data which might be useful in daily air service. [...]
>
> The JL-6 in which I will fly, will carry mail from the Atlantic to the Pacific Coast, which will therefore make it the first transcontinental air mail trip ever flown across the United States.

Every leg of the route had been flown before, but never with the idea that each location would have to sustain heavy air traffic. The entire western part of the path had never been flown as an airmail route, so it required particular attention. As it turned out, more than one airport at which the expedition landed proved unsuitable.

Two other purposes were served beyond that of the Post Office. *First*, the US Army Air Service was interested in cooperating with the Post Office. The Army would fly one of their JL-6s across the country at the same time as the airmail flight, then leave it on the coast to be used for forest fire patrol near San Francisco. They would gain experience in long-distance flying using the JL-6. In addition, the Army was very active in promoting the New York to San Francisco route. *Second*, Hollywood producer, Cecil B. DeMille, also owned one of the world's first passenger airlines, Mercury Aviation. DeMille planned to use a small fleet of JL-6 aircraft to establish regularly scheduled flights to multiple destinations. He ordered one and it was this airplane that actually carried the mailbag to San Francisco before the the plane was delivered to DeMille in Los Angeles.

One of the participants, E. E. Allyne, notes that it was a record-setting event in another way. This was the first round-trip transcontinental passenger flight.

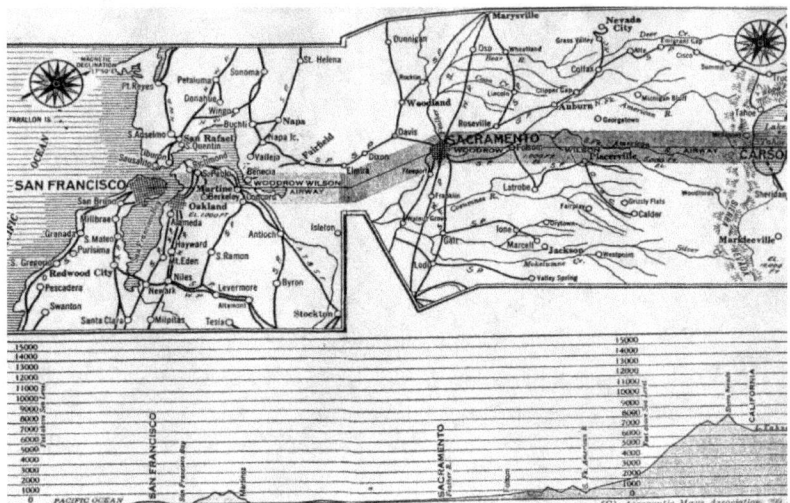

Map of the final stage of the Woodrow Wilson Airway. PHOTO/EBC

Another important accomplishment that only made page twelve news was the fact that when the Larsen flotilla completed its mission, the end-to-end survey of the Woodrow Wilson Airway was finally complete. The airway, started in 1917, laid out an 80-mile-wide passage between New York and San Francisco that was selected in late March 1920 to serve as the backbone for coast-to-coast airmail.

Who Went—Key Personnel

The key participants and their assignments remained stable for most of the expedition. The first two days involved some variations, and at different times several people joined and left the flight, but this list provides a picture of the major participants:

Plane 1

+ Bert Acosta, pilot
+ Ernie Buehl, mechanic and copilot
+ Eddie Rickenbacker, passenger
+ Edmund E. Allyne, President, Aluminum Castings Company of Cleveland, passenger
+ John M. Larsen, manufacturer of the JL-6, passenger

Plane 2—the "camera plane"

+ Samuel Custer Eaton, jr., pilot
+ Harry S. Myhres, mechanic and copilot
+ Leon B. Lent, General Superintendent of the Aerial Mail Service, passenger
+ John A. Brockhorst, representative of the International News Service, passenger

Plane 3 - the Army plane (crashed at Omaha)

+ Capt. Harold E. Hartney, pilot
+ Lt. Charles Colt, copilot

Safety Issues

Although safety issues arose associated with the JL-6, these were not directly related to Buehl's story. One has to ask if a discussion of them belongs in this book. However, so many instances of JL-6s catching fire in midair created a scandal that echos to this day. Because he worked with Larsen, Buehl gets associated with scandal.

Engine fires caused JL-6 aircraft to crash almost from the moment they were put into service. On 12 May 1920, a fiery crash killed the JL-6 crew of two men. On 31 August, another JL-6 went down in flames, but the crew members survived. On 1 September, two pilots were killed, and then on 14 September two more died. In mid-September 1920, the Air Mail Service grounded all JL-6 aircraft until the cause of the engine fires could be determined and corrected.

Obviously, despite the claims that had been made, the all-metal construction of the JL-6 did not guarantee safety from fires. Although the JL-6 was made of fireproof metal instead of fabric, it was soon discovered that an engine fire could cause the aluminum plate separating

Buehl's Position

Although Buehl's position is listed here as "co-pilot," in 1920 people did not refer to the second man in the cockpit as the "co-pilot." His job title was "mechanic." Because either "co-pilot" or "mechanic" might be misleading, each having different implications now versus the way the terms were used then, one simply has to choose one term and then explain what is meant. "Co-pilot" is used in this book because Buehl's major duty when flying was to monitor the mechanical performance of the airplane, which is much of what a co-pilot does today. Although he sometimes would take the controls while they were airborne, he never took-off or landed the airplane. In response to a direct question relevant to this point, in 1926 Buehl said, "I have never been called a pilot." At the time, he identified himself as a mechanic.

the engine from the cockpit to quickly melt, allowing a gasoline-fueled inferno to enter the cockpit.

There was, and still is, a lot of speculation about why the JL-6 caught fire. One explanation claimed that the engine overheated when using benzol for fuel. A second explanation had it that rubber tubing in the fuel system was incompatible with the use of benzol as fuel. It would corrode and then leak. A final explanation blamed a modification made to the fuel system by Larsen and his chief engineer, Charles B. Kirkham.

Who Knew About It?

Thinking about the fires plaguing the JL-6, it becomes obvious to ask who was responsible. There was the possibility that Larsen and Kirkham were introducing modifications to the F-13 that they knew were defective and then callously ignoring the problems. After all, the Junkers F-13s in Germany were not having this problem. In fact, this was the charge bitterly made by Hugo Junkers: the problem was that Larsen introduced unauthorized modifications that caused the fires.

Rickenbacker knew enough to be worried. Buehl said he and Rickenbacker, a former mechanic, often visited about the BMW engine but they never spoke openly about his concerns. However, Rickenbacker frequently hinted about his anxiety in relation to the design of the fuel system. According to Buehl, Rickenbacker could easily see that the fuel line had to run two feet between the gas pump and the carburetor and that the connections were hard-soldered. He knew this was a problem waiting to happen.

Years after the trip, Buehl read Rickenbacker's autobiography. Naturally, Buehl was interested to read what Rickenbacker had written about their transcontinental trip. It struck him that in the book, Rickenbacker discussed the weakness in the fuel line. In his book, Rickenbacker indicates that he became aware of the problem only after he learned of the first mid-air fire of a JL-6, which occurred days after he and Larsen completed their transcontinental flight. Until then, he had been assuring everyone that the JL-6 was "fireproof." In his book, he correctly blamed the rigid fuel line, which would "break under pressure and vibration." Fuel then spilled into the engine compartment, and the engine, "starved of fuel, would backfire, which would, in turn, ignite the spilled gasoline." Concluding his discussion of the issue, Rickenbacker wrote, "I will never understand how we completed our trip without burning up."

The truth is that everyone on the transcontinental flight was aware of the hazards. Addressing a meeting of the Experimental Aircraft Association in 1986, Buehl shared that on the 1920 transcontinental flight, everyone in his plane clearly knew of the risks well before mid-air fires were downing the Post Office planes. Rickenbacker, Larsen, and Allyne were nervous about it the whole trip. Buehl said that they were constantly in a state of tension, "waiting for it." As Buehl commented, "that was not a healthy way to fly."

Illustrating his point, Buehl told of how during the trip, while flying over a mountain range, Acosta adjusted the carburetor to accommodate the higher altitude but did not operate the controls smoothly. The correct procedure at about 15,000 feet was to push in the adjustment lever until the "engine sneezes" and then back off a bit. In this case, Acosta operated the control too quickly and it caused the engine to sputter. Everyone in the passenger cabin panicked.

Reviewing the hypotheses one by one:

The hypothesis that the use of benzol caused the problems was not true. Everyone on the transcontinental flight was aware of what some might call the "benzol problem," but it was really a gasoline problem. Failure at take-off occurred because pilots were not correctly adjusting the fuel to the engine. More than one crash or near-crash occurred when a pilot attempted to take off using gasoline instead of benzol. During this trip alone, participants observed as H.E. Hartney, who in 1920 was one of the military's best pilots, lost two airplanes in quick succession because of this error.

It also happened to S.C. Eaton, an experienced aviator who was employed directly by Larsen. On 13 August, Allyne's log recorded that Eaton was barely able to clear the telegraph wires at the end of the airfield at Tucson because the engine "was heating badly [...] Plane would not rise further and motor spurts hot water in the faces of the pilots. We fly at this level for three or four minutes when motor quits." The problem started, Allyne records, when Eaton "erred in turning the wrong fuel valve, using gasoline when he intended to use benzol."

Why was benzol used in the first place? The answer was that these were high-compression engines designed to operate on synthetic German fuel. It was impossible to operate them at full power when using unmixed gasoline as the fuel. The US Army Air Service studied this issue closely and concluded that "A mixture of one-half petrol and one-half benzol gives the best engine results." Experience showed that the engines could cruise well using unmixed gasoline and really only needed benzol for take-offs.

The somewhat more complex procedure associated with take-off in a JL-6 led pilots to get mixed up and make mistakes. This would be a true example of Murphy's Law: "If there's any way they can do it wrong, they will." Kirkham and Larsen finally made this fuel mixture error impossible by replacing the high-compression pistons in the BMW engines with low-compression pistons. Using low-compression pistons, the engines could operate with ordinary gasoline.

The hypothesis related to the use of rubber tubing was wrong. The fuel system of the early JL-6 was made entirely of metal tubing. On the airmail flight, Buehl knew that the fuel line vibration was an issue. Vibration embrittles copper, and the normal vibration of the engine was enough to do this. Therefore, for every twelve hours of engine time, Buehl drained the fuel line and heated it with a blow torch to anneal it — to remove accumulated stresses in the metal. Nobody knew he was doing this, but he said he was just doing it as "a good practice." Later in the trip, following some difficulty with the fuel pump that they experienced in New Mexico, Buehl purchased a bit of rubber tubing and quietly replaced most of the copper line between the fuel pump and carburetor. Buehl said he made the modification but "didn't tell nobody nothing."

The problem identified with the fuel delivery system was solved by the use of rubber tubing, not created by it. The modification Buehl made to the fuel line was later endorsed in official recommendations from U.S.A.A.S. testing at McCook Field. Their report stated, "Breakage of gas lines was prevented by the installation of flexible hose connections."

It was true that Larsen and Kirkham made modifications to the fuel lines. Indeed, thinking it would improve safety, Larsen ordered significant changes to the fuel system. Carlos Warner, Larsen's superintendent, stated that "an entire new gas system was fitted." Testifying in court, Larsen referred to photos while he explained what he had done:

The fuel tanks are located inside the wing here and on the other side. There was piping to the tank and from the tank, a double set of piping. That piping through vibration crystalized and broke and it would cause a back-fire, spark, or a fire and it would be finished. We got up a system where we would have just one pipe to the tank and no return pipes at all. [We] Made the piping very short and the piping extremely good.

Once modifications were made to the JL-6, replacing metal tubing with rubber, it recovered a good reputation among people who knew it. For example, Eddie Stinson, a celebrity aviator who later developed his own airplane manufacturing company, purchased four of the aircraft from the US Airmail Service in February 1922, and in June of that year, he even hired Eddie Rickenbacker to ride along on a three-month national tour demonstration flight.

The decision to drop the JL-6 was not due to the fires experienced early in their use. Once the problems were worked out, the JL-6 was again seen as a superior choice. In fact, among the buyers of the unused fleet of JL-6s were the pilots and engineers most familiar with the issues, including Lent, Kirkham, and Hartney.

It was the problem of supply from Germany that made it impossible for the Post Office to use them. After mid-October 1920, it was impossible to get new ones in the US.

Canada

B uehl helped to open the routes into Canada nearly to the Arctic Circle. Arriving in Canada in January 1921, working conditions were terrible. Buehl was among the first few aviators who had to work out solutions to the challenges of making airplanes work in the far north.

HEADING   NORTH

EDMONTON, CANADA.   MARCH 1921.

JL-6 taking off for Edmonton. PHOTO/EBC

One begins to get a hint of the impact of what he was involved in by noting the importance of mining to the Canadian economy, and particularly the significance of the export of mineral fuels to the United States.

In 1920, worldwide, three major new oil fields were discovered: one in Columbia, South America; one in Wyoming; and one in the Canadian far north. The Canadian discovery has continuing economic importance to this day. In 2021, the value of the crude oil alone that Canada exported to the United States was nearly $80 billion (US dollars). This does not include natural gas and oils obtained from bituminous minerals, which would add another $24 billion.

By the time Buehl was working in Canada in 1921, there was a considerable incentive to develop the resource. There was a growing worldwide demand for gasoline, with the price shooting up 600 percent in just a few years.

The presence of oil in northern Canada had been generally known since the eighteenth century. In 1789, explorer Alexander Mackenzie reported natural gas was discharging in one location at a rate of ten

Even today, aviation is of vital importance to villages in the far north. In the early 21st century, Buehl's granddaughter, Rosanna, traveled widely in the subarctic and arctic to work in both winter and summer, and the only practical way to get around was to fly. (Four passengers are preparing to load. Rosanna is second in line. PHOTO/AUTHOR

million cubic feet per day. The value of this wasted gas was estimated in 1921 to be worth three million dollars per year.

The challenge of developing this region was daunting. Getting a geologist into this far north region was difficult. Also, given the amount of area to explore, it was hard to know the extent of the oil deposits. The area around Fort Norman, where oil was just naturally seeping out of the ground, was an obvious place to start looking. Most deliberate exploration and drilling in the region, though, did not produce much except disappointment.

The importance of aviation to opening this region is noted in an article in the *New York Herald*. The author of the article says: "The hard factor is the problem of the enormous distances to be traversed. Fort Norman is 1,500 miles from the outskirts of settlements." In 1920, under the best of circumstances, it would take three months to travel into and out of the area around Fort Norman. In 1921, using airplanes, it was possible to make the trip in and out in six days. Opening the region by airplane and ocean-going boat was noted to be crucial in order to explore the resources there.

The Discovery Well

In May 1920, geologist Theodore A. Link and his driller, A.W. Patrick, left Edmonton, headed for Fort Norman, a hamlet located at about 65° N, 125 ½° W. The "Discovery Well" was just north of Fort Norman, at about 65 ¼° north. They took the railroad to Peace River and from there had to travel by water 1,600 miles to their destination. Carrying drilling equipment, including well casings, along with all of their camp equipment, food, and supplies, travel was challenging. Overland, they tried to use Caterpillar-type tractors to move equipment, but they did not work because the ground was too soft. Draft horses were the only option for moving large equipment.*

---

* Since 1996 its name was officially changed; now it is listed as Tulita. In this book, though,

Suitability of the JL-6

When one understands the difficulty of even accessing the site, one immediately sees why airplanes were needed. It was not only a matter of the distance involved.

Several challenges related to geography might not be obvious to those who have not traveled in this region. Subarctic regions such as this are generally more easily traveled during the winter because the land is firm, whereas during the summer, the surface thaws and is mushy. Overland travel in the summer is difficult or even impossible.

Structure from the Discovery Well, looking out over the Mackenzie River. PHOTO/EBC

Locating near water was noted to be an advantage during the summer because the aircraft could be fitted with pontoons as landing gear. Hopping from one area of open water to another makes summer travel possible.

The JL-6 was designed so that the airplane could have its landing gear easily refitted. It was a simple operation to replace the wheels with skis or with pontoons. In the winter, being near a frozen river is an advantage. A long-enough stretch of frozen water provides a safe landing space, one where the landing gear is not going to get caught in underbrush.

In seasonal transition times when ice is thin, the sturdy all-metal design of the JL-6 provided a particular advantage. As one Canadian authority said, when landing on thin ice of a frozen lake, "a fabric covered machine might suffer serious damage by going through the ice," but the JL-6 "would emerge almost unscathed and after drying out could be put immediately back into operation."

we use the old name, Fort Norman, because that is the name used in all of our source material.

Working Conditions

As a part of Larsen's team, Buehl flew two JL-6 aircraft to Canada and then trained local pilots and mechanics to keep them operating. While training Canadian technicians, he worked alongside them to solve the early problems of integrating the new equipment into their work environment.

JL-6 *on skis.* PHOTO/EBC

Buehl and the teams working to open the first routes into the Northwest Territories had to contend with at least three challenges that made their jobs tough. *First,* the weather could be deadly. *Second,* the distances and the remoteness of the locations they worked in added a level of risk. *Third,* it is dark for most of the hours of the day during the winter. One of the defining features of living above the Arctic Circle is that the sun does not rise at all during the winter; for 24 hours per day, one experiences the darkness of night. In the subarctic, where Buehl was working in the winter, one sees the sun for only a little while each day. One depends a lot on artificial light.

The conditions were ferocious.[†] One writer, reporting years later, got a little of the story: "Buehl described it as 'brutal work,' with the temperature often 52 below zero and the water-cooled motor covered with ice formations." Certainly, Buehl, with his military training and experience as a veteran of the Bavarian Alpenkorps, was as well prepared for this world as anyone is likely to be who was not born to it.

Buehl told an illuminating story of how they would have to manage

---

† Commenting late in his life about his work with Larsen, Buehl noted the irony that in 1920 they were flying across the Mojave Desert at the height of summer and then in 1921 they were working in the Canadian subarctic in the depth of winter.

Provisions for Larsen's trip north. Note that they have packed everything one might need in the far north, except for a radio! Basic broadcast stations serving the far north that could allow pilots simply to get accurate weather reports were a decade away from when Buehl was working in Canada. Looking at this photo, one has the impression that Larsen is trying to look tough, while Buehl is just hoping he does not look ridiculous. PHOTO/EBC

during the winter. As they were just getting operations established, there were no heated buildings to house the airplanes. The plane was out in the weather, so if they did not drain the oil, it would freeze and they would not be able to start the engine. Once the oil froze in the engine, there was not much to be done.

It was not enough just to throw a blanket over the engine when stopping for more than a couple of hours. Every night they would have to drain approximately eight gallons of oil out of the engine crankcase and (he said) "take it to bed with us" to keep it warm. The next morning they would get up and pour it back into the engine. If the oil froze anyway, Buehl and his crew would have to thaw the large can of oil near the fire inside the living quarters before they could do anything.

Remoteness was an issue all by itself. Any flight required good provisioning in case of an emergency. However, any safety equipment or emergency supplies carried would reduce the size of the payload, which further increased the expense of flying in the far north.

Access to airplane fuel was a concern from day one. Between Peace River and Fort Norman, a fuel cache was established at Hay River, necessary because the distance required the airplanes to refuel along the route. To establish fuel dumps along the route, Larsen arranged for two large motorized boats in the summer to carry gasoline and supplies north from Peace River.

Delivering the JL-6 to Canada

Buehl accompanied a team of four Canadians and two American aviators as they flew two new JL-6s to Edmonton, a large and sophisticated city where Imperial Oil had corporate offices.

The aircraft, the *René* and the *Vic*, left Mineola, New York, bound for Edmonton on 3 January 1921. At the end of the first day, they stopped at Virden, Manitoba. The next day, the *Vic* was able to take off safely and make it to Saskatoon. On 5 January, the *Vic* was delivered to Edmonton.

The *René*, though, crashed into a fence at Virden during a heavy snowstorm at the start of the second day from New York. The landing gear was damaged, so it had to be repaired before continuing. It was shipped to Brandon for repairs. It took until 24 January before the *René* could continue.

With H. S. Myhres as the pilot and Buehl the co-pilot, the *René* took off that morning. A radiator leak was discovered shortly after they took off, so they had to put down again in Saskatoon for repairs. This took until 26 January.

On 26 January, Canadian pilot, George Gorman, replaced Myhres as pilot while Buehl continued as co-pilot for the flight to Edmonton. Taking off just before noon with two passengers, they arrived in Edmonton only 155 minutes later. The record-breaking speed of the trip was so fast that it caught nearly everyone in Edmonton by surprise. There were very few people at the airfield to greet Gorman and crew upon arrival.

Through the month of February, Buehl overhauled the airplanes in Edmonton. By early March, they were ready to be tested in service.

Reaching Peace River

From Edmonton, Buehl and others took the planes to Peace River, where they were hangared only a little way from a place where Alexander Mackenzie had made his winter camp in 1793. The hangar was located at the confluence of the Peace and Smoky Rivers, on the west bank of the Smoky River.

Buehl did much of his work at Peace River, located at about 56° North and 117° West. In 1921, it had a population of 980 and was already a hub of oil field activity. There were railroad tracks to Peace River, but at that point the steel stopped. The Arctic Circle begins only about 10° north of this location [About 690 miles.].

The plan was next to fit the airplanes with skis at Peace River and then take them to Fort Vermillion and Fort Norman. Preparing for emergencies, oil and fuel would be cached "in small installments at points further north."

On 5 March 1921, at 3:00 PM, a JL-6 aircraft arrived at Imperial Oil's base at Peace River. The people of Peace River scrambled on short notice to get out to the airfield to see the planes land. Citizens placed a large, dark cross on the snow on Shaftsbury Flats, where the airplane was to land, and lit a smoky fire so that the pilots could see the direction of the wind on their approach. Mayor Grimshaw greeted the crew when they disembarked.

At least 20 Peace River school children skipped school in order to be present for this event. Many of the children volunteered to help remove the wings from one plane and push it into the hangar. The other plane was moved close to the hangar but was left outside until the next day.

Buehl and Gorman delivering the René to Imperial Oil in Edmonton. The René was delivered in record time. They made it from Saskatoon to Edmonton so quickly that the people who planned to welcome them had not yet made it to the airfield. PHOTO/EBC

The importance of the landing at Peace River was explained: "In the annals of the far North it will go down in history as the dawn of the era of actual beginning of the development of the great oil wealth."

The Broken Propeller

After returning from Canada, Buehl told a story of being stranded in the Northwest Territory following a bad landing in the snow, resulting in a broken propeller. Even when he was an old man in his late eighties, this story was in circulation as one of the most popular stories about Buehl. By that time, Buehl was no longer telling this story, but the people around him repeated it a lot, often mixing up details or unconsciously adding embellishments.

Here is how the story went, as told by others. After crashing and breaking his prop in a very isolated location near the Arctic Circle, Buehl had to make a new prop for his airplane. The story was vague on the details, though.

There were so many questions that nobody asked. From the way the story was told, one got the impression that Buehl was all alone in the middle of some snowy waste, that he had to cut down a tree to get the

CHAPTER 3: The Larsen Years · Canada   79

wood (Do suitable trees grow that far north?). There was no mention of woodworking tools (why would a mechanic carry woodworking tools?). Maybe he used his folding Buck knife to whittle a precision prop? What happened to the prop? Did anyone keep it? When Buehl was asked about the prop he always said that it was not a very good propeller so it was just thrown away when the plane got home.

Here is the story as it actually happened: On 28 March 1921, two JL-6s appeared in the sky over Fort Simpson, a village located at about 62° north, 121° west. The first of these planes, the *René*, piloted by Captain George Gorman, experienced a bad landing, nose-diving into the drifted snow, breaking the prop, wrecking the landing gear, and damaging a wing tip. The second plane, the *Vic*, piloted by Elmer Fullerton, landed safely. However, the *Vic* was having engine trouble, so they transferred the prop and landing gear from the *Vic* to the *René* and straightened the wing tip. The next morning, Gorman attempted to fly the repaired *René* out to get help, but he nose-dived on takeoff and broke this propeller, too.

That evening, the general handyman at Fort Simpson, a fellow

Man with a dog sled. PHOTO/EBC

named Walter Johnson, proposed to make a new propeller. Using some oak sleigh boards, Johnson was able to go into his shop and come out two-and-a-half weeks later with two good replicas of the original prop. Mechanic William Hill assisted Johnson.

In the meantime, the crew from the airplanes were able to repair the *Vic*'s engine. With the repairs, they were able to get the *Vic* in the air on 15 April 1921. They took about another week while getting ready to fly back to Peace River. They made it back to Peace River safely on 21 April 1921 using their homemade prop.

As it happened, Buehl, was in Peace River when the fliers from Fort Simpson landed. Buehl learned the details of the story there. Before anyone else heard about these events, Buehl absorbed the story while it was still fresh in the participant's minds. Since it was a great story, he told it many times, and eventually he became personally associated with it.

One final note: the homemade prop really was discarded after they got the *Vic* got back to Peace River. Later, as the story became more widely known in Canada and people asked about the prop, a search

Airmail Milestone

Historian Philip Godsell wrote that the event at Fort Simpson was also remarkable because it marked the first airmail to travel from the Canadian northwest to cities in the south. Official, regular airmail started in 1929. Up until then, remote outposts would get mail delivery by dog sled.

Just as Gorman was leaving Fort Simpson, Godsell handed him a letter addressed to the Winnipeg office of the Hudson Bay Company. Godsell noted that under normal circumstances, a letter from Fort Simpson would not reach Winnipeg until late August, but in this case it arrived only a few days after he had sent it.

was mounted to find it. In the end, both props that were made in
Fort Simpson were finally located in 1945. These are now housed at
Canada's National Aviation Museum.

The Slow Collapse of Larsen's Business

It would have been impossible for anyone outside Larsen's inner
circle to know how much trouble the business was in. By 1921,
Larsen was not selling any new airplanes because he had not received
any new stock from Germany since the fall of 1920. He was selling
or leasing used JL-6s and he was thinking hard of a way to stay in the
aviation business.

Larsen kept promoting the JL-6 as though he had an endless supply
to sell. One has to ask why? Lacking any practical reason to pretend
that his business was still viable, he may simply have been attached
to the romance of aviation. In the short time he had been promoting
the JL-6, he had developed enviable social connections and prestige,
and may have felt he would lose those if he went back to making re-
frigerators and working out better ways to freeze fish.

The JL-12

In a baffling attempt to see if he could salvage his business, Larsen
modified a JL-6 by filling it with as many machine guns as it could
hold. He called it the JL-12 Attack Plane, and he hoped to sell it to the
War Department. It had a 400-horsepower Liberty engine, could fly
141 miles per hour, and could cruise for 400 miles. Its purpose was to
swoop down on infantry, spray them with bullets, and then speed away.

When work started on the aircraft in the spring of 1921, as many
as ten people were working on the JL-12. By the time the JL-12 was
demonstrated, the crew at Larsen's airfield had been reduced to only

three: Buehl, superintendent Carlos Warner, and night watchman John Dinkelmeyer. This number does not include any of the pilots, who were brought in as needed, and it does not include anyone working in the downtown office. Buehl was the only machinist.

The airplane was shown several times in Washington. For the final demonstration, an officer from the War College asked to see the machine guns firing. The War College issued ammunition and agreed to ensure that no one would be in the area where they were actually going to fire the guns. During the demonstration, the JL-12 came out of the sky at high speed from 2,500 feet and then, flying at between 75 and 150 feet above the Potomac River, fired all of its down-pointing guns for about three seconds. The effect was dramatic. Encompassing an area about three or four hundred yards long and as wide as a street, the water in the river appeared to be seething and boiling, its level raised significantly.

At the conclusion of the demonstrations, there seemed to be a promise of orders to follow. It was Larsen's understanding that the Army would buy "two or three of these planes to start with." Ultimately, no orders were received. Apparently, some unfavorable opinions surfaced about the JL-12. One test pilot said the plane was "nose heavy." Another said the airplane had stability problems.

If he had received orders, one wonders how Larsen expected to fill them, given that he had no more F-13s to convert into JL-12s.

The Larsen Race in Omaha

Immediately following the demonstration of the JL-12, on 26 October 1921, Larsen and his team flew three JL-6s from Washington, D.C., to Dayton, Ohio, and from there to Kansas City, arriving on 27 October. Between Dayton and Kansas City, the JL-6s broke several records: an altitude record while overloaded with eleven passengers, a speed record while carrying seven passengers, and a record for long-distance flight. Among Larsen's passengers during these flights was Augustus Post, president of the Aero Club. Larsen bragged that by the time they reached Kansas City, the JL-6 held "every record except altitude for a single man."

From Kansas City, Larsen's team flew to Omaha to participate in a contest sponsored by the National Aero Congress to coincide with its first annual meeting. Larsen endowed the prizes. There would be a total of $6,000 in cash awarded. The owner of the winning airplane would receive from Larsen $3,000 cash and a four-and-a-half-foot-tall silver trophy with two silver figures standing on a globe, holding a gold JL-6 above their heads. The globe had an airplane propeller mounted at the equator, symbolizing "the ability of aircraft to move the earth." The second-place plane would receive $2,000, and the third-place $1,000. The competition was identified in the newspapers as "the Larsen race."

The idea of the race was to test airplanes for a combination of both speed and economy. The challenge considered speed, fuel consumption, and the load carried. Explaining his idea for the race, Larsen expressed his hopes for the future of aviation to the *Washington Times*, which reported that,

> ...we actually have in our possession planes that can carry freight or passengers as cheaply as some other modes of transportation. [Larsen] feels that once this fact is established, then the government will take care of the essentials such as landing fields and organized airways and soon regular lines will be in operation.

The course of the race took fliers from Omaha to Loveland, Iowa, then to Calhoun, Nebraska, and back to Omaha. Each airplane had to carry at least 400 pounds of dead weight and make eight trips around the course. The total distance was about 250 miles. Of the eighteen airplanes entered, three were owned by Larsen. Flying for Larsen were B.H. Pearson, Max Goodnough, and Eddie Stinson. Buehl was the mechanic for Pearson.

Pearson's plane carried six people as its load, including Larsen himself and Buehl. Guests aboard were Grace O'Brien, who was the daughter of a friend of Larsen's, John Markel, a Nebraska automobile dealer, Edward Rice, a ten-year-old aviation enthusiast, and J.T. Armstrong, a newspaperman.

Pearson's airplane was the fastest of the Larsen entries, but it was forced down near Loveland, Iowa, eleven minutes after completing the fifth lap of the race. A washer on an engine valve had come loose, but Pearson was able to land safely in a nearby farm field.

On 8 November, the scores were finally computed, and the winners were announced. The two Larsen airplanes that finished the race placed second and third. Pilot Earle F. White won the race with a score of 4,671 points. White's airplane was owned by C.B. Wrightsman, an oil tycoon from Tulsa. Larsen's pilot, Max Goodnough, scored only 31 points less. Eddie Stinson placed a distant third, with 4212 points.

Going into the race, Larsen had every reason to believe that he would sweep all of the prizes himself. After all, he had studied the possible competition and knew that the JL-6 led all other aircraft in efficiency. He had been so confident he would win that the trophy depicted a JL-6.

After the scores were tallied, Larsen grew suspicious. He investigated and very easily turned up evidence that the Wrightsman-owned airplane had secretly carried a concealed gasoline tank. Wrightsman's pilot reported only the fuel used from the amount officially carried, without adding in the amount used from the concealed tank. Larsen moved to block the contest committee from awarding the prize. The Aero Club took several months to investigate, but when they announced their judgment in August 1922, they agreed that Wrightsman had cheated and ordered him to return the prize.

No sooner had Larsen filed his complaint than Wrightsman started looking for a way to get revenge. He would do what he could to destroy Larsen.

Wrightsman

While Larsen was wealthy by ordinary standards, he was in the minor leagues compared to Wrightsman, and they both knew it. Unfortunately, Buehl got caught in the middle between these two quarreling titans.

Charles Bierer Wrightsman was the son of C.J. Wrightsman, an extremely wealthy and influential, pioneering oilman from Tulsa, Oklahoma. C.J. was described as one of the first wildcatters. Drilling in a place not known to have oil, wildcatting was a very risky business from a financial standpoint, but it had the potential to be enormously remunerative. C.J. Wrightsman was the rare wildcatter to strike it rich.

A fraud case brought against him in 1915 exposes C.J.'s harsh, unpleasant character. He was happy to add to his personal wealth by buying junk debt and then squeezing the desperate borrower for what in official documents was called "an extremely onerous interest rate." He passed along his business sense and predatory values to his son C.B. Wrightsman.

C.B. Wrightsman's story is particularly lurid. He was described in one source as an exceptionally vulgar, abusive man who cheated at polo, chiseled on his taxes, concealed vital information from investors in Standard Oil when he was president of the company, and who swindled his own father. When C.J. Wrightsman became ill and thought he was going to die, he transferred the titles to his oil wells to his son. C.B. refused to return them when his father unexpectedly recovered.

Born in 1895, as a young man he was a jet-setting playboy before jets were invented. (In a curious aside, his son-in-law, Igor Cassini, was the one who coined the term "Jet Set."). He spent quite a bit of time lounging by his swimming pool in Los Angeles and playing with Hollywood starlets. Later, C.B. was involved with the oil business, first by acquiring mineral rights in the southwest United States. Eventually, he became president of Standard Oil of Kansas.

Socially, C.B. and his family were able to use their wealth to bootstrap their way into the American aristocracy. Using the family's resources of extreme wealth, his wife cultivated her knowledge of fine arts and, over time, became a bona fide world-class expert. She maneuvered her way onto the boards of directors of prestigious arts institutions, including the Metropolitan Museum of Art. C.B. was happy with this because it gave him access to powerful, old-monied families who ordinarily would not have associated with him. In Wrightsman's obituary, *The New York Times* stated that he had amassed "one of the most important private art collections in the world."

World Record for Sustained Flight

On 7 November 1921, Larsen was named as defendant in a damage suit related to the crash of one of his airplanes in Omaha, and on 8 November, he had apparently lost the trophy in the race he had all but rigged to win. In spite of his mounting troubles, though, he kept promoting the JL-6. Through all of this, Buehl could see the business dwindling away, but he just assumed Larsen knew what he was doing and that he had a plan. All he could do was to keep working while he waited to see what Larsen was going to do.

In late December 1921, Larsen sent Eddie Stinson and Lloyd Bertaud aloft to challenge the record for sustained flight. They were able to stay in the air for 26 hours 19 minutes. This beat the previous record by more than two-and-a-half hours. It was a hard-won achievement, and it attracted a lot of positive attention. It was headline news in the *Washington Times*. After Stinson and Bertaud landed, they received a telegram from the chief of the United States Air Service, General Patrick, congratulating the two.

They certainly deserved the accolades. They had flown day and night over Hazelhurst Field, on Long Island, in terrible weather. It had been snowing hard, and visibility was limited. Much of the time, they were not able to climb above 100 feet in the air, so they had to dodge church steeples. At times, the gale-force wind was so fierce that when facing into it, they hung practically motionless. The air temperature in their open cockpit often was near or below zero degrees Fahrenheit. Neither pilot was equipped with electrically-heated clothing, and the JL-6 heating system worked only intermittently.

At 2:00 AM, a malfunction occurred in the system delivering oil to the engine. In the cold, the oil had con-gealed in the supply line. Stinson had to remove his glove in order to punch a hole in the emergency oil tank in order to draw from it to manually fill the main tank. Oil was delivered to the engine in that manner for the remaining nine hours of the flight.

Upon landing, it was discovered that four of Stinson's fingers were frozen, and both fliers were covered with oil. There is a darkly comic element to this: men want-ing to shake hands with the pilots had to be waved off for fear that they would

Stinson is clowning for the camera before his record-setting flight in December 1921. (L to R) unknown, Stinson, Buehl. PHOTO/EBC

further injure frozen fingers. Also, although excited well-wishers im-mediately surrounded them, it was a half hour before either of them could hear well enough to converse, having been temporarily deafened by the continuous roar of the engine. People offered congratulatory statements, but Stinson and Bertaud, experiencing only a ringing in their ears, heard none of them.

Once the two had recovered, they were able to tell their story. In spite of the obvious dangers, the flight was remarkable for its monotony. They did not dare sleep for fear that when they woke up they would be so chilled they would not be able to take over the airplane's controls. They ate very little because they were afraid that they might become sick, but they drank a lot of coffee. All together, they flew 2,600 miles, covering a distance that easily would have taken them across the Atlantic.

Larsen continued receiving favorable publicity, and was even listed in the 1922 *Who's Who in American Aeronautics*. However, his business had already fallen apart. A suspicious person might wonder if all of this, including the race in November, was done just to provide background cover for what was to follow in several weeks.

Buehl recognized that setting this record was a big event. It was among the events he mentioned in his application for his first mechanic's license in 1927. He was chief mechanic for the flight.

Behind the Scenes at Larsen's Business

It is shocking to learn by late 1921 just how flimsy was the nature of Larsen's business. Behind the scenes, Larsen's aeronautics business was a sham. From the beginning, he had been pretending to manufacture airplanes when in fact, he was just importing airplanes and assembling them with small modifications. The German-manufactured airplanes arrived unassembled in crates, and they were bolted together according to the instructions that came with the kit, as one does when assembling Ikea furniture. The process from unpacking to delivery might have taken three days. Some of the first airplanes were delivered to the buyers from what Larsen called his "factory" on Long Island with no modifications at all. To call this "manufacturing" was like warming a can of Campbell's soup and calling it "cooking."

The shops consisted of two larger hangars and a smaller one at Plain Edge, Long Island. They had been built largely from lumber salvaged from the shipping crates in which Junkers had packed the airplanes when they were sent from Germany. There was no machinery of the sort used in factories: no lathes, no shapers, no milling machines, no drill presses. There were only small hand tools such as files and hammers, but most of these belonged to the workmen Larsen employed.

About this time, Larsen had largely stopped paying creditors. The airfield was under lease, and he was not keeping up with payments. He was behind on rent payments on his New York City apartment, too. His landlord in the city sued for back rent and won a judgment against him for $1,405.97. By early February 1922, his combined balance at two banks was actually less than $1,700. All the evidence indicates that his indebtedness exceeded his cash resources.

The Plotting

On Wednesday, 7 February 1922, Buehl got a call from Larsen inviting Buehl to join him at his apartment in New York City at 91st Street and Riverside Drive. Buehl was on friendly terms with his boss, so everything about the invitation seemed normal. It was about 8:00 PM when Buehl knocked at Larsen's door, and the cook let him in.

Larsen and Buehl talked about general topics and the work they were doing. Soon Larsen admitted to Buehl that things were not going well. He was not able to obtain new airplanes or even parts and materials from Junkers. They talked about what would come next.

Their future together was not a new topic for them to talk about. As early as December 1921, the two of them had been visiting about new businesses Larsen was planning. Larsen planned to establish two new businesses, the Larsen Air Navigation Corporation and the J.L. Air Service Corporation.

The Air Navigation Corporation would involve a management role for Buehl as chief mechanic in Chicago, and Larsen would bring Buehl's brother Fritz from Germany to work there, too. Fritz had already done some work for Larsen to research the market value of German motors in Europe. Larsen said he had facilitated arrangements with Washington to get permission for Fritz to move to the United States.

That evening, Larsen stated that to focus his efforts on the new businesses, he needed to get rid of the aerodrome on Long Island, which he said he didn't need anymore. Then Larsen came right out and told Buehl to set fire to the hangars on Long Island. He said he would pay Buehl $1,500 to set a fire that would burn the buildings and their contents.

Larsen gave detailed instructions: use lots of gasoline and make sure it gets spread around. The floor was made of wood planks, so the gasoline would soak in. Larsen stored some of his personal property at the airfield, including an automobile, his Locomobile, at the airfield, and it was in one of the hangars. His motorized speed boat, the *Firefly*, was also in a hangar there. He told Buehl to be sure to splash some gasoline on the car and the boat. He should set up a blowtorch as though he were going to use it to do some soldering. Later, when people asked, Buehl could say that he accidentally knocked over the torch and it started the fire. It would be a good idea to save at least one airplane in order to allay suspicion. Buehl himself should stay away from the flames so he would not get hurt.

As they were discussing the plans to burn down the aerodrome, Buehl asked Larsen if he had raised his insurance coverage. Larsen

These hangars at Larsen's field were what he referred to as his "factory." PHOTO/EBC

told Buehl, "No." However, a letter to one of his insurance companies showed that Larsen did, indeed, order an increase in his insurance coverage just before the fire. The increase was confirmed by the insurance company on 3 February 1922. Larsen also replaced the automobile insurance on his Locomobile to obtain higher coverage, which was confirmed on 3 February, only four days before the fire.

While Larsen was directing Buehl to set the fire, he was also conspiring with Carlos Warner to arrange things in the background. He had already ordered Warner not to be present at the airfield on the day of the fire. Buehl was not aware of Warner's involvement.[‡] In the end, the night watchman, Dinkelmeyer, seems to have been the only one of Larsen's employees at the airfield entirely left out of the scheming.

Buehl left Larson's apartment at 11:00 PM and took the 11:30 train to Hempstead, where he was living.

The Fire

On 8 February 1922, the day after Buehl met with Larsen in New York City, fire broke out at Larsen's airfield, destroying two hangars and some aircraft. It was reported that an accident involving the use of a blowtorch started the fire, and a high wind made it impossible to extinguish before it had burned down the hangars.

Larsen had directed Buehl to light up the hangars at his first opportunity. Impatient to hear the hangars were on fire, Larsen called Buehl every 15 to 30 minutes that morning. It was necessary to speak indirectly to one another at this point. The telephone was on a party line and there might be people listening.

Larsen called, demanding to know what Buehl was doing, and each time Buehl would tell him he was engaged in some normal activity. From this, Larsen would infer that Buehl was not carrying out the plan. The first time he called, Buehl explained that Dinkelmeyer was

---

‡ Note that Warner was specifically charged in another related case.

still there, which agitated Larsen. During each subsequent call, Larsen was more and more annoyed to learn that Buehl had not yet started the fire. Each time, he pressured Buehl to "get busy" right away, but Buehl could not bring himself to light the fire.

In spite of the exhortations from Larsen, Buehl was having trouble gathering his resolve. Larsen called just before 2:00 PM, demanding to know why Buehl was not carrying out the plan. When Buehl told Larsen he did not want to do it, Larsen chided him for being silly and reiterated that he needed Buehl to do what they had talked about.

After that, Buehl proceeded by morally compartmentalizing each action leading up to setting the fire. No single action taken by itself was immoral, so he controlled his doubts. In this way, he went about setting up what he needed to do to carry out the plan, including taking the unusual step of pulling an airplane into the hangar without first draining its gas tank, a violation of company policy. Buehl, of course, brought it into the hangar specifically so that there would be plenty of gasoline to spread around. He opened the valve in the gas tank and let the gasoline spill onto the wooden floor. As the gasoline drained, he collected several pails of gasoline and splashed them around the shop. Then he lit the fire.

Party Lines

Party lines used to be very common because there was not enough switching capacity to allow every telephone customer to have a personal number. It would be common for four families to share a number, with each family having a coded ring so that they would know who should pick up. Many times, another person on a line, wanting to place a call, would inadvertently pick up their phone while the line was already in use. As it was, it was also very common for neighbors to quietly pick up and just eavesdrop. It was a great source of news, gossip, and entertainment. In this case, it was a great way to spread misinformation.

Within a few minutes, some passers-by stopped and helped as Buehl acted as though he were trying to save whatever he could. Buehl's clothing was burned, and he suffered burns himself as he ran into the buildings. As the fire spread, Buehl tried to call the Fire Department from the field, but by then the telephone wire had burned off. He ran about 300 or 400 yards to the neighbor's home, that of a farmer named Stiler. He alerted Stiler and then ran back to the airfield. In the end, the fire consumed almost everything, burning the buildings to the ground within about half an hour.

There had been six airplanes in the hangars: three JL-6s, the JL-12, a Bristol fighter, and an Avro. Buehl pushed out as much as he could. He got two JL-6s out of a hangar that was not yet burning. One of these was the airplane Stinson and Bertaud flew to set the duration record. Larsen's Locomobile and his speed boat, along with business papers related to the Aircraft Company, including all invoices, were consumed by the fire. The following day, *The New York Tribune* said the fire started in the woodwork and canvas covering the hangars. Given the severity of the fire, it seemed surprising that several airplanes had been saved.

Buehl at the helm of Larsen's speed boat, the Firefly. The name seems more amusing now than was probably intended. PHOTO/EBC

It emerged later that Larsen had taken more papers from his office to his home in New Jersey. These were burnt up when Larsen's home in New Jersey caught fire, subsequent to the airfield fire. Numerous other papers were taken by Larsen to Germany when he left the US after the fire.

After the Fire

There was never any debate over who started the fire. It was Buehl. In an affidavit prepared on 11 February, he admitted causing the fire but said it was accidental. Following the script Larsen gave him, he said he had been working on a radiator in the middle hangar when the torch he was using to solder a radiator "overflowed." The affidavit was prepared at Larsen's Madison Avenue office and witnessed by Carlos Warner and Eddie Stinson.[§]

In the affidavit, Buehl said he had arrived that Wednesday morning at Larsen Field before 9:30 AM. Soon after arriving, he was alone at the field. Buehl gave the story that he had several things to do that day. One was to work on Larsen's car. Therefore, Buehl started his day with jacking up the automobile, pulling out the plugs, and draining the gasoline. Next, since one of the airplanes had a leaky radiator that needed repair, he prepared the radiator for soldering. The torch he was using to heat his soldering irons overturned, igniting the blaze.

Once claims had been filed, insurance adjusters came to the airfield and talked with several people involved. The process began of cleaning up and evaluating the losses. The JL-12 Attack Plane, which Larsen valued at $85,000, was destroyed. Larsen had insured the plant and its contents for $250,000, and by early 1923 the insurance company had paid out $190,000.

It was about a month after the fire, on 9 April 1922, Larsen met Buehl at the airfield office, which had not burned down. Buehl received the agreed-upon $1,500 for setting the fire in the form of ten $100 bills and one $500 bill. Buehl also learned that Larsen was going to put his plans on hold for a year or two since he had decided to research European aviation while waiting for Congress to pass legislation he

§ It is likely that this event strained the relationship between Buehl and Stinson. One gets the sense that as Buehl signed the affidavit Stinson cooly observed and any warmth between them was gone. Stinson, of course, was never part of the plotting so he would have had no way to understand what was happening.

deemed necessary to his business future. During this time, neither Fritz nor Ernie Buehl would be needed.

Buehl used $700 to purchase a second-hand Dodge Roadster. He planned to get married so he used $396 to buy a diamond engagement ring for his fiancée and then deposited the balance in a savings account at a bank in Hempstead.

Warner received a similar deal to the one Larsen offered Buehl. He was paid for his participation and then laid off after the fire, but after charges were first filed against John Larsen, Warner was rehired "at wages greatly in excess of what he had recently been receiving."

Before the fire, Larsen had transferred the refrigeration business to Harry, and after that Harry continued to do business in John Larsen's name. As part of the deal with Buehl, Larsen said he would recommend that Harry employ Buehl. Harry did, in fact, subsequently hire Buehl to work in his factory, building refrigeration equipment. As an aside, Fritz never was able to move to the United States.

Larsen was allowed to travel to Europe after the fire, and was even in Europe during parts of the trials that followed. By July 1922, while John Larsen was in Europe, Harry Larsen was collecting insurance payments and transferring the money abroad to his father.

Amundsen

The story about Roald Amundsen is about as strange an interlude as one could imagine in this story. Just before the fire but during the time Larsen was planning to burn down his business, in early January 1922, Roald Amundsen had approached Larsen to talk about equipping an attempt to fly over the North Pole in a JL-6.

Amundsen was chronically broke and could not have afforded a new airplane. He spent most of his time between expeditions in two activities: dodging the creditors who had loaned him money for his previous expedition, and trying to raise money for his next expedition. (Amundsen did pay off his creditors, eventually). In this instance, he approached Larsen with the request that Larsen simply give him a JL-6.

Amundsen viewed the JL-6 as a well-tested aircraft, shown to be suited for use under polar conditions, a dependable workhorse in sub-arctic Canada. But Amundsen had one particular JL-6 in mind. He wanted the one Stinson and Bertaud used to make their record-breaking endurance flight. While the airplane was not new, as far as Amundsen was concerned it had proven capability under difficult conditions. He was also aware of the publicity value in saying that his JL-6 was the same airplane used to set the endurance record. Later, Larsen would admit that he was not sure exactly which airplane was delivered to Amundsen, but he did nothing to contradict Amundsen's publicity announcements.

There were several reasons why it worked to Larsen's advantage to give Amundsen a JL-6. At the time, Amundsen and Larsen may have considered each other countrymen after a fashion. Norway and Denmark were culturally and politically very close because when Norway gained independence from Sweden in 1905, Prince Carl of Denmark became king of Norway. After giving Amundsen the JL-6, Larsen's standing in his native country increased. In gratitude for facilitating Amundsen, Larsen was knighted by the king of Denmark.

In addition to this connection and the friendliness it produced, Larsen knew he was going out of business, so he agreed to this arrangement: Larsen would give Amundsen an airplane, but Amundsen would have to pay any expenses to have it modified to his specifications. Larsen would arrange for the work, and all parts and labor would be provided at cost. They settled on $10,000 as the amount Amundsen would pay for the modifications.

After the fire, Larsen knew he would have no work for Buehl or for his superintendent, Carlos Warner. As part of the deal, Larsen would be able to ship these two far away, making it inconvenient for anyone who might want to question them about the fire. It was arranged that Buehl and Warner would leave Larsen's employment and be picked up by Amundsen. Buehl would accompany Amundsen to Point Barrow, the jumping-off point for the flyover attempt. It was expected that Buehl would be gone for about a year or a year-and-a-half.

According to the plan, when Buehl's work with Amundsen was finished, Harry Larsen would employ Buehl until John Larsen returned. At that time, Buehl would work with John Larsen again in his new enterprise. Buehl never worked for Amundsen for long enough to be paid by Amundsen himself. All of the money Buehl was paid during the time he worked on the *Elizabeth* flowed through Larsen. Also, Larsen promised to pay Buehl $75 per week if he would accompany Amundsen to Alaska.

Amundsen named his new airplane the *Elizabeth*, after Kristine Elizabeth Bennett. Publicly at the time, Amundsen explained the name was given to honor an old aunt. Actually, it was named for a married woman whom he had been trying to impress for more than ten years.

Buehl and Amundsen and the North Pole

Buehl spoke of working with Roald Amundsen as the famous explorer who planned an attempt to reach the North Pole by airplane. However, the story Buehl's friends and acquaintances told was bigger: they claimed he was Amundsen's pilot for an expedition over the Pole. Later in Buehl's life, a local newspaper repeated the story, saying that Buehl "piloted two polar flights for Roald Amundsen, the Arctic Explorer, in 1922."

Amundsen genuinely was a remarkable person. When put in proper

Kristine Elizabeth Bennett

Amundsen met Bennett in 1912 during a lecture tour. She talked to him, asked him questions about things that interested him, and listened attentively to his answers. He was, after all, a fascinating adventurer of international reputation. She demonstrated a momentary interest in him and smiled at things he said. Amundsen was blown off his feet.

Whatever their relationship may have been in the beginning, it quickly became one-sided. When they were apart, Amundsen thought about how nice it felt to be near her. Thinking about Bennett turned into dwelling on her. There is little evidence that Bennett did much to encourage Amundsen, but for years he maintained the idea that they were somehow involved.

perspective, nearly everyone's achievements look fairly ordinary, but not Roald Amundsen's. Arguably the greatest Norwegian explorer since Leif Erikson, Amundsen could count among his many accomplishments being the first to lead an expedition to reach the South Pole, and although it was disputed at the time, we now know he led the first successful attempt to reach the North Pole.

A little fact-checking reveals some problems with the legend associating Buehl with Amundsen. To begin, Buehl would have been an unlikely choice to be Amundsen's pilot. He was not regarded by anyone at that time as a pilot; he was a mechanic. Further, there is no mention of Buehl in any of Amundsen's articles or books related to his polar flights. Nothing in what Amundsen wrote, nothing in any book anyone else has written, mentions Buehl. Every member of Amundsen's polar expeditions is listed somewhere, right down to the camp cook, but Buehl's name does not appear. Buehl, in fact, was not a member of any team that even came close to the North Pole.

A reason why documentation is scarce related to Buehl's participation is that at most he worked for Amundsen for a matter of hours, not weeks or even days, and furthermore, the expedition itself failed. Amundsen's leadership of the 1922 expedition does not represent his better work. It was not characterized by the meticulous planning that had gone into the Antarctic expedition, perhaps because he was distracted by a complicated personal life.

To be fair, Buehl never actually said that he, personally, made it to the North Pole. What Buehl said was that he had met Amundsen, had worked with him, and had flown with him for the 1922 attempt, all of which was true.

The Short Flight and Then Crash of the Elizabeth

Amundsen and his party left Larsen Field on Long Island at 8:18 AM on 10 April 1922, expecting to fly the *Elizabeth* to Cleveland. Amundsen hoped to pause there for several hours to visit with some friends, then fly to Chicago to spend the night. From Chicago, his route would take him to Seattle, with multiple stops in between.

The party included: H.T. Lewis, Oscar Omdal, and Buehl. Lewis was the pilot, demonstrating the aircraft to Omdal, who would be flying the *Elizabeth* in the Arctic later that year. The cross-country flight would allow the expedition team to learn more about the airplane, and it would generate publicity for the expedition.

Carlos Warner was going to take the train to Seattle, where he would join the others. From there, they would all board a ship to Point Barrow. It was explained that Buehl and Warner were along to ensure that the airplane was ready for the flight over the Pole to Spitzenburg, Norway.

Unfortunately, on the day the party left Long Island, the *Elizabeth* crashed and was damaged beyond repair. They did not even get as far as Pittsburgh. This was the only time Buehl flew with Amundsen.

Many accounts explore the reason for the forced landing. "Ran out of gasoline" was commonly offered as an explanation. Amundsen and some others said the crash was caused by "an overheated motor." Even Buehl, recalling the event more than 60 years after the fact, blamed an overheated motor. In this case, Buehl's recollection was likely contaminated by what he had heard from others.

The local newspaper reports, recorded at the time of the crash, are more likely to have the story right. These sources indicate that Lewis, an experienced and highly skilled pilot, was forced to land because the aircraft got caught in a violent hail storm. Lewis had to put the plane down in a soft field, the landing gear caught in the soil of the field, and the airplane flipped over. Given Lewis' skills as a pilot, the "hail storm" explanation is much more likely than any of the others offered.

In a story remembering the crash of the Elizabeth, *The Clarion Republican* looked into the written records of what happened that day near their community:

> *Thirty-eight years ago this week (10 April 1922) the all-metal mono-plane shown above was damaged on a forced landing on the Cosgrove farm, a short distance east of the Miola church.*
>
> *It was a Junkers JL-6, owned by the famous Arctic explorer Captain Ronald [sic] Amundsen, and piloted by H.T. "Slim" Lewis of Belle-font. Lewis was slightly hurt, the only occupant to be injured at all. The exploration party was flying from New York to Seattle, intending to continue by ship to Alaska. The airplane, named "Elizabeth" passed directly over Clarion, headed due north at the time, and encountered hail.*
>
> *When the pilot landed to escape the storm, the airplane nosed over on to its back. One wing was badly damaged and a relief plane from the government field at Bellefont came to Clarion to assist in repairs.*

The wreck of the Elizabeth PHOTO/EBC

Continuing the Attempt

Following the crash, Larsen submitted a claim for insurance on the Elizabeth. He had not fully insured the airplane, but was able to collect $8,000, nearly enough to recover Amundsen's costs for the modifications made to the aircraft.

Because Larsen had no more JL-6s in his inventory after the first one crashed, he approached the military to allow Amundsen to use one of the airplanes they had purchased. He gave the government a bond that said he would replace it with the same plane or another like it. This new plane was picked up at the Navy Yard in Philadelphia and brought back to Long Island to be fitted with the instruments and attachments Amundsen required. Buehl began working on it promptly to install the equipment Amundsen wanted. It appears that the money to pay for this flowed through Larsen, who continued to help Amundsen. Amundsen had to raise some more money for modifications to this aircraft.

In June 1922, the second airplane was shipped in pieces to Seattle, where the *Maud* was moored. Amundsen took the new airplane in boxes to Wainwright, Alaska, where it was assembled.

Buehl did not travel with Amundsen this time because by June he was working with Harry Larsen in New York. However, Amundsen had hired the highly experienced Canadian pilot Elmer Garfield Fullerton. Spoiling what would have been a very good hire, Amundsen quickly fired Fullerton over a personal issue.

It is difficult not to speculate how differently the 1923 attempt might have turned out if Buehl and Fullerton had been working in Alaska with Amundsen then. Fullerton and Buehl had flown JL-6s together and probably had as much experience operating the JL-6 under the fierce conditions Amundsen would face as any other pair of aviators alive at the time.

Omdal crashed this airplane on a test flight in Alaska, wrecking the landing gear. Amundsen blamed the gear for being flimsy. This is possible. Landing gear was one of the items Larsen upgraded when converting an F-13 to a JL-6, and this airplane was an unmodified F-13. However, it is more likely either that Amundsen's team had not installed it properly or that Omdal, who was relatively inexperienced in flying the JL-6, just brought the airplane down too hard. This was certainly Larsen's opinion.

There were reports that the second aircraft was old and known to have an unreliable engine when it was delivered to Amundsen, but these stories are not accurate. Larsen and Junkers argued in the press over who had sold Amundsen an obsolete aircraft, but Junkers finally offered Amundsen yet another aircraft. Amundsen peevishly declined the offer.

Soft Landings

Larsen's early specifications for the JL-6 claimed that it was unlikely that the airplane would nose over in landing on soft ground, but it had happened before, on 28 March 1921, when George Gorman accidentally flipped the *René* during a landing in soft snow at Fort Simpson, Canada.

The airplane was not old. The factory number of the replacement airplane was 568, an airplane that had been delivered to New York on 28 August 1920. The 568 was part of a shipment that included airplanes 561, 566, and 567. Within that batch, Larsen himself used the 566 to take to Canada in 1921, marked as the N-CADT, and the 561 was the *Vic*, an airplane proved in service in Canada. These were among the latest airplanes delivered to Larsen. Unlike the others in that shipment, though, the 568 was delivered in unmodified condition to the U.S. military. Because it was unmodified, Larsen considered it to be a Junkers F-13 and not a JL-6. Buehl, who worked on this airplane, confirmed this. He described it as "brand new, but without Larsen's reinforcements on it."

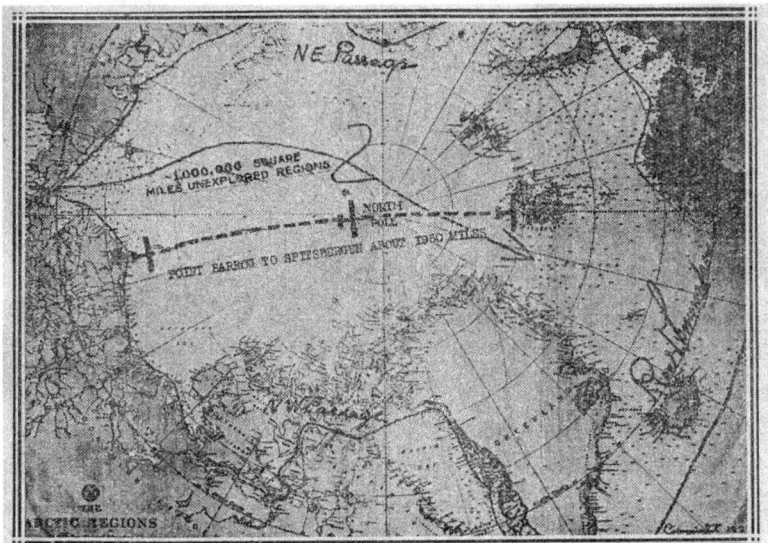

AUTOGRAPHED MAP OF AMUNDSEN'S PROPOSED FLIGHT TO NORTH POLE, showing route famed Norwegian explorer plans to follow in air route of 2,000 miles from Point Barrow, Alaska, to the tip of the earth and on to Spitzbergen. He will use a metal monoplane, the Elizabeth.   (C. N.)

Amundsen's proposed route from Point Barrow, Alaska, to Spitzbergen. PHOTO/EBC, PUBLIC DOMAIN, BUT NEWSPAPER SOURCE IS MISSING

Timeline: Amundsen

JANUARY 1922 Amundsen approached Lars-
    en, asking for an airplane.
8 FEBRUARY 1922 Date of the fire. After this, Bue-
    hl prepared the first JL-6 for Amundsen.
9 APRIL 1922 Buehl was let go by John Larsen.
10 APRIL 1922 Buehl was picked up by Amundsen
    and was to accompany him to Alaska. The
    first JL-6 crashed, so Buehl prepared an other-
    wise unmodified F-13 for Amundsen. It was not
    planned for Buehl to accompany this second
    attempt, but Buehl worked on the modifica-
    tions of the second JL-6 Amundsen received.
MARCH 1923 Larsen's knighthood was men-
    tioned in newspaper accounts about the
    Commercial Union Insurance trial. The
    honor was described as "recent."

The End for Larsen

Following the fire and the failure of Amundsen's expedition, Buehl worked for Harry Larsen at a factory on 14th Street in New York City that made refrigeration equipment.

In the meantime, C.B. Wrightsman was lurking, still looking for revenge on Larsen for exposing his cheat in the October 1921 Larsen Race. Suspecting that the devastating fire at Larsen field was actually arson, Wrightsman hired the Schindler Detective Agency to look into it. Soon, the detectives focused on Buehl, and soon after that, Wrightsman had the evidence he needed to trigger legal proceedings against Larsen.

One of Schindler's employees spent weeks developing a relationship with Buehl, eventually trapping him into a meeting directly with Schindler himself. In the course of this meeting, Buehl confessed to setting the fire. Schindler offered to protect Buehl from prosecution for his role in the crime, but he neither threatened nor paid Buehl for his cooperation.

Schindler moved Buehl from Hempstead to the city, where he was kept for about five months under 24-hour surveillance by detectives until a state prosecutor could formally depose him. The detectives wanted to ensure that Buehl would not wander away before he was formally deposed. They also wanted to make sure that someone from Larsen's side did not tamper with his testimony, either by harming him or bribing him to change his story. From 25 October, Buehl was entirely unemployed. Until 26 February 1923, he was required to live off his own savings, paying all of his own expenses.

During these five months, Buehl could only stay at his hotel or go to movies. He was not allowed to have a job. Hour by tedious hour passed slowly for almost half of a year. After giving the deposition before the New York Supreme Court's appointed Referee, he was given enough money to cover his rent plus ten dollars per week in exchange for checking in with Schindler. This arrangement lasted for another month before Buehl found work and could support himself again.

Only after he was formally deposed did Buehl learn that Schindler and the other detectives were working for C.B. Wrightsman, the aviator who had won the Omaha race by cheating.

Following his deposition before the Referee, Buehl was summoned to testify before the Grand Jury in Mineola, New York, on 29 May 1923. It was in the course of this testimony when he was questioned by Robert Kelly Prentice, an attorney for Globe & Rutgers Insurance Company, that the insurance company first heard of Buehl's confession. Globe & Rutgers had already initiated civil actions against Larsen, and Prentice informed the district attorney that there might be cause for a criminal action against Larsen.

John Larsen was brought to trial for insurance fraud. His motive was clear. By late 1921, Larsen was running a worthless business. The loss of his agreement with Junkers in 1921 left him with no source for new inventory. The business being a dead loss, on 9 Feb 1922, he ordered his aerodrome burned and then made a fraudulent insurance claim.

Buehl testified for the prosecution. It came out in testimony that Buehl had not profited in any way from his part in the crime. He did not keep the money he had been paid for the crime but returned it to the insurance company. In addition, he had been forced to exhaust his personal resources while waiting to be deposed. Further, he had been engaged to a woman, but in the pressures associated with depositions and trials the relationship collapsed.

In the end, Buehl's testimony was not found to be believable. The reason he was not believed is itself implausible. The idea was that Buehl could not be believed when he confessed to arson because that would mean he had lied before under oath when he claimed the fire was an accident. He lied once; maybe he told the truth before but was lying now? (False confessions are not unknown, but Buehl was not coerced in any way. However, it is common for people to deny having committed a crime because they fear the legal consequences).

The Outcome

Neither Larsen nor Buehl was ever convicted of a crime. Buehl confessed under oath to cooperating in insurance fraud. Larsen successfully denied under oath that any such thing had taken place. At minimum, one of these men perjured himself. Neither was punished.

Because he cooperated fully with law enforcement, and because the evidence supporting his testimony was strong, Buehl was released with a clean record. His role in the arson did not count against him when he applied for U.S. citizenship.

After the cases were closed, Larsen left North America and returned to Europe, where he lived out the rest of his life. He continued to work in the field of refrigeration, and filed several international patents related to dairying and to fish preservation. Among other things, he is known as the man who introduced Danes to the American-style popcicle. He passed away peacefully on his estate in Denmark on 15 February 1950.

Why Did Buehl Do It?

Buehl's association with Larsen ended shamefully, for Buehl and for Larsen. When Larsen's business in aviation was all but dead and Buehl was nearly his last employee, he ordered Buehl to burn down the airfield, and for some reason Buehl did it. Why?

The end of their relationship was painful for both of them. At some level, they had a good relationship together. Buehl was grateful to Larsen for many things. With the loss of the relationship, Buehl was at loose ends. He missed the nonintuitive combination of both stability and adventure associated with Larsen. On the one hand, Buehl was well-paid and earned a steady paycheck for doing things he liked to do. On the other hand, the work was often challenging, demanding the world-class skills he could deliver. He got to go a lot of places, and he got to hobnob with celebrities. With Larsen, Buehl got a front-row seat to see aviation at its leading edge.

Having to testify against Larsen was painful for Buehl. There was a small but telling moment during the trial in which it came out that Buehl had spoken in a mildly disrespectful way about Larsen in a letter to Fritz. What he said was no worse than what many young people might say when wanting to assert some independence from someone older and more powerful, but even in the adversarial context of a trial, Buehl was ashamed and embarrassed when the letter came out. What he had written did not reflect how he actually felt, and he did not want Larsen to hear it.

For his part, Larsen lost a man he liked, and he had respected Buehl for both his skills and discretion. Indeed, he treated Buehl more like a nephew rather than strictly as his employer. He had included Buehl in his life. He must have been genuinely and personally hurt when Buehl testified against him. But, if Larsen actually did treat Buehl somewhat as he would a nephew, one has to ask what kind of uncle invites his nephew to join him in a high-stakes criminal activity? Whether he himself ever admitted it or not, Larsen was a crook. Beyond the puffery and self-aggrandizement associated with the way he did business, arson and insurance fraud appear to have been part of his way of life.

For Buehl's part, it could have been hoped that he was simply naïve and had been set up. Perhaps he did not know that the fire was part of an insurance fraud scheme? But on examination of the evidence, there is no way he could have missed it. At 24 years of age, Buehl's character was tested, and he failed the test.

Buehl failed because he misapplied a set of values that had served him well all of his life to that point: when his employer ordered him to burn down the hangar, Buehl did it because he believed he was doing his duty. Buehl was young and even for someone of his own time he had an unsophisticated sense of duty.

It is hard for us today to enter into the mind of a young German Catholic who was born before the beginning of the twentieth century. Defiant individuality was not as celebrated in Buehl's time and place, and he was not surrounded by a culture in which people were as deeply cynical of authority as we are in the early decades of the twenty-first century.

We all have a duty to follow lawful orders from people who are in authority over us. A social superior, a man of international reputation, had given Buehl an order, and he carried it out. Larsen denied to Buehl that the fire was to be part of an insurance fraud, and Buehl, not in the habit of questioning authority, wanted to accept Larsen's premise that they were burning the airfield simply because Larsen "did not need it any longer."

It seems that Buehl deliberately convinced himself that the order from Larsen was somehow lawful. After all, Buehl reasoned, someone who owns a thing has the right to dispose of it for any reason he chooses, and it is not illegal to burn trash. The problem was, one does not collect insurance money for burning trash. Also, Buehl could see that Larsen wanted to conceal the arson. Buehl should have asked himself, why conceal a lawful activity? If he asked himself that, then he had to deliberately ignore the obvious answer.

On 8 February 1922, Buehl agonized about setting the fire. His testimony in court reveals his internal conflict. To help him over the barriers of conscience, Larsen gave Buehl a detailed script for what to do and some rationales for why it should be okay.

Larson was concerned that gasoline leaking from a tipped-over torch would not be enough to ensure that everything burned in the fire Buehl would set. He wanted Buehl to splash extra gasoline around the building, paying particular attention to certain items. Larsen obviously wanted the JL-12 attack plane to burn, but he also wanted his own automobile to burn. Larsen had placed many business letters and other papers in the automobile.

Although it is a strange thing to do so, taking the activity in isolation, one finds there is nothing immoral about splashing some gasoline around. The strangeness of this activity would have been a little hurdle for Buehl to clear, but the practice he got from overcoming the mild inhibition blocking him at this step would have made it easier to go on to the next steps. He overcame his inhibition against doing this strange thing with gasoline by repeatedly imagining himself doing it until it no longer seemed too strange. Mental rehearsal was crucial. One of the key ways we form our behavior is through practicing what we are going to do.

Revealing his ambivalence, though, it took Buehl hours to carry out what really was a very simple plan. Following the script, he would set up some evidence so the fire would look like an accident. He would place a radiator that needed some work on a steel bench, as though he were going to solder it. He would place a gasoline blowtorch nearby, as though he were going to use it to heat his soldering irons. There was nothing wrong with setting things up to solder a radiator.

He had to know he was setting up a lie, though. Buehl knew that after the fire the arrangement of evidence should look as though the torch had been knocked over accidentally while he was performing a routine task. The purpose was to encourage investigators to conclude that gasoline had spilled from the lit torch and the whole place had caught fire as a result. He ignored the implications.

In the meantime, Larsen was calling Buehl. He initially called to ask, "Are you alone there?" At that moment, there was one other person on the grounds, the night watchman. Half an hour later, Larsen called again to find out if Buehl was alone. This time he was. "Are you carrying out the plan?" Larsen asked. Later, when he heard nothing further from Buehl, Larsen called at least two more times with similar questions, each time urging Buehl to act. Buehl even argued with Larsen, saying that he did not want to carry out the scheme, but Larsen pressured him and repeated the rationales for why it was okay for Buehl to set the fire.

For all the talk about blaming the fire on a lit torch falling off a workbench, Buehl later admitted he never actually used the torch. He just lit a match and threw it on the floor. There was so much gasoline on the wooden floors and splashed on the walls that the whole place went up immediately. By the time he started the fire, Buehl was a practiced expert in compartmentalizing his actions, so lighting a match was little problem for him. He had lit many matches before and he never felt badly about any of them.

Through the hours before lighting the fire, Buehl said he felt as though he were in a trance. In the final moments, at the point of the last step, he could have walked away if he had just decided to keep his matches in his pocket. Instead, he took the tiny but important step forward of placing his matches in his hand. At this point, his focus narrowed so much that every other consideration left his mind. Standing there with the crime entirely set up and with the matches in his hand, the tension Buehl experienced was so uncomfortable he would have done nearly anything to make that feeling stop.

It takes a fraction of a second between a decision and an action, a little time for the brain to process a decision and then act. An impulse to just get it all over with entered his mind, and since he had spent the past hours making everything ready, and since he found himself armed with matches in hand, within the next 400 milliseconds the deed was done. He lit the match and threw it on the floor.

Two hundred milliseconds after he saw the fire spreading, Buehl realized what a terrible mistake he had made. The realization came too late. Buehl said, "As soon as I see the fire, I was sorry it happened and I tried with Pyrene⊄ to stop it until I set my own pants on fire."**

As much as Buehl wanted to undo what he had done, rushing around to try to put out the fire and limit the damage, the whole thing was now out of his control. The last moment he was in control was the moment just before he struck the match. Further, he had been in control every moment up to then, but instead of doing anything other than carrying out each step leading up to the fire, he had

---

⊄ Pyrene was the brand name of a fire extinguisher that used carbon tetrachloride, a very toxic substance now banned from use.

** It is impossible to avoid the taunt: "liar, liar, pants on fire."

stuck to the plan, each harmless step by harmless step. Later in his life Buehl knew better, but at the time he failed to consider his personal responsibility.

Buehl confessed to the crime. In doing so, he followed every step he knew of Catholic confession and penance. He admitted his responsibility, he felt remorse, he accepted punishment, and he made restitution. He never did anything similar again.

What Buehl Said

Buehl never once talked about the fire with anyone in his family. It was the dark secret he hoped everyone had forgotten and hoped no one would ever discover. As a result, his family had no idea why, for example, he ended up in Philadelphia.

The only whisper of a hint found in Buehl's scrapbooks that there had been a fire was a tiny seven-line clipping from the *New York Times* that simply stated the losses.

Selected Sources

Aerial Age. "The Larsen Trophy - News of the Month." Aerial Age Company, August 1922.

Allyne, Edmund E. *First Round Trip Transcontinental Passenger Flight: July 29th to August 22nd 1920.* self-published, 1921.

Andersson, Lennart, Gunter G. Endres, Rob J. M. Mulder, and Gunther Ott. *Junkers F13: The World's First All-Metal Airliner.* EAM Books EEIG, 2012.

Bellingham Herald. "All-Metal Monoplanes on Flight from New York to San Francisco." July 29, 1920.

Billings Gazette. "When Fear and Hysteria Swept through Billings and Montana." February 20, 2018.

Bown, Stephen R. *The Last Viking: The Life of Roald Amundsen.* First Edition edition. Boston, MA: Da Capo Press, 2012.

Bristol Daily Courier. "Flying Dutchman Airport Sold to Development Co. Korman Pays $625,169 for Bensalem Site." August 10, 1960.

Buck, Olga. "Eddington's Buehl Airfield Home to Oldtime Flying Dutchman." *Bucks County Sunday Press.* December 13, 1953.

Buehl, Ernest H. "Handwritten Draft of Response to Correspondence from K.M. Molson." Molson wrote to him on 22 June 1977.

Chicago Tribune. "Larsen Accused of Paying $1,500 to Burn Factory: Aircraft Plant Was Heavily Insured." March 7, 1923.

Clarion Republican. "Famed Explorer Wrecked Plane in Miola Field 38 Years Ago This Week," April 7, 1960.

Decisions of the Railroad Commission of the State of California. Vol. 7. State of California, 1915.

Department of Commerce. "Application for Mechanic's License." Department of Commerce, Aeronautics Branch, February 26, 1927.

EADS. "EADS History of Aviation 1910 to 1919 - Junkers F 13." Corporate history, February 16, 2008.

Edmonton Bulletin. "Larson [Sic] Plane Zoomed down Thursday 3 P.M. Flying Time from New York Was Twenty-Eight Hours and Twenty Minutes." April 1, 1921.

Edmonton Bulletin. "Larson [Sic] Plane Zoomed down Thursday 3 P.M. Flying Time from New York Was Twenty-Eight Hours and Twenty Minutes." April 1, 1921.

Edmonton Journal. "Edmonton Flyer Makes Saskatoon." January 4, 1921.

Edmonton Journal. "Land near Site of Old Winter Camp." February 28, 1921.

Edmonton Journal. "Mammoth Monoplanes Are Being Fitted with Skis at Peace River for Flights Further North." March 5, 1921.

Edmonton Journal. "Monoplane Rides Wintry Blasts on Jump from Saskatoon." January 5, 1921.

Edmonton Journal. "Oil Company Well Satisfied with Results Long Flight and Will Carry out Original Scheme: Monoplanes Will Be in Commission 12 Months of the Year Carrying Mail and Materials to Northern Points." January 6, 1921.

Edmonton Journal. "Speed Records Smashed by Monoplane." January 26, 1921, Last edition edition, sec. 1.

El Paso Herald. "Great Metal Bird,

Filled with Men like Trojans' Horse, Drops out of Skies before Crowd at Fort Bliss." August 16, 1920, Evening edition.

Ernie Buehl Talks to the Experimental Aircraft Association, Pennsylvania Chapter 76. Videotape, 1986.

Evening World. "Monoplane in Which Explorer Amundsen Narrowly Missed Death in Drop to Earth. Amundsen Is Hurt When Plane Falls," April 11, 1922.

Fleischman, John. "Where Did Max Miller Die?: One Man's Search for the Place Where the U.S. Air Mail Service Lost a Star." *Air & Space Magazine*, August 2015.

Flying Magazine. "JL-6 (Advertisement)," August 1920.

Gazetteer of the Northwest Territories. Prince of Wales Northern Heritage Center, 2015.

Glenbow Museum, Calgary, Canada. "Glenbow Museum Archives Photographs."

Godsell, P.H. "Mail Flown South – 1921." *Airmail Study Group Newsletter* 9, no. 3 (December 2001): 32–35.

Grand Forks Daily Herald. "All-Metal Monoplane Arrives Here Enroute to Ft. Norman, Alberta." March 20, 2021.

Grand Forks Daily Herald. "Aviators Are Delayed Here." March 22, 1921.

Grand Forks Daily Herald. "Harry Meyers Visits Minot." March 24, 1921.

Grand Forks Daily Herald. "John M. Larsen Made Defendant in Damage Suit at Omaha, Neb." November 8, 1921.

Grand Forks Daily Herald. "John M. Larsen Monoplane Arrived in Saskatoon on Wednesday, Telegram Says." March 31, 1921.

Grand Forks Daily Herald. "Larsen Expects to Leave Today." March 29, 1921.

Grand Forks Daily Herald. "Monoplane to Be Ready Soon." March 26, 1921.

Grand Forks Daily Herald. "Receive News of Monoplane." April 12, 1921.

Grand Forks Herald. "Aviators Guests of Club; Served in War in Opposing Armies." March 23, 1921.

Grand Forks Herald. "Big Purse Offered in Last Air Race of National Aero Congress." November 5, 1921.

Grant, R. G. *Flight: The Complete History.* Reprint edition. New York: DK Publishing, 2007.

Gross, Michael. *Rogues' Gallery: The Secret Story of the Lust, Lies, Greed, and Betrayals That Made the Metropolitan Museum of Art.* First paperback., 2010.

Hearings before the Subcommittee of the Committee on Post Offices and Post Roads United States Senate, 66th Congress, Second Session on H.R. 11578." Washington, D.C: Government Printing Office, 1920.

Hofmann, Angelica. "Der Konstrukteur Otto Reuter." Hugo Junkers - Ein Leben für die Technik., December 11, 2012.

Hofmann, Angelica. "Werknummernverzeichnis der Junkers F 13." Die Junkers F-13, February 6, 2013. (web page)

Hugo Junkers - Ein Leben für die Technik. "18 Februar 1921: Junkerspilot Emil Monz tödlich verunglückt," March 18, 2014. (web page)

J.L. Monoplane in 1,200 Mile Nonstop Flight." *Aircraft Journal* 7, no. 2 (July 12, 1920)

JL Corp. "Preliminary Specifications of J.L.6 Airplane." Unpublished typed sheet, n.d.

Junkers, Hugo. Flying machine. US1576977

A, filed June 28, 1920, and issued March 16, 1926.

Kansas City Kansan. "Conclave Plans Hold Attention of American Legion," October 28, 1921.

Laut, A. "The Struggle to Make Canada's Oil Fields Pay." *New York Herald,* July 21, 1921.

Lent, Leon B. "United States Air Mail Survey Flight New York - San Francisco." U.S. Postal Service, n.d. RG 18 Stack area 190, row 39, compartment 16, shelf 1. National Archives.

Lewis, W. David. *Eddie Rickenbacker: An American Hero in the Twentieth Century.* Reprint edition. Baltimore, Md: Johns Hopkins University Press, 2008.

Macready, J.A., and Harold R. Harris. "Performance Test of Junker SL-6 with 185-H.P. B.M.W. Engine." Air Service Information Circular, Vol. 2, No. 173, 1/15/1921. McCook Field Report Serial No. 1414. Engineering Division, Air Service, October 22, 1921. Smithsonian Libraries National Air & Space Museum.

May, Denny. "The Wop May Chronicles – Stories about Wilfrid Reid (Wop) May." (web page)

Molson, K. M. *Pioneering in Canadian Air Transport.* Winnipeg, Ont: J. Richardson, 1974.

Morning Bulletin. "Communication with Far North No Problem Now." April 30, 1921.

Mulder, Rob J.M. "Mr Batts Flies in Norway." European Airlines, June 20, 2010. (website).

National Aviation Hall of Fame. "Acosta, Bertrand 'Bert' B."

New York Times. "$50,000 Loss in Airplane Fire." February 9, 1922.

New York Times. "Air Mail Starts to Pacific Today." July 28, 1920.

New York Times. "All-Metal Plane Stirs Fliers Here: JL-6 Monoplane Looked upon as Revolutionizing Present Design and Construction," June 20, 1920.

New York Times. "Charles Bierer Wrightsman, Philanthropist, Is Dead at 90," May 28, 1986, sec. Obituaries.

New York Times. "Denies He Plotted to Burn His Plant." June 21, 1923.

New York Times. "Dozen Airplanes Carry Racegoers," July 16, 1920.

New York Times. "New Aeroplane Record: Six-Passenger Car Flies 120 Miles in 59 Minutes 34 Seconds," June 1, 1920.

New York Times. "Plane Builder Wins Suit," February 1, 1924.

New York Times. "Says Plane Maker Ordered Plant Fire." March 7, 1923.

New York Times. "See Plot to Brand Larsen as Firebug: Allegation Denounced as Phase of Conspiracy Following Aviation Contest. Suit to Recover Insurance. Confession of Incendiarism by German Said to Have Been Extorted by Threats." June 19, 1923.

New York Times. "Writes as He Flies in 248-Mile Race: Col. Wilson Dashes off Letters While Winning All Metal Monoplane Contest," June 13, 1920.

New York Tribune. "Defense Society Says U.S. Buys German Planes. Camouflaged Machines of All Metal Type Imported by Larsen and Sold as Mail Carriers, Is Charge." September 3, 1920.

New York Tribune. "First German Plane Flown Here Crashes: New Commercial Machine Driven by Enemy Pilot Smashed in Fall as Allied Mechanics Refuse Help." March 27, 1920.

New York Tribune. "First Transcontinental

Air Mail Starts Today." July 29, 1920.

New York Tribune. "German Inventor Here to Exploit Metal Monoplane. Professor Junker's Machine Will Be Handled by Firm Headed by J. M. Larsen; Flies to Atlantic City." May 30, 1920.

New York Tribune. "Planes Worth $50,000 Destroyed in L.I. Fire. Blaze from Blow Torch Razes Two Hangars of J.L. Aircraft Corporation." February 9, 1922.

New York Tribune. "U.S. Flyers Make Record for Duration: Stinson and Bertaud Battle with Frostbite and Exhaustion; Stay up 26 Hrs., 19 Mins., 35 Secs." December 31, 1921.

New York Tribune. "White Larsen Race Winner: Tulsa Pilot given First Place; New Yorker Is Second." November 8, 1921.

Norwich Bulletin. "Making Trip to Wedding in All-Metal Airplane." June 19, 1920.

Office of the United States Trade Representative. "Canada-US Trade Facts 2017." Office of the United States Trade Representative.

Omaha World Herald. "Lack of Washer Lands Big Plane," November 5, 1921, Evening edition.

Omaha World Herald. "Pilot Planes Finish Wilson Airway Route," August 18, 1920.

Omaha World Herald. "Safe on Land after Peril in Air," November 5, 1921.

Passenger Manifest Listing Emil Monz 13 May 1920.," May 13, 1920.

Passenger Manifest Listing Ernest Buhl 13 May 1920," May 13, 1920.

Pittsburgh Press. "Wreck of Amundsen Monoplane." April 12, 1922.

Pope, Nancy A. "DeHavilland DH-4."

Smithsonian National Postal Museum.

Prince of Wales Northern Heritage Centre. "Oil & Gas Industry | High Resolution Photo Gallery." (web page)

Rickenbacker, Edward V. Rickenbacker: An Autobiography. First. Englewood Cliffs, NJ: Prentice-Hall, 1967.

Riverside Enterprise. "Just Returned from Aerial View of Shamrock IV Winning Second Cup Race." July 27, 1920.

Robbins, Jim. "Pardons Granted 88 Years After Crimes of Sedition." The New York Times, May 3, 2006, sec. U.S.

Robie, William and National Aeronautic Association (U.S.). For the Greatest Achievement: A History of the Aero Club of America and the National Aeronautic Association. First Edition edition. Washington: Smithsonian, 1993.

Rock Island Argus and Daily Union. "All-Metal Plane near Flight End." June 22, 1920.

Salt Lake City Tribune. "Pioneer Airplane Carrying U.S. Mail Arrives in City from Cheyenne in Four and One-Half Hours." August 5, 1920.

Saskatoon Phoenix. "All-Metal Aeroplane Jumps 360 Miles in Two Hours 50 Minutes." January 25, 1921.

Spark, Nick T. "The Fastest Man on Earth: Why Everything You Know About Murphy's Law Is Wrong (Part 1 of 4)." Annals of Improbable Research 9, no. 5 (2003).

Stangeland, Hallvard. "Roald Amundsen's Expeditions from 1918 to 1926 in Media and Politics." Master's thesis, University of Oslo, 2011.

State Sedition Laws: Their Scope and Misapplication." Indiana Law Journal, Military, War, and Peace Commons, 31, no. 2 (1956): 17.

Sun and New York Herald. "1,200 Mile

Flight Ends near Phila. All Metal Monoplane Comes from Omaha without a Stop. New Record Is Made.," June 28, 1920.

Supreme Court Appellate Division. National Union Fire Insurance Company of Pittsburg, PA vs. John M. Larsen, Harry E. Larsen and Carlos H. Warner. New York, 1923.

The Globe and Rutgers Fire Insurance Company against General Adjustment Bureau (Defendant-Appellant). Supreme Court of New York, Appellate Division-First Department, 1926.

The Globe and Rutgers Fire Insurance Company against General Adjustment Bureau - Case on Appeal. Vol. 5902. New York Supreme Court Appellate Divison—First Department Papers on Appeal from Order, 1923.

The Globe and Rutgers Fire Insurance Company against John M. Larsen. Vol. 5929. Supreme Court of New York, Appellate Division-First Department, 1924.

Washington Times. "Prize Cup for Planes given to Aero Club," October 22, 1921.

Washington Times. "U.S. Flyers Break Endurance Record: Sustained Air Record Is Broken at Gotham." December 30, 1921, Final Home Edition edition.

Who's Who in American Aeronautics. Aviation Publishing Corporation, 1922.

Windsor, Henry Haven, ed. "Trophy for Airplane Efficiency." In Popular Mechanics Magazine, 37, no. 2:323. Popular Mechanics Company, 1922.

Wüstenbecker, Katja. "German-Americans during World War I." In Immigrant Entrepreneurship: German-American Business Biographies, 1720 to the Present. German Historical Institute, September 25, 2014.

Young, Patrick. "Inside the Mind of a Know Nothing." Long Island Wins (blog), November 16, 2011.

Young, Patrick. "The 14th Amendment and Birthright Citizenship for Children of Immigrants." Long Island Wins (blog), July 9, 2016.

Chapter 4

Early Pennsylvania Years

Brock & Weymouth, 1923–1926

Once he was allowed to work again, Buehl moved to Gladys Avenue in Hempstead, Long Island, and worked at nearby Mitchell Field. During that time, Buehl met Ralph K. Smith, a pilot for Brock & Weymouth, one of the pioneering companies in the field of aerial mapping. When Buehl was able to help Smith with a German aircraft engine, the quality of his work led Smith to recommend him to Arthur Brock. Buehl accepted a job offer to become chief mechanic for Brock & Weymouth. In July 1923, he moved to Philadelphia, where he would be responsible for maintaining the company's fleet of Fokker airplanes.

After the excitement of the previous four years of his post-war career, working at Brock & Weymouth must have seemed boring. It is easy to guess that aerial mapping seemed dull compared to flying celebrity passengers across the continent and participating in record-setting events. However, a little less stimulation may have been welcome in his life after the bruising he got during his separation from Larsen.

Aerial mapping is not at all boring, though, if one keeps in mind how it was that aviation became important. During World War I, people seriously focused on what to do with airplanes, and two

Ralph K. Smith, the pilot who invited Buehl to Philadelphia
PHOTO/EBC

uses emerged. Carrying messages quickly over long distances was one important early use. But aerial map-making emerged just as early and, for a time, achieved even greater importance.

The reason these uses became important in the sequence they did had to do with the capabilities and capacities of early airplanes. These vehicles were small and could not carry much cargo, but they could easily lift a camera to a useful altitude for taking pictures and making maps. There were plenty of sophisticated problems to overcome to per-

fect aerial photogrammetry, but by 1923 Brock & Weymouth had solved them and was making excellent maps from pictures taken from small airplanes. On the other hand, by 1923, the Post Office was limited to using deHavilland DH-4s, with a load capacity of only 400 pounds.

(above) The old way of taking an aerial photograph—stick your camera out of the door and just take a picture of the ground.

(below) A Brock & Weymouth Fokker C-II airplane with its aerial camera mounted in the belly. It is the camera that is visible through the door. PHOTOS/EBC

A comparison with Thomas Edison's invention of the electric light bulb further illuminates the issues. About the time Edison was working on the problem, several other people also invented electric light bulbs, but none of these bulbs caught on. Edison's unique insight was that for light bulbs to work, there needed to be a large-scale infrastructure of generators and electrical distribution networks. Similarly, using airplanes to deliver airmail had to wait for the building of extensive, coast-to-coast infrastructure. Using airplanes to take pictures that can be processed and converted into high-quality maps, on the other hand, required the support of little more infrastructure than one might find in a well-equipped office in, for example, downtown Philadelphia.

Explorer Roald Amundsen illuminated the importance of aerial map-making in a 1922 interview:

"Our present knowledge of the earth, its form, size, the configuration of its surface features, their measurements and representations on maps as we see them today is the result of many centuries of strenuous endeavor and conquest over obstacles. Yet, at the present time, only one-seventh of the earth's land surface has thus far been accurately mapped, and it would take at least two hundred years to complete the task—with the usual methods.

"Aircraft will make it possible to do in twenty years what would require two hundred years with the usual methods."

Brock & Weymouth was the first firm in the United States to use aerial photography for commercial mapping. The Brock brothers, Arthur and Norman, along with Edward Cahill, were "the first to create an aerial camera that was mounted in the plane instead of holding the camera over the side."

The abstract for a paper published by the American Society of Civil Engineers says,

The Brock and Weymouth Mapping Instruments which were designed and built in Philadelphia in the early 1920's were a unique development. The "Brock Process" started a new era in American surveying and was the forerunner for many currently used photogrammetric methods.

An issue of *Prop Wash*, the employee newsletter of Aero Service Corporation, says that Brock & Weymouth began their "pioneering photogrammetric work" in 1924, when Buehl was there. Brock & Weymouth "produced the first accurate photogrammetric maps in the United States and Canada."

The photograph on the next page is one that Buehl had in his collection. It shows what he referred to as "strip mapping." The original of the photograph is trimmed to about 6 by 8 inches, is sepia in tone, and appears to be a contact print from the original glass plate, which would have measured 6.5 by 8.5 inches. Small trapezoidal marks at the bottom and top corners of the image are the shadows of tabs that held the plate in the camera magazine. The aerial camera used by Brock & Weymouth held 46 glass plates in its magazine.

During his work with Brock & Weymouth, Buehl traveled to Canada to participate in a mapping project in Quebec. The purpose of the project was to develop rail spurs from a gold mine to nearby smelters. The Fokker c-11 they used was shipped to Canada by rail and then assembled. After the flights were done, the airplane was disassembled and shipped back to the United States.

When Buehl worked for Larsen, he traveled in western Canada numerous times. His presence in eastern Canada for Brock & Weymouth attracted attention, though. It is unclear why this happened eight years after the War, but his German accent and German passport

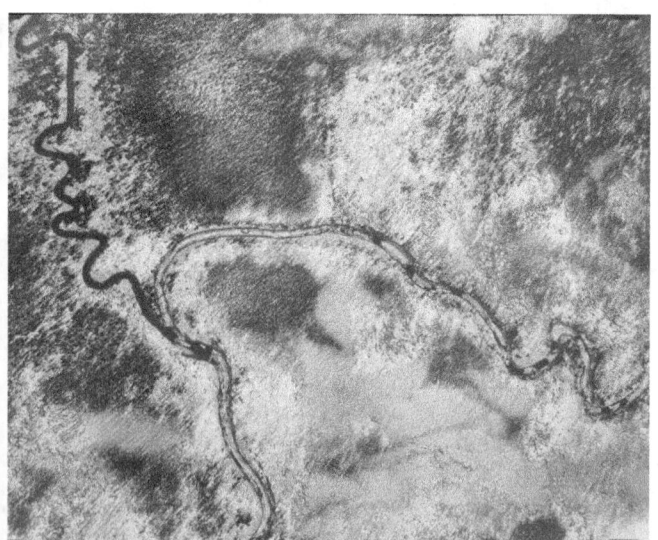

seemed suspicious, and Ernie was detained for a day or two by Canadian authorities. Buehl said he was locked in a boxcar until they could investigate him. After that, when he had to go to Canada, Brock & Weymouth sent him with travel papers explaining his purpose for being there.

Aerial photo of the type used by Brock & Weymouth. The shot is pinpoint sharp, making it possible to count every tree in the landscape. PHOTO/EBC

Marriage

During his tenure at Brock & Weymouth, Buehl met Anna Manso and they married. It was a difficult marriage. According to people I met, she did not support him to advance in his career, and she even worked against his success. It is difficult to speak of this aspect of Buehl's life, but I find it necessary to do so because understanding a little about his wife clarifies a few things about Buehl.

Anna was born on 8 August 1900 in Loivos, Portugal, to this day a place remote from any major population centers. Her childhood was a long nightmare. Early in her life, her mother died and her father moved to Brazil, leaving the little girl with elderly relatives. Anna was treated as a household servant and in this role was disciplined very harshly. Finally, when she was six years old, she was sent to Brazil to join her father. Contrary to her dearly-held hope, her father had little interest in her and all but abandoned her once she arrived in Brazil. Anna concealed this story and nearly every other story about her origins.

There were two stories of how Anna got to Philadelphia. The first story notes that Anna was a plucky young woman who sold her very

(left) Anna Manso Buehl in 1924.

(right)Anna Manso before cutting her long hair. Anna came to dislike this photo and tried to destroy it.
PHOTOS/EBC

long hair to get money for passage to the US. This was not what really happened, but it was believed within the family. Anna did nothing to contradict this story.

There is nothing wrong with the true story of how she came to Philadelphia, but it is not as heroic-sounding. A generous American couple hired her to look after their daughter while they were in Brazil. Her employer was an engineer who worked for Bethlehem Steel and had been temporarily posted abroad, along with his family. When the family returned to the US, they brought Anna with them. She and the family sailed on the *SS Vasari* from Buenos Aires, Argentina, on 26 February 1918, arriving in the United States on 21 March 1918. The passenger manifest for that voyage shows that she traveled "first cabin."

In the arrival documents, she is listed as 17 years old, 5 feet 4 inches tall, and having brown hair and brown eyes. She had no identifying marks, had a sun tan, and was in good health. The record shows she could read and write, and was listed as being employed as a domestic. (Anna was sensitive about being referred to as having been a domestic. She insisted she had been an "au pair.")

When it was time for her to separate from the family that had brought her, they helped her to attend a trade school so she could enter a career as a beautician. She moved to Philadelphia, where she lived at the Columbia Hotel at 19th and Wallace Streets. This was where Buehl first lived in Philadelphia and where they met. They married on 6 December 1924. She was 24, and he was 27. After getting married, they moved into a larger apartment at the Columbia Hotel.

The story of her early years of abuse and neglect is supported by indirect evidence from the way her personality

Buehl's 1923 automobile license, giving his exact address on Wallace Street. PHOTO/EBC

developed. A background of being raised in severely abusive circumstances is associated with the sort of personality we found in Anna.
Her personality was characterized in part by an extreme need to get
people to express admiration for her.

Her need for admiration was so great that if she imagined the
slightest neglect, she would become angry, jealous, and demanding.
She was capable of being so imperious in how she dealt with people
she knew that at least one close friend of the family believed she was
descended from European nobility.

Buehl wrote a poem describing his marriage. It was undated but
relates to the time in the early 1960s after his children were grown up

A Poem by Ernest Buehl

My Home once a Beauty and of Representation
In there I reared two Children of my Creation
The Years went by in Health and Happiness
And the Children grown to adult Eagerness.
So, all at once in the same old Year
Twice Wedding Bells one could hear
Now gone is the laughter and Noise
Somewhat perplexed I stand and poise —
My Wife with all her ambition and Correction
She lost two Prospects of her Perfection
So I am left the old Boy with all his faults
Now nothing I do is right and brings Squalls
My Partner try to change me till she is hoarse
As I grow older things are getting worse
Who wants to be perfect and feel so above
As in a House of Correction there isn't any Love.

and he was alone in the home with Anna. It expresses feelings consistent with those he shared with me privately during conversations in the 1980s.

༄

A couple of points related to Anna's personality and behavior become relevant later in the story about Buehl. First, some documentation one might expect to find in the materials Buehl saved over the span of his career is missing, and that is because Anna destroyed it. Anna was very jealous of her husband and the attention he received. She attacked friendships he had with prominent people, and she attacked his collection of photos and memorabilia when the items involved someone famous. For instance, she destroyed nearly all of what he had from Rickenbacker. Second, it says something about his character: he remained married to Anna and behaved as a faithful husband for their whole marriage. It is to his credit that he remained with Anna.

It would be unfair to Anna only to note only her eccentricities and rough qualities. It can be said that she liked young children and was able to provide a certain amount of good guidance to them. Also, when first getting to know her, she could be interesting and engaging.

Philadelphia Rapid Transit

There is a curious story that appears briefly in a book called *Aviation and Pennsylvania*, in which it is stated that in 1926 Buehl was tapped by André Priester to maintain the engines in the aircraft operated by the Philadelphia Rapid Transit (PRT) Air Service. All evidence says this story is not true.

The PRT Air Service was established by Philadelphia businessman Thomas Mitten in 1926, when the United States was celebrating its sesquicentennial. The PRT flew a route between Philadelphia, the first capital of the United States, and Washington, DC, the present capital.

When Mitten decided to use Fokker Trimotor airplanes for the service, Anthony Fokker recommended fellow Dutchman André Priester as general manager. According to the story, Priester then selected Buehl to maintain the aircraft, which, according to the story, were equipped with BMW engines.

The short-lived PRT air service operated only until late fall in 1926. When it shut down, the story says that both Priester and Buehl were set "adrift." Priester went on to become the chief engineer for Pan American Airlines, which was just getting started then. As for Buehl, he is said to have "barnstormed" for a little while, billing himself as "The Flying Dutchman," before establishing his Flying Dutchman Air Service in northeast Philadelphia, a mile north of Bustleton Air Mail Field.

There are some problems with this account, though. Most of the problems are circumstantial.

Buehl was working for Brock & Weymouth between the time he left Larsen and the time he and a partner set up Flying Dutchman Air Service. He was never "adrift" or without employment. Also, he never did any barnstorming, particularly if by "barnstorming" we are talking about stunt flying. He could fly an airplane, but in 1926 his skills as a pilot were not good enough.* In 1926, Buehl made his living at Brock & Weymouth working as a mechanic, not as a pilot.

Another significant problem with the story is that the Fokker Trimotors used by the PRT were equipped with Wright Whirlwind engines, not BMW engines. The rationale given in the book for Buehl's selection was his expertise with the BMW engine. Since these were not used, the story's authenticity becomes more unlikely.

---

* Even after he developed sufficient skills to perform barnstorming stunts, he would not perform these maneuvers because he felt they were too stressful on the airplane.

The Flying Dutchman Takes Off

Flying Dutchman Air Service

Buehl was an adequate pilot in 1928, when he started Flying Dutchman. He was good enough to pass the test to get the commercial license he needed, but he was not evaluated as excellent. He became an excellent pilot later.

This is the earliest picture we have of Flying Dutchman Air Service. Buehl is standing at the wing-tip of a KR-31 Challenger, which may be his or may be the one belonging to his partner.
PHOTO/EBC

Working for Brock & Weymouth gave Buehl a five-day workweek. On the weekends, he was free to do what he wanted. During this time, Buehl and another man started talking about opening a flying service, and sometime in late 1927 or (more likely) early 1928, they began piloting passengers. They were operating out of Lincoln Highway Airport, a little airport that disappeared before 1930. Another name for this field was Lincoln Airways Inc., Field. The location given on the application was described as "Roosevelt Boulevard and Bensalem Pike," an intersection which also no longer exists. Buehl never mentioned the name of his partner.

As Buehl told the story in later years, the other man purchased the small biplane they used in the business. Buehl said it was a KR-31 Challenger. The partnership between the men was simple: the other man would provide the airplane if Buehl would do the flying. They would split the money they took in. In other words, the partner had all the capital investment, while Buehl contributed all the labor. In a short time, Buehl quit his job at Brock & Weymouth and went to work for his new partner.

It was his partner who promoted Buehl as the "German ace." This promotion was entirely cooked up as a sales gimmick. There was no point in trying to conceal Buehl's German heritage. As soon as Buehl started to speak, it became obvious to everyone who met him. In a climate infused with anti-German prejudice, the partner saw a way to turn Buehl's German-ness into a virtue. They would imply Buehl's high degree of skills by advertising "Come see the German ace." For his part, Buehl, who personally did not like being billed in this way, would go along with the story by not directly contradicting it.

Whats in a Name: The Flying Dutchman

The name, Flying Dutchman, is a play on words with respect to Buehl's nation of origin: it does not refer to "Dutch," as relating to Holland, it refers to *Deutsch*, the word Germans use to identify themselves. It is also a nickname used by Anthony Fokker, who actually was Dutch, years before Buehl got tagged with it.

At a deeper level, it brings to mind the legend of the Flying Dutchman. In the beginning, the legend involved a ghost ship, cursed to wander the oceans forever. By the time Wagner wrote his opera, The Flying Dutchman, the legend had softened significantly. By Buehl's time, the association with a curse faded so much that Dutch Airline KLM picked up the story in their advertising, emphasizing the fun and intrigue of world travel. Buehl's logo featured a sea-going ship that picks up a theme of the legend.

The business logo Buehl used for Flying Dutchman Air Service PHOTO/EBC

His partner was likely the one who also came up with the name of the business. Putting together the idea of the German ace with the well-known story of the Flying Dutchman, they had a promotional package that sold itself. It was a name that was already familiar to people, and it was easy to associate the name with Buehl. Of course, sharing the nickname with Anthony Fokker did not hurt Buehl at all.

The partner was a young man named Thomas Trivigno.[†]

Trivigno was born in Italy in 1900. His family immigrated to the U.S. in 1905, and he became a naturalized citizen. In 1930 he gave his occupation as "aviator." Receiving instruction at Pitcairn Flying School, he applied for a student pilot's license in August 1927. In October 1927, Trivigno purchased a used Curtiss JN-4C (a model known as a "Canuck").

The evidence indicates that Buehl and Trivigno joined up sometime during the three months between October 1927 and January 1928. Buehl's Pilot's Log Book for 1928, the earliest one we have, shows that in January of that year, he was flying Trivigno's Canuck. Buehl used the airplane routinely from 8 January until 14 March 1928.

In mid-March 1928, Trivigno purchased a KR-31 Challenger. Buehl test-flew the new airplane at Crescent Field in Camden on 14 March and then took delivery of it on 17 March. From that point forward, Buehl only flew the KR-31. He used the Challenger to offer sky-rides, passenger flights, and lessons. Weekends usually produced much better revenue than weekdays. Average (median) revenue for a weekend was $75, while for a weekday it was $12.

Trivigno was also flying the Challenger. He flew it when preparing for his private pilot's license exam, and his first solo flying experience

---

[†] In 2011, it was reported in Smithsonian Air & Space that Buehl's partner was E.C. Malick. Supporting this, there are circumstances that could have brought Malick and Buehl together. Malick was licensed significantly before Buehl, they lived within easy walking distance of one another in Philadelphia, and there was an overlap in occupations. However, after visiting for several years with Malick's biographer, Mary Groce, we agreed that he was never Buehl's business partner. The partner was certainly Trivigno.

was in this airplane. There is no evidence one way or the other that Buehl instructed Trivigno. It is known that Trivigno started his instruction at Pitcairn, and he likely continued there. Buehl likely gave Trivigno some informal tips. Trivigno was tested for his "private" rating on 23 June 1928, and that day he flew the Challenger for his flight test.

Ironically, Saturday 23 June, the day Trivigno took his flight test, was also the day Buehl realized he did not need a partner. That day, the weather was unfavorable. The temperature was a cool 63°F, and it was breezy and raining in Philadelphia. It was not bad enough to

A page from Buehl's Pilots Log Book showing when he acquired his Challenger. PHOTO/EBC

keep airplanes grounded, but people did not come out for sky rides in an open cockpit biplane on cool, rainy days. Also, Buehl did not have full use of the airplane that Saturday because Trivigno was using it. Revenue was only $12.

According to their routine, at the end of each day of operation, Trivigno would show up at the airfield, they would discuss the day, Buehl would turn over the day's revenues, and Trivigno would pay him. That Saturday, Buehl commented apologetically about how little money he took in. Trivigno replied, "That's okay. We made enough to cover the payment on the airplane."

At that instant, Buehl realized his partner had borrowed money to buy the airplane they were using. Buehl quickly figured out that he could just as well borrow money and buy his own airplane. Buehl liked the idea of being an independent businessman. On Saturday, 7 July 1928, he flew his own Challenger for the first time, recording revenue for the day of $65.

> *Timeline: Partnership*
>
> **1927, AUGUST 10** Trivigno applied for a student license. He is flying at Pitcairn.
>
> **1927, OCTOBER 3** Trivigno acquired the JN-4C Canuck.
>
> **1928, JANUARY 8** Buehl is flying the Canuck.
>
> **1928, MARCH 15** Buehl receives his limited commercial license
>
> **1928, MARCH 17** Buehl takes delivery on Trivigno's Challenger.
>
> **1928, MAY 5** Trivigno sells the Canuck.
>
> **1928, JUNE 23** Trivigno applies for his private pilot's license.
>
> **1928, JULY 7** Buehl has his own airplane, a Challenger. The partnership is dissolved.

The Challenger

As Buehl told the story, the dealer agreed to sell a KR-31 to Buehl for $2,570. (In 1928, a new Ford Model T cost $290). Buehl gave him 10% to hold the airplane and then had ten days to pull together the balance. He took out two additional mortgages on his home and began approaching everyone he knew who might lend him a little money toward the final sale price. For nine days, he drove to the homes of everyone he knew and rang their doorbells to ask people to lend money to him.

Finally, with enough cash in hand, mainly in fives and tens, Buehl and Anna drove to the dealer and Buehl presented him with the money. Counting it out, the dealer found that the amount was five dollars short. Buehl told him not to worry about it; he had the money in his car and would go to get it. He walked back to the car and asked Anna how much money she had with her. Anna refused. "Oh, no!" she said. "No more! No more!" She finally admitted that she had $6.80. "Just give me five! You know I am good for it!" he insisted. She finally, very reluctantly, gave him the money along with a "bad look."

Ernie and Anna Buehl in 1928 beside his new Challenger. His 1927 Fairchild KR-31 Challenger was Buehl's first airplane. He borrowed money to purchase the Challenger. PHOTO/EBC

Buehl composed himself, went in, and casually handed to the dealer the last $5.00, leaving them with $1.80 in their pockets. At that point, about a year away from the start of the Great Depression, Buehl's commercial assets were the airplane, about $12 worth of gasoline, and over $2,000 in debt. As one writer later put it, Buehl showed that "one man with a big dream can parlay $1.80 in cash, one airplane, three mortgages on his home and a rented airstrip into one of the best flying schools in Pennsylvania."

When Buehl told the story, he added tension by emphasizing how little money he had left in his pocket after purchasing the Challenger, less than two dollars. He made it sound as though he and his wife were going to have to skimp on meals for a while and maybe even visit with the landlord about being able to pay the rent on time. Reviewing the story and adding in what we know from his records, here is what we find: on Saturday, 7 July 1928, he purchased the Challenger. By the end of the same day, Buehl pocketed $65. The next day his revenue was $105. For the days on which he recorded revenue, half the time Buehl took in between $8 and $26 on weekdays, and on weekend days he took in between $38 and $100. He was able to pay off the debt quickly, and on 8 May 1929, he purchased a second airplane. Clearly, buying the Challenger was not a risky investment.

Buehl's First Licenses

People in his later years saw Buehl primarily as a pilot, but in his early years he did not see himself that way. After all, for years he was not hired as a pilot. There were a lot of outstanding pilots, but early in his career he was a world-class mechanic. He did not rush to get his pilot's license.

He taught himself to fly in 1914 and he would pilot an airplane from time to time, but not commercially. There was no formal training, and in the early days it was common for pilots not to be licensed. He did not need a pilot's license because he could fly as much as he wanted without one.

It is hard to know what changed for Buehl. One thing we know is that he and Frank Mills became acquainted. Mills had purchased a BMW-powered airplane and hired Buehl to work on it. It is possible that Mills bartered flying lessons for the help with his BMW engine. In any case, Buehl took his first formal flying lessons with Mills, and that led to Buehl's first pilot's license. It was issued in 1926, and it was for hydroairplanes. Mills operated the Philadelphia School of Aviation at Essington, on the banks of the Delaware River. There were never any runways there, as the facility specialized in the operation of "flying boats." The aircraft would simply land in the river.

The United States itself did not begin to issue civilian pilot licenses until April 1927. Therefore, Buehl's 1926 license predates anything that would have been available to him from a United States civilian regulatory authority. It also predates by about a year any evidence that Buehl was planning to become a pilot.

The license itself is dated 21 September 1926, and it is signed by Orville Wright. It says:

"Fédération Aéronautique Internationale
National Aeronautic Association of U.S.A. Inc.
Certificate No. 824
The above named Association, recognized by the Fédération Aéronautique Internationale, as the governing authority for the United States of America, certifies that Ernest H. Buehl born 30 day of April 1897 having fulfilled all the conditions required by the Fédération Aéronautique Internationale, for a Hydroairplane Pilot is hereby brevetted as such."

Buehl's first pilot's license. PHOTO/EBC

His license has a surprisingly low number, until one considers that this was a license for piloting hydroairplanes. Before 1926, the FAI granted thousands of licenses in the United States for those who wanted to fly conventional airplanes, but many fewer for hydroairplanes. That is why Buehl's license number is so low.

This was the license to show to the newspapers. A reporter might ask to see his first license, and Buehl would pull out this one. They would see Orville Wright's signature and wrongly assume that Wright himself gave Buehl flying lessons. He did not mind the confusion. The promotional value was real, even if the implication was misleading.

Of more direct importance for Buehl's business than his FAI license was his United States Transport Pilot license. He had an instructor's rating, so he could teach. This license number was 1918, and again some newspaper reporters were confused, thinking 1918 was the year he was licensed. He was actually licensed by the CAA in 1928. He received his "limited commercial" license on 15 March that year. In July, he received his Transport Pilot's license.

Given that Buehl had been working with his partner at least since January 1928, does that mean he was doing commercial work without a proper license? The answer is no. He did not log any revenue from work with his partner until 17 March that year, two days after he had the license.

Buehl's Aviation Licenses

- United States Transport Pilot license, number 1918
- Pennsylvania Transport Pilot license, number 54
- United States Mechanic's License (Airplane and Engine), number 260,
- Pennsylvania Mechanic's License, number 10

It can be admitted that his scores on his flight test in 1928 were not impressive. His skills were good enough to pass, but he got "fair" ratings in several areas. This should not be surprising: Buehl was largely self-taught. Observational learning is powerful, though. He likely learned a lot when he sat in the co-pilot's seat while working with Larsen. With the opportunity to fly across the continent with Bert Acosta, Buehl really saw what an airplane can do, as well as refining his navigational skills.

His formal instruction was with hydroairplanes, which would not feature the same skills that would be taught if he were flying land-based airplanes. His background had gaps, and as of late spring 1928 he still needed to polish his skills. Two years later, in his 1930 flight check, his scores were uniformly "excellent." By that time he had logged 912 hours total of solo flying time and about 1400 hours flying as a co-pilot.

His licenses as a mechanic were more important to him than his pilot's licenses. In his work as an aviator, he was first respected for his mechanics skills. After all, he was recruited from Munich to New York as a mechanic, then recruited to go to Philadelphia as a mechanic. Most of his great adventures were flown as a mechanic, not as a pilot.

His mechanic's license showed he was rated for airplanes and airplane engines. Buehl applied for his US mechanics license in February 1927. He listed significant experience on many engines: Rapp, BMW, Benz, Mercedes, Argus, Austro-Daimler, Siddley Puma, ox-5, Hispano, and Liberty. His experience in airplane structure and rigging included work on: Junker, Fokker, Bristol, Aeromarine, and others. In his application, he mentioned that he was the chief mechanic on the 1919 world altitude record flight and the 1921 endurance record flight. Also, he served as flight mechanic for five coast-to-coast flights and two flights from New York to Peace River, Canada.

Flying School

The flying school took its first students in early 1928, about half a year after Lindbergh made the first solo transatlantic flight.

Years later, he advertised that Flying Dutchman was "Philadelphia's oldest flying school."

Previously it was noted that Buehl's reputation as an aviator was built primarily on his skills as a mechanic. This was true in the earlier part of his career. Over time, he built another solid reputation as a flight instructor. The thing is that Buehl was a good pilot when he started the flying school, and within a couple of years he became an excellent pilot.

(above, top) Buehl and some of his early students.

(above, bottom) Promoting the flying school. PHOTOS/EBC

It is said that teaching someone else is one of the best ways to sharpen one's own skills, and this was true for Buehl. By 1930, he had years of focused practice on skills his students would need to pass their flight checks. He had to learn these skills beyond the level of intuition most pilots need. He had to develop explicit knowledge at a level that would allow him to explain it to others. A couple of years after he opened his flying school, Buehl's own skills became increasingly refined, and he became an outstanding teacher.

After buying the Challenger in July 1928 and separating from his partner, Buehl approached "a farmer on the [Roosevelt] Boulevard" who "rented me a 40-acre rhubarb field" to use for an airport. This would have been close to Northeast Philadelphia Airfield and several other small airports in northeast Philadelphia.

Buehl offered sky rides to the curious, and he offered flying lessons.

The claim to operate the "oldest" flying school in Philadelphia was true in a narrow, hair-splitting sense. Buehl did not claim to have opened Philadelphia's first flying school. That particular honor went to his friend and first teacher, Frank Mills, who established the Philadelphia School of Aviation in 1916.

The Philadelphia School of Aviation was closed on December 8, 1941, the day after the Pearl Harbor Attack, as was every other private air facility in the region, and it did not reopen promptly after the war. This interruption in service at the Mills facility gave Buehl the opening to make his post-war claim for being the "oldest" flying school in Philadelphia.

In spite of this competitive one-upmanship, there existed considerable mutual respect between Buehl and the Mills family. Buehl went to Frank Mills for help getting his license, and later Buehl helped Frank Mills' son, C. Robert (Bob) Mills get his license. Just as Buehl had been flying for years before he came to Frank Mills' school for instruction, Bob Mills was already an exceptional pilot before he came to Buehl's school. Bob had flown in World War II and in 1944 was awarded the Distinguished Flying Cross. Bob merely lacked the license he needed to pursue a civilian career in aviation.

According to Harry Silcox, who wrote several books about the history of the northeast Philadelphia area, at his flying school in the 1930s "Buehl taught over three thousand" students how to fly. This seems like a large number and we cannot verify it. It is important to note with caution that many details Silcox wrote about Buehl are wrong. However, it is easily confirmed that Buehl employed several trainers, and he managed a lot of students at Somerton. The number is possible.

First Airport

Buehl referred to his first airport as "Boulevard Airport." He described things as going well for him there, until one day he was pulling the prop on an airplane for a student and the student neglected to turn the magneto switch to off. The engine kicked back, and Buehl got a broken right arm. Once his arm was set, he found he could fly left-handed, so he went back to work.

This airport lasted only for a very short time. He was there for only about two months before he had to move. Buehl recorded that "someone wants to start a big airport," which would include the 40 acres he was renting. The farmer from whom he was renting directed Buehl to vacate.

An airport had been operating near this location since 1918. In that year, the earlier airport was operated as Bustleton Field, and it was the site of the first regularly scheduled US Air Mail delivery, 15 May 1918. In 1928, a group of investors acquired 80 acres and opened what they called William Penn Airport. It has often been suggested that Buehl first operated Flying Dutchman out of William Penn, but it appears to be the case that it was William Penn Airport that displaced Buehl from that location.

Buehl quickly approached "a landowner on the Bustleton Pike" and was able to negotiate a longer-term lease for 115 acres. This new location became his Somerton Airport. With the stability of a lease, he could afford to improve the airport and build hangars.

ॐ

The 1950 USGS topo map shows a "Boulevard Airport" at the corner of Roosevelt Boulevard and Red Lion Road. This likely occupies the 40 acres Buehl rented in 1928.
PHOTO/USGS

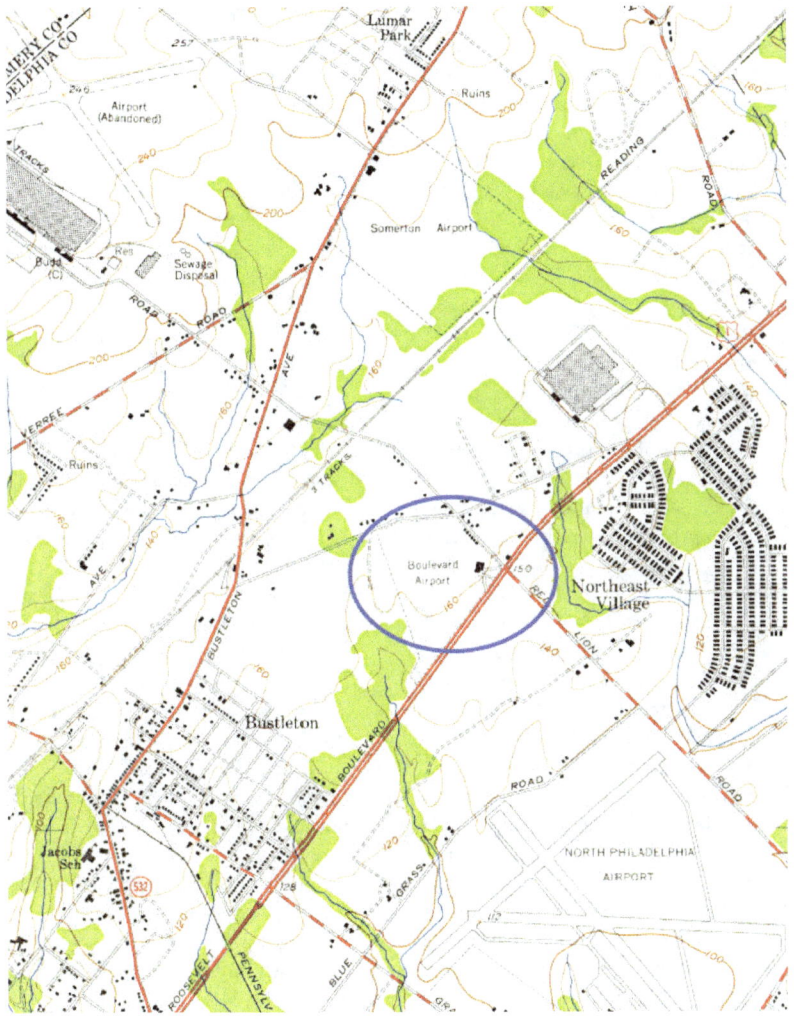

Selected Sources

Aero Club of Pennsylvania. "History | Aero Club of Pennsylvania." (web page).

"Application for Identification Mark—Form R-15." Department of Commerce, Aeronautics Branch, October 3, 1927.

Beadle, J.B. "Travel Document for Brock & Weymouth," August 13, 1926. EBC.

Buck, Olga. "Eddington's Buehl Airfield Home to Oldtime Flying Dutchman." *Bucks County Sunday Press*. December 13, 1953.

Buehl, Ernest H. "Checkbook Autobiography," n.d. Probably when he was in his early eighties, he summarized some highlights of his career in the pages of an unused checkbook register.

Buehl, Ernest H. "Handwritten Draft of Response to Correspondence from K.M. Molson. Molson Wrote to Him on 22 June 1977," June 22, 1977.

Buehl, Ernest H. "Untitled Poem," n.d.

Burtch, Robert C. "History of Photogrammetry: Early Developments." The Center for Photogrammetric Training, Ferris State University, August 24, 2008.

Department of Commerce. "Application for Mechanic's License." Department of Commerce, Aeronautics Branch, February 26, 1927.

Department of Commerce. "Application for Pilot's License (Trivigno)." Department of Commerce, Aeronautics Branch, June 23, 1928.

Department of Commerce. "Application for Pilot's Rating (Buehl, 1A Land Rating)." Department of Commerce, Aeronautics Branch, September 26, 1930.

FAA Airmen Certification Branch, AFS-760.

Department of Commerce. "Application for Transport Pilot's License (Buehl)." Department of Commerce, Aeronautics Branch, June 9, 1928. FAA Airmen Certification Branch, AFS-760.

Ellis, Walt. "C. Robert Mills: A Tribute." Philadelphia Seaplane Base [9N2], 2008. (web page)

Ernie Buehl Talks to the Experimental Aircraft Association, Pennsylvania Chapter 76. Videotape, 1986.

Evening Public Ledger. "Amundsen Will Chat with Rest of World While Drifting or Flying over North Pole." June 19, 1922.

Freeman, Paul. "Abandoned & Little-Known Airfields: Pennsylvania —Northeastern Philadelphia Area." Abandoned & Little-Known Airfields, n.d.

Friedel, Robert, and Paul B. Israel. Edison's Electric Light: The Art of Invention. Updated edition (June 8, 2010). *Introductory Studies in the History of Technology*. Johns Hopkins University Press, 2010.

Gebhart, Ed. "Flying Was in Bob Mills' Family, and in WWII, It Came in Handy." *Delaware County Times*. August 2, 2002.

Hart, Mike. "Hand-Propping Demystified." AVweb Features, March 29, 2015. (web page)

History. "Model T—History," August 21, 2018. (web page)

Maksel, R. "The Unrecognized First." *Smithsonian Air & Space*, March 2011.

"Petition for Naturalization—Ernest Buehl." United States Department of Labor, September 26, 1928.

Prop Wash—Aero Service Corp. "The Brock Award," October 1956.

Quinn, Alfred O. "Brock & Weymouth Photogrammetric Mapping Equipment." *American Society of Civil Engineers, Journal of the Surveying and Mapping Division* 103, no. 1 (September 1977): 47–52.

Robie, William and National Aeronautic Association (U.S.). *For the Greatest Achievement: A History of the Aero Club of America and the National Aeronautic Association. First Edition* edition. Washington: Smithsonian, 1993.

Silcox, Harry C. Remembering Northeast Philadelphia. *American Chronicles: A History Press Series.* Charleston, SC: History Press, 2009.

Smith, Frank K., and James P. Harrington. "Pennsylvania Aviation Matures." In *Aviation and Pennsylvania.* Franklin Institute Press, 1981.

The Globe and Rutgers Fire Insurance Company against General Adjustment Bureau—Case on Appeal. Vol. 5902. New York Supreme Court Appellate Divison—First Department Papers on Appeal from Order, 1923.

Tubis, Harry. "The Brock Brothers and the Brock Process." *Photogrammetric Engineering and Remote Sensing* 52, no. 8 (August 1976): 18.

Young, Clarence M. "Letter Accompanying Delivery of License 1918," March 15, 1928. FAA Airmen Certification Branch, AFS-760.

Young, Clarence M. "Letter Accompanying Delivery of Transport License 1918.," July 30, 1928. FAA Airmen Certification Branch, AFS-760.

CHAPTER 5

Vision for Aviation

Buehl approached his airports and flying school with a particular mission in mind. He wanted to democratize aviation. He was guided by a vision, widely shared at the time, of everyone owning an airplane. Families would live in homes with an attached hangar as well as an attached garage: Walk out your front door in the morning, hop in your airplane, taxi out to the runway next to your home, and then fly to work. Airplane ownership should be as common among the general public as boat ownership on Cape Cod.

He carried his democratic mission through his time at Somerton and into his time at Eddington. As a simple example, Buehl sold Piper aircraft. One might ask why Piper? Why not sell Beechcraft? The answer is that more people could afford to get into flying through Piper. Piper was the "Ford" of flying machines, whereas Beechcraft might be thought of as more the "Cadillac." When he established Somerton, Buehl did not have his sights on business fliers. He wanted everyone to fly.

THE SKYSEDAN

This beautiful experimental airplane is built to answer all the travel needs of the postwar family. The Skysedan is a four-passenger, low-wing monoplane powered by a 160 h.p. engine. Handsomely designed inside and out, it has a top speed of 140 mph, cruises at 125 mph and lands, with flaps, at 50 mph. Its maximum cruising range is 500 miles.

PRELIMINARY
SPECIFICATIONS

Length Overall	26'
Height Overall	7'
Wing Span	34' 8"
Total Area (sq. ft.)	200
Chord	95" Root 47.5" Tip
Weight Empty (lbs.)	1250
Useful Load (lbs.)	1050
Gross Weight (lbs.)	2300
Baggage Compartment	
Front Seat	13"x14"x40"
Rear Seat	8"x16"x40"
Baggage Capacity	100 lbs.
Rate of Climb (Full load)	570 ft.
Top Speed	140 mph
Cruising Range (miles)	500
Landing Speed (with flaps)	50 mph
Absolute Ceiling (solo)	15,600 ft.
Gas Consumption (at cruising)	10 gal. per hr.
Gas Tank Capacity	40 gallons

Specifications Subject to Change.

Buehl saved this specifications sheet for a Piper product called the "SkySedan." According to Piper, it was "built to answer all the travel needs of the postwar family." PHOTO/EBC

Somerton Airport 1947 PHOTO/SKYPHOTOS

Somerton

In September 1928, Buehl became a citizen of the United States. That same year, he opened Somerton Airport. Despite the onset of the Great Depression in 1929, it was a happy time for Buehl. Although economic conditions were dismal, he was rapidly able to build a successful business. It was reported that during the Depression, Somerton was the only private airport in Philadelphia to make any money.

Located within the city limits and only sixteen miles from City Hall, Somerton Airport had a 115-acre flying field of smooth, sodded, level ground. The land now is occupied by housing developments.

How could Buehl make money at his airport during the Depression when others could not? There were at least three major reasons:

A 1950 map showing Somerton, marked in the top half of the image, a little to the right of midline. Also visible are North Philadelphia Airport in the lower right corner, Boulevard Airport just to the north of North Philadelphia Airport, and the abandoned Budd Factory Airfield on Red Lion Road. PHOTO/USGS, PUBLIC DOMAIN

Service bill to Abby Wolf for work on his OX-5 powered airplane. PHOTO/EBC

First, he was the best. Not just good. The best. He could make things happen that other people could not. A little story told by Brigadier General Abby Wolf illustrates: Wolf's personal airplane was powered by an OX-5 engine. He was having trouble keeping it running, so he took it to the mechanics at Pitcairn. This was no surprise. Pitcairn was not just another little airport; it was a notable aircraft manufacturer. They developed a variety of aircraft and held a number of government contracts. Pitcairn even received the Collier Trophy in 1930. If anyone could fix it, Pitcairn's mechanics should be able to do it. However, the Pitcairn mechanics could do nothing. Perhaps it was the notoriously frustrating Berling magneto that put the problem beyond the

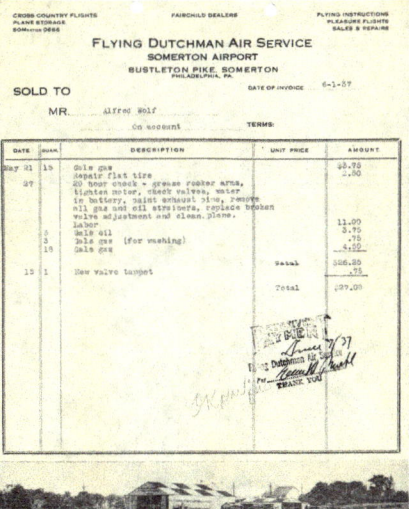

reach of their skill? In any case, the mechanics there recommended Wolf take his airplane to Buehl. As they said, Buehl had the rare ability to keep an OX-5 running well in all seasons. When Buehl quickly solved the problem, Wolf became a fan of The Flying Dutchman.

Second, Buehl was a creative and persistent promoter. He created a persona that attracted other aviators. Naturally, it took no effort for a visitor to get Buehl to talk about his early exploits in the air. He was friendly and outgoing, and he actually knew a lot of the early aviators others only read about in the newspapers. A visit to Somerton always held the promise of a good story about his adventures and the

Buehl's QB pin. The Quiet Birdmen was a secret drinking club made up of accomplished aviators. Membership was by invitation only. The name "Quiet Birdmen" was deliberately ironic, as was the idea that it was "secret." This was a boisterous group. PHOTO/AUTHOR

glamorous people he had met when flying. He took his listeners back to the romance of early aviation. Over time, people would come to the airport just to see what Buehl was going to say or do next.

Third, Buehl had his vision for aviation, in which he invested all the energy he had. He saw his work in aviation as his purpose in life. All of this represented something much bigger to Buehl than just a way to make a living. He was passionate about flying. He thought about it all the time, whether he was "working" or not.

Buehl with instructors and students at Somerton. PHOTO/EBC

To encourage his vision to become reality, Buehl sold good, affordable airplanes, and he would teach anyone who wanted to learn how to fly. The cost for a good used plane would be as low as $600. If someone purchased a new airplane, the cost would include flying lessons.

At Somerton, Flying Dutchman offered private flying lessons and, as World
War II approached, also provided instruction through the Civilian Pilot Training
Program (CPTP). According to a brochure
Buehl published to advertise The Flying
Dutchman Air Service, "Usually a person
learns to fly in 15 to 20 lessons of ½ hr.
periods. Cost for ten one-hour instructions
$125." Even if a student did not have the
money, Buehl would train them. Some of
his students would later recall the time
they spent clearing trees from the airport
in order to earn lessons.

*It was a time when a boy and his
dog could come to the airport after
school and spend some time flying.*
PHOTO/WAYNE KLAW

Buehl also broke racial barriers by training black pilots. C. Alfred
Anderson, later known as "The Father of Black Aviation," was his
student at Somerton. Few others in the entire nation would help a
black pilot to become a professional aviator, but Buehl would.

To attract students who might become steady clients, Buehl offered
sky-rides. Bill Lokes, a former employee of Buehl Field, recalled a
story Buehl told once when the two of them were driving together.
The story illustrates how competitive the airport business was at that
time. Bill wrote:

> *I remember Ernie telling me a story of flying out of his airport in the
> early days. There was another (rival) airport almost across the street.
> A drunk came into the office and got Ernie. Taking Ernie outside,
> the drunk pointed up and offered $10 if Ernie would fly him through
> "that" cloud. Ernie accepted and flew through the cloud several times.
> Each time he felt a bump. After he landed, he noticed the guy from
> the other airport had been flying through the same cloud at the same
> time. Ernie flew over to the other guy's airport and they got into an*

argument over whose cloud it was. Ernie claimed it was his since it was over his airport!

Buehl worked hard to develop attractions to get people to stay at the airport for as long as he could hold them. If they simply showed up at the airport with some vague impulse to try a lesson, they might leave if they had to wait for an instructor to become available. But if Buehl could keep them entertained, they would be more willing to hang around the airport until an instructor was free. This increased the chances that they would actually complete the lesson. Also, just by hanging around the aviators there, they would begin to absorb more of the excitement of flying.

Events might include Buehl showing off simple stunts in the air, or even giving parachute-jumping demonstrations. A story Buehl told was of the son of a family friend who wanted to pay his bill by providing a parachute jumping demonstration. The young man explained that he wanted to make the jump because some months earlier he had

(left) Pleasant sitting areas in front of the office encouraged people to spend more time at the airport. PHOTO/WAYNE KLAW
(right) Parachutist prepared for a demonstration at Somerton. PHOTO/EBC

published a story in his church bulletin, saying that he had made a parachute jump, but the truth was that he had never jumped before in his life. He felt badly about telling this lie, so he wanted to make it true. As he explained, if he could make this one jump, he could tell himself that he had just reported the facts "a little early."

Nickname

The danger of parachuting was exaggerated in nearly everyone's mind, other than in the minds of those who actually engaged in parachuting. Parachutists got so used to being questioned by onlookers at demonstrations that they began to refer to outsiders to the sport as *wuffos*.

The name is said to have arisen when, one after another, the onlookers at a parachute demonstration in a southern state approached the parachutists and asked, "Wuffo you want to jump outta a perfeckly good airplane?"

Buehl would probably count as a *wuffo*. We do not have any stories of him trying a parachute, and he seemed to be very nervous about this event he arranged.

Parachutist prepared for a demonstration at Somerton. PHOTO?EBC

Buehl was very concerned about allowing the young man to jump, but finally said he would agree to do so if the fellow could find a four-leaf clover in fifteen minutes. As Buehl told it, "The first thing I know I seen about twenty of my students lookin' for a four-leaf clover!" Before the time was up, the student approached Buehl saying, "Here it is, a four-leaf clover!" Buehl was forced to allow the jump to go forward, but he directed the pilot to go up an additional 1000 feet, to ensure that this inexperienced jumper would have a little more time to open his parachute. After the young man landed, he admitted to Buehl that he and some others had glued an extra leaf to an ordinary clover. This was the last time Buehl had a parachute demonstration.

Ground activities included performances that were completely irrelevant to flying but that would attract people to the airport and give them something to talk about. There were "performers" whose "talent" involved being buried six feet underground in a glass-topped coffin for a week or two at a time. The coffin would have a donation slot, and visitors could chat with the buried person: "Hello. How are you?" People would come to the airport, look into the simulated grave, and then stick around to visit with others about what it all meant.

It was easy to arrange this particular sort of attraction. There were people who made a bit of a living by being buried alive, and they were always looking for places to perform. In that business, there were even records to be set for how long one could remain buried. Buehl did not like this sort of performance. During World War I, he spent enough time in trenches and tight little tunnels that he developed significant claustrophobia and a fear of being buried alive. Even though Buehl thought it was creepy, it was popular, so he set up these performances more than once.

Buehl told a story of a woman who was buried at the airport, determined to set a new endurance record. She was buried with great fanfare on Sunday and intended to stay down for two weeks. Unfortunately for her plans, it began to rain Sunday night. Monday morning, it was still raining. Buehl was quite concerned because he could see that the hole was going to fill up with water. He checked on her at night to make sure she was okay, and she indicated that she wanted to remain buried. However, as it continued to rain and the hole really did fill, she had to adjust her position in the coffin in order to keep her nose out of the water. At that point, Buehl ended the display and had her "exhumed."

Buehl was always ready to feed a nice story to the local newspapers. As an example of exactly the kind of thing a newspaper would love to print in the Sunday features section, one story he gave to the *Philadelphia Evening Bulletin* involved a dog, an airplane, and an odd little "hook": the owner of the dog wanted to try taking his nearly deaf dog up in an airplane because someone had told him that it might restore some of the dog's hearing. From a newspaper's perspective, this type of feel-good story nearly tells itself. The caption just about says it all: " 'Flying the Dog' in Doctor's Test. 'Punch,' Dalmatian pup in the arms of his master, Charles R. Bechtle, takes off at Somerton Airport in a plane piloted by Ernest Buehl, president of the Flying Dutchman Air Service, to determine whether rapid changes in altitude may remedy the dog's deafness." From Buehl's perspective, this was free publicity that would make people think of his airport when they thought of flying.

C. Alfred Anderson and the Tuskegee Airmen

It was not widely documented at the time. No news clippings Buehl saved mention it. It was, though, one of Buehl's most important personal contributions to aviation. From August 1931 to February 1932, Buehl helped C. Alfred "Chief" Anderson to obtain an Air Transport License (ATL), enabling him to fly as a commercial pilot and to train others. Anderson went on to become the Chief Flight Instructor for the Tuskegee Airmen, a group of fighter pilots who demonstrated exemplary performance in combat. Anderson has been described as "The Father of Black Aviation." Anderson's Air Transport License was awarded in February 1932.

Born in Bryn Mawr, Pennsylvania, on 9 February 1907, C. Alfred Anderson wanted to fly, but prejudice in aviation was so strong that Anderson was unable even to get a ride in an airplane. Certainly, anyone in the Northeast, with its virulent racism and active Ku Klux Klan, would have been sticking his neck out by agreeing to train a black pilot.

Opportunities to learn anything about aviation hardly existed for black students, and did not improve for many decades. Perhaps the earliest "class in aviation" available to African-Americans was offered at the Negro Manual Training School in 1910, but the instruction was limited. The students learned the principles of airplane propulsion by studying a "model which travels along a wire, its motor being driven by electricity." Instruction that involved actual flying was difficult to find anywhere in the country for black students.

Anderson applied to the Drexel Institute Aviation School, but was rejected for admission because of his race. Later, he joined the National Guard to become a pilot but was rejected for the Air Corps for the same reason.

After much persistence, Anderson was able to enroll in Pitts Aviation School, where they would teach him about mechanics and give him some ground schooling, but they would not give him flight instruction.

To supplement what training he was able to get at Pitts, Anderson spent a lot of time at Philadelphia Air Transport Company (PATCO) Airport, in Norristown, Pennsylvania. He discretely listened to the pilots as they would talk about flying, quietly picking up what practical knowledge he could. Instructors there finally said they would teach

Anderson how to take off and land, but they would not allow him to use any of their airplanes for this instruction.

The only way he was going to be able to learn to fly was to purchase his own airplane. So Anderson saved and borrowed and was finally able to purchase a Vielie Monocoupe. In spite of whatever the instructors at PATCO said, he had to train himself how to take off and land. This led to some very expensive and painful trial and error. Also, he could not find anyone who would help him accumulate cross-country flying experience. Ingeniously, he worked out an arrangement with a white pilot, Russell Thaw, who would rent the Monocoupe and allow Anderson to accompany him. Thaw provided some informal instruction while he flew.

Compounding the difficulty of getting the practice and hours of experience he needed to qualify for a private pilot's license, at many airfields Anderson was not allowed even to get out of his airplane once

Buehl's granddaughter, Rosanna, with Colonel Roosevelt Lewis (ret.), one of Anderson's last students. Lewis was very helpful in filling out the story of the relationship between Buehl and Anderson.
PHOTO/R. BUEHL

he had landed. At a number of airports, he was chased by broom-handle-wielding employees and was threatened with violence. Still, by means of his exceptional resolve, Anderson was awarded his private pilot's license in 1929.

Anderson was not the only aspiring black pilot who had trouble finding instruction. Lincoln Payne, a young black aviator who ended up studying with Buehl, talked about his difficulty finding instruction. He, too, needed help getting enough hours and experience flying cross-country. Payne told a story of trying to get some help from the chief pilot at the largest airfield in

Philadelphia, who asserted the following explanation of why he was not going to help Payne: although he personally had no problem working with a black student, "the other pilots were mostly Southerners," and "he was quite sure they would not tolerate the presence of 'colored fellows' as students. Therefore, it would be safer for me to seek some other school." Payne then found Buehl, who gave him the training he needed so he could receive his license on 13 December 1930.

The next step for Anderson was even harder. Anderson wanted to earn the Air Transport License so he could fly commercially and train others. Although there were several who held private pilot's licenses, there were no black pilots who had the Air Transport License. The ATL was the gateway to entering the profession, and white pilots guarded it zealously.

Being self-trained, Anderson had gaps in his skills. Doing what he could, he continued to find opportunities to study what he would need to know for the written part of the commercial exam, but there remained many practical things he did not know about managing and handling an airplane in the air.

Anderson needed financial help to pay for the lessons he needed. The Quaker City Lodge of Elks, which was founded in 1926, became interested in Anderson. This was the Improved, Benevolent Protective Order of Elks of the World (IBPOEW). The white-run BPOE did not admit black members until 1972. It was the mission of the IBPOEW to promote civil rights, and at a time when many unions were segregated, they worked to improve employment opportunities for blacks. To advance their mission, the Quaker City Lodge had the idea to help a black pilot become licensed to instruct other black pilots so that they would be qualified to fly the air mail. Post Office jobs were considered to be quite good: they paid well compared to most other jobs available to blacks at that time, the work was steady, and in general postal employees were fairly treated. The involvement of the Elks brought a focused push to get Anderson licensed. They paid the $4,255 for Anderson's instruction and licensing fees.

No one knows for certain how Anderson found Buehl. Before Anderson came to Buehl, though, he knew Buehl was approachable. Anderson was not the first black student Buehl trained, so word got around. The connection, I believe, was Lincoln Payne, whom Buehl helped to become licensed in 1930. Significantly, Payne was a member of the Elks. Many sources say that Buehl and Anderson met in 1929, which is entirely possible. Payne likely would have been Buehl's student at that time and may have introduced them.

Here is how Anderson talked in an interview about working with Buehl:

> *Of all things I met a man by the name of Ernest Buehl. He was a pilot in the First World War in the German Air Force—he was known as the 'Flying Dutchman.'* Someone told me that if I went to see that man he would probably help me qualify to get this license. Sure enough, when I went to him to talk about it he said, 'Sure, I'll give you instruction.' He gave me instruction in spins, steep turns, and perfected me so I could go take a flight check for the Transport license. Well, when we went to take this flight check the inspector didn't want to give it to me. He said, 'Well, I've never given a flight check to a colored boy, and I'm not going to do it now!' I remember Mr. Buehl became very hostile with the man, and threatened him, 'You're going to give him the flight check—he deserves it—he's qualified and I demand that you give him the flight check or else you're going to have to deal with me!' The inspector decided to give me the flight check.[...] After it was over Mr. Buehl asked him how I did. He said, 'Well he did okay with his flying, and he got a 100% on his written test—I'll give him an 80% and that will pass him.' So that's how I happened*

---

* The only combat Buehl saw during the war was as a rifleman in the trenches. See the earlier chapter about World War I

to get the first Air Transport License ever issued to a black in the United States.

Given the violent prejudices of the time, one has to ask why Buehl would have risked helping Anderson. Fortunately, a couple of interviewers asked Buehl why he agreed to help Anderson. A remarkable account of Anderson's career appeared in *People Magazine*. It provides a clue about Buehl's motivation in working with Anderson:

> *At last he found a teacher, Ernest Buehl, a German immigrant. "In them days a colored man in an airplane, it just never was known," says Buehl, now 92. "Anderson had been to all the other airports surrounding Philadelphia. People really condemned him and called him names. But, oh boy, how he would like to fly."*
>
> *Anderson credits Buehl with refining his technique and with forcing a federal examiner to give him his commercial pilot's test. "When the government agent came," Buehl recalls in accented English, "he took me aside and he called me everything under the sun because I would even attempt to get that man into an airplane. I finally tell him, 'Look, I'm a foreigner. I'm a citizen by the paper. That guy's born here.' And I threatened to make a little trouble for this guy. So he finally took him up and kept him up a considerable time longer than a white man. He really put him through the works."*
>
> *Anderson, then 25, was awarded aviation's top license; for many years, among a handful of black aviators, he was the only one to hold it.*

In an interview in *Flying*, Buehl touched again on his motivation to train Anderson. The writer described how Buehl shared with him his painful experience of prejudice. As the article explained, Buehl's experience "did not leave him bitter, but rather a man determined to avoid having the same thing happen to some other American." Buehl told the writer: "He [was] a natural pilot and smart, too. He made 100 on the CAA exam, and the examiner took me aside and said he couldn't give him a 100 because "y'know, he's colored." I told him the airplane couldn't tell the difference."

The way the story is often told, it sounds like Buehl physically threatened the CAA examiner but that was not true. Buehl, a battle-hardened combat veteran, could be quite forceful when he needed to be, but he was a talker, not a fighter. Significantly, he gave some thought to selecting the inspector whom he would ask to examine Anderson. He chose a man he believed would be the most likely to give his student a fair chance. So strong was racial prejudice at that time, though, that Buehl had to put a good professional relationship on the line and even threaten to make trouble. Still, it would have been out of character for Buehl to have physically threatened the examiner.[†]

After Getting the License

After Anderson was licensed in February 1932, he and Buehl stayed in touch. Anderson and Lincoln Payne started a flying club at Somerton in April 1932. It was called the Challenger Aviation Club. They had 14 members in addition to Anderson and Payne, and they housed two airplanes at Buehl Field.

In 1933, Anderson was still in the area, and he was taking members of the local Boys Club that met at PATCO, in Norristown, to tour Somerton, to introduce them to Buehl.

The story is often told in a way that implies Buehl physically threatened the examiner, but that is not true. Of course, this is a staged "fight" and has nothing to do with the conflict Buehl found himself in with Anderson's examiner. PHOTO/EBC

---

† This was not the only time Buehl threatened to make some trouble for someone who was practicing racial discrimination. William Ferguson and his wife, a black family he worked with and came to know well, needed a bank loan and they were having trouble with the bank. Buehl found out, and since this was the same bank Buehl used, he wrote a letter endorsing Ferguson's character and honesty. He went further, too, and stated he would change banks if the Fergusons did not get the loan. The bank backed down and issued the loan.

Anderson did some demonstration flights and began training other black airmen, including Dr. Albert Forsythe, a physician from Atlantic City, New Jersey who had had to go to Canada to escape US racism in order to pursue a medical degree. He became interested in aviation and sought out Anderson, who introduced Forsythe to Buehl.

For Forsythe, the connection to Buehl was important. Forsythe needed an airplane, and it is said that, due to his race, he would have had "extreme difficulty" buying one without Buehl. Buehl sold Forsythe a Fairchild 24, a small cabin monoplane, which they named "Pride of Atlantic City." Buehl provided some initial lessons, and Anderson finished the training for Forsythe. Soon after, Forsythe and Anderson flew this airplane from New Jersey to California and back, making the first transcontinental flight by black pilots. They made their flight a deliberate protest against racism. Upon their return, Forsythe wanted to take a "South American Goodwill Tour," so they needed a more powerful airplane. Buehl used his connections to help them purchase a Lambert monocoupe, the "Booker T. Washington."

In 1935, Buehl hosted "the first flying circus staged by colored aviators in this vicinity" at his Somerton airport. It was organized to "stimulate interest in aviation" among people of color. Anderson helped to organize it, and it was co-sponsored by the Education Equality League, which had been founded in Philadelphia to desegregate public schools, hire more black teachers, and to obtain representation on the school board.

In 1940, Anderson was tapped to be the chief trainer in the program for black pilots at Tuskegee Institute. On 29 March 1941, Eleanor Roosevelt was visiting the Infantile Paralysis (polio) Unit at the hospital at Tuskegee when she heard about the flight program. She asked to be taken out to the airfield to see for herself. Anderson recalled:

The first thing she said was, 'I always heard colored people couldn't fly airplanes, but I see you're flying all around here.' And then she said, 'I'm just going to have to take a flight with you.' Of course, all her escorts ran out there and they were all very much opposed to it—'No Mrs. Roosevelt! You can't do that!' Well, she just made up her mind she was going to do it and got in the airplane. You don't argue with the First Lady, so we took off and made the flight, and then when we got back down she said, 'Well, I see you can fly all right!' It wasn't long after that that President Roosevelt's administration decided to have this program called the 'Tuskegee Experiment."[‡]

Famous photo by Prentice Herman Polk of C. Alfred Anderson and Eleanor Roosevelt preparing to take off in a Piper Cub from Kennedy Field. PHOTO/ PUBLIC DOMAIN

Racism, Aviation, Anderson, Buehl, and the Seed of the Civil Rights Movement

Even though for his whole life Anderson honored what Buehl did for him, it is still necessary to directly deal with Buehl in the context of racism and white supremacy. The reason why it is necessary is because the question arises about Buehl in the literature about the Tuskegee Airmen.

In his excellent book about the Tuskegee Airmen, *Freedom Flyers*, J. Todd Moye reports that Buehl believed in "white supremacy." This is an idea that immediately conjures images of mobs of hooded KKK vigilantes burning crosses in people's yards and enforcing racist ideas.

Moye describes Buehl as "a willing instructor with an unlikely background," referring to Buehl's background as a German immigrant.

---

‡ Contradicting Anderson on one point in the story about Eleanor Roosevelt, the decision had already been made to establish a facility to train black pilots at Tuskegee before Mrs. Roosevelt took her famous flight with Anderson in March. The key decision had already been announced in January of that year

The fact that Buehl's involvement in training Anderson would, at first glance, seem "unlikely" or unusual, immediately suggests that the story deserves a close look, but Moye devotes only one paragraph to it.[§] Of course, Anderson himself was not the topic of Moye's book about the Airmen, and Buehl's role is just a detail in the story of Anderson, so it is understandable that he did not explore it more deeply. Moye documents this aspect of Anderson's training by citing just one source, albeit a strong one, an oral history interview given by Anderson in 1981.

After reading Moye's book, there are questions one has to ask: Was Buehl a "white supremacist"? Was he a racist? These questions immediately lead to the deeper question of why Buehl would agree to help a black man he did not know in an era when it was dangerous to do so.

Before proceeding, it is necessary to remind white readers who came to political awareness after the 1960s of the climate of racism in the United States before that time. Even with the resurgence of naked racism in the early decades of the 21st century, it is hard to picture what it was in the 1950s and earlier. It is also necessary to insist that this is not "black history." The history of slavery and racism is the history of all Americans. As our heritage, it still touches us all.

Slavery—and the racism that had to go with it as part of its moral justification—forms a central theme in the history of the United States. Slavery had to be addressed in the writing of the Constitution itself, and the deep legacy of racism is one we still face every day in the United States.[ℭ]

---

§ Perhaps it is not too unlikely that a German would have feelings on these issues. Albert Einstein, another German immigrant, spent a considerable amount of effort speaking out against racism in the United States. He pointed out that because he did not grow up with the US prejudices against blacks, he did not take them for granted. He explained: "The more I feel an American, the more this situation pains me. I can escape the feeling of complicity in it only by speaking out."

ℭ Article 1, section 2 deals with how to count citizens of the United States who were not "free persons"—who were, to put it plainly, slaves. Amendment 14 was added after the Civil War, primarily to clarify that everyone born in the United States, including those descended of slaves, are citizens having full rights and privileges.

In the days when Buehl agreed to train Anderson, racism was expressed openly and was so virulent in the US that the uniformed pilots of the Tuskegee Airmen, who were commissioned officers in the US Army Air Force, were expected to give up their seats on public transportation to *any* white, including German prisoners of war.

After the War, the Airmen returned home to the US to the daily reality of legalized discrimination and prejudice. In Europe, they had felt for the first time that they were identified as Americans rather than as members of a race. Many career officers, including General Benjamin O. Davis, Jr., admitted that they preferred overseas assignments to being posted in the United States. As much as they loved the US, the harassment they faced in every part of our nation made life difficult. Coming back to the US, they were less willing to put up with racial discrimination.

In 1945, at Freeman Field, in Seymour, Indiana, black officers were not allowed to use the Officer's Club or even to go into the PX to buy a candy bar. At the same time, German prisoners of war were allowed to come and go freely on the base. A group of black officers decided to challenge the policy of segregation on base. In small groups, they entered the whites-only Officers Club, asked to be served, and were subsequently arrested. This so-called Freeman Field Mutiny "is generally regarded by historians of the Civil Rights Movement as an important step toward full integration of the armed forces and as a model for later efforts to integrate public facilities through civil disobedience."

It is possible to make a case for the argument that Buehl played a limited but significant role in setting the stage for what played out later in the civil rights movement, leading in the next few decades to the enfranchisement of black voters. Of course, Buehl's action in the early 1930s in training Anderson was taken a long time before the emergence of the civil rights movement in the 1960s, or even the Freeman Field

Mutiny in 1945, so it can be argued that the effect is too distant from the supposed cause to make a firm link. However, there certainly was a connection between the training of black officers for the Air Force and the Freeman Field Mutiny. In turn, the Freeman Field Mutiny certainly served as a model for effective resistance to segregation. The help Buehl gave Anderson to get his commercial pilot's license certainly affected the training of the black Air Force officers who came out of the Tuskegee program. Therefore, it is a reasonable argument.

Classifying people by race was very common in those days, and it was applied to everyone. The taxonomy of race split people into many more categories than we think of today, and it was not based entirely on skin color. It was believed at that time that the French were one race, Germans another, the Irish another, and so on. (I would have been described as the product of uncertain miscegenation, a mixture mainly of races found in the British Isles). Of course, the strongest racial prejudices were based on visible characteristics, such as the shape of one's nose or the shade of one's skin.

Buehl would have been identified at that time as a representative of the German race, and people's perception of him would have been influenced by stereotypes about Germans. According to the thinking then, Germans are genetically predisposed to being disciplined, orderly, blunt, humorless, loud, and war-mongering. Therefore, even though he was white, he himself was the target of racism, and he would have understood this fact in precisely that term, *racism*.

Buehl knew what it was like to be the target of prejudice. As a German immigrant, Buehl often found himself in the crosshairs of prejudicial suspicion and sometimes hatred. It is hard to recall now, but at the time Buehl arrived in North America, the newspapers were full of anti-German rhetoric. He himself faced a wall of prejudice.

In milder instances occurring even in the 1960s and 1970s, Buehl recalled flying his Challenger to various aviation events and being snubbed. When people saw his interesting antique aircraft, they would wander over to talk with him but then turn and walk away as soon as they heard his German accent.

Anti-German prejudice was not only a US phenomenon. Even the British royal family came under pressure to change its dynastic name from the House of Saxe-Coburg and Gotha to the House of Windsor precisely because of this issue. As an example from Buehl's life, when he was working in Canada he was briefly imprisoned because his accent alone aroused suspicion. This occurred sometime between 1923 and 1926, when he worked for Brock & Weymouth.

In a stronger example, in 1920, Buehl observed the way Emil Monz was destroyed by anti-German prejudice in the US. It was one of the first lessons John Larsen gave both Buehl and Monz: you may not be able to lose your accents, but you must do everything else you can to avoid being identified as the "Hun." In the end, though, Monz was humiliated and eventually committed suicide.

According to his granddaughter, Buehl was a product of his own time. He was not a native speaker of English, so he used the vocabulary he learned from the people around him, some of it race-based. For example, we have a recording of him using the phrase "nigger in the woodpile," meaning there was something suspicious in the situation. It was a phrase that was in common use at the time. However, Buehl does not seem to have ever intentionally disparaged people of color.

His granddaughter believes her grandfather regarded black people in much the same way that he regarded people from any other group to which he did not belong. Buehl, like most people, valued his own background and experiences in life more than those of others, and even imagined these to be a bit superior. Being German is better than being Italian, but being southern German is better than being northern German, being Catholic is better than being Protestant, and so on. However, Buehl did not strongly adhere to any of these beliefs, and they did not much influence how he dealt with others. He certainly did not believe it was necessary to carve out some kind of legal protection for white people.

The statement briefly quoted by Moye in *Freedom Flyers* was particularly confusing because it did not seem to fit with anything else Anderson ever said about Buehl, and it did not fit with how Buehl conducted himself. It is hard to reconcile that with the fact that in the early 1930s Buehl appears to have been the only white pilot in the northeast willing to provide advanced training to a talented black aviator. It was necessary to track down the source, to listen to the original tape recording of Anderson responding to his interviewer.

In 1981, Dr. James C. Hasdorff, interviewing Anderson for the us Air Force Oral History project, directly asked Anderson why Buehl agreed to train him. Anderson's response was confusing:

"Well, I often wondered about that. Because he was with Hitler, during the war, you know, and, they, they were, uh, they were, he'd be, he, he, he'd always, uh, was in favor, you know, supremacy, white supremacy, and I wondered myself why he, uh, decided to do that, but he seemed to me to have no objection whatsoever."

As he responds to Dr. Hasdorff's question, Anderson is heard to be fumbling for words. He states that he often wondered about this himself. In parts of his response, his volume dropped as he tried out various phrases to express what was in his mind. At these points it is difficult to make out what he was saying. Even an expert transcriptionist could make errors when listening to this part.[**]

In the interview, Anderson tossed Buehl, Hitler, World War I, and white supremacy into a confusing salad of facts. The pronouns Anderson uses confuse everything even more. To isolate the references

[**]   It was necessary for this author to slow Anderson's speech in this section of the recording by as much as 80% to catch his words (this is possible without changing the pitch of his voice), and to amplify parts of what he was saying so that it could be heard. This was possible by using Adobe Soundbooth cs4 software.

for the pronouns, the references are highlighted: **Buehl** (bold), *Hitler* (italic), and GERMANY (small caps) in order to untangle the message.

Anderson: "Well, I often wondered about that. Because **he** was with *Hitler*, during the war, you know, and, THEY, THEY were, uh, THEY were, *he'd* be, *he, he, he'd* always, uh, was in favor, you know, supremacy, white supremacy, and I wondered myself why **he**, uh, decided to do that, but **he** seemed to me to have no objection whatsoever."

When introducing himself to Buehl in 1931, Anderson would have been hearing about Hitler and escalating racism in Germany, and he must have wondered if Buehl, a German immigrant, shared the same racist attitudes. Anderson was pleased to find that the stereotype of the German racist did not apply to Buehl.

It is impossible to associate Buehl with Hitler. Although Buehl and Hitler both fought on the German side in World War I, they were in different units, deployed in opposite ends of Europe. Further, Buehl left Germany before Hitler got started in politics and, in fact, Buehl later spent World War II doing his best to fight Hitler's Nazis by training American military pilots.

Buehl was not a believer in white supremacy. He was not a racist. The reason why he helped Anderson was because he was a flag-waving patriot for his adopted country. Without qualification, he believed in American ideals of equality for all citizens, and he believed in fairness.

Buehl standing at an award ceremony in the 1960s as a black pilot is honored. We do not know the name of the black pilot. PHOTO/EBC

World War II

On 8 December 1941, the day after the Pearl Harbor attack, every civilian airport in the Philadelphia region received a telegram telling them to remove the propellers from their airplanes and close their airports. This included Buehl's Somerton Airport. These facilities were too near the coast, and indeed the coasts were vulnerable. In the Atlantic and the Gulf of Mexico, Nazi submarine activity within US waters had already resulted in the sinking of mer-

Group picture at Franklin & Marshall. Buehl is standing in the front row, on the left.
PHOTO/EBC

chant ships almost as soon as they left their harbors. There was concern that small airports might be misused. When flying restrictions were lifted at the end of the war, Buehl re-opened Somerton Airport.

While Anderson was training pilots at Tuskegee, for two years

CHAPTER 5: Vision for Aviation *World War II* **169**

during the War, Buehl trained aviation cadets for the Navy at Franklin & Marshall College at Lancaster, Pennsylvania. According to one newspaper article, when Buehl was training cadets, "He used some thirty planes for instruction work with over 1,400 students." Decades later, his wife recalled that those two years during World War II were the only time in Buehl's life that he worked regular hours, and the only time during their marriage that she could count on him being home on time for dinner.

While Buehl had family in Germany, people for whom he was

deeply worried throughout the entire duration of the war, he was a loyal citizen of the United States, and he did all he could to ensure the success of the US military effort to defeat the Nazis. In his mid-forties in 1941, he probably could have avoided serving the US as a trainer of aviators, but he decided to serve anyway, setting aside personal considerations in favor of doing the things his adopted nation needed him to do. Buehl chose to do his duty.

Unlike Buehl himself, his brother Fritz was a committed Nazi, as was another brother, Karl. This is a formal portrait taken in 1936 of Fritz in the uniform of a "Brown Shirt." Buehl was aware of his brothers' activities in Germany. PHOTO/EBC

A curious side note: although Buehl faced anti-German prejudice for years before this, he never mentioned any problems associated with being of German

origin when doing this work for the War Department. Of course, he worked as part of the Franklin & Marshall faculty and was not directly employed by the US government.

Post War

The post-World War II years were good for many small airport owners. The government paid for flight instruction for soldiers returning home, and many returning GIs wanted lessons. Also at this time, manufacturers were offering a variety of inexpensive aircraft.

Despite the general prosperity, Somerton closed for the last time in 1952 because Buehl lost his lease on the land. When he first started, the owner, a farmer, had leased it to him at a very favorable price. According to Pennsylvania law, though, if a tenant leased land for 25 years, he acquired the right to purchase it. Buehl's lease was written for 24 years and eight months. At the end of this term, the farmer refused to sell to Buehl or to renew the lease. The land would bring a much better price if sold for a housing development.

In February 1952, a picture appeared in *The Breeze Newspapers*, showing Buehl in the cockpit of his Challenger, preparing to take off for the last time from Somerton. The accompanying brief article stated that Somerton Airport closed permanently on Saturday, 23 February 1952, at 11 o'clock, when Buehl flew his 1927 Challenger from there to his new airport at Eddington.

Eddington

As it became evident that he would not be able to continue to operate out of Somerton, Buehl purchased 138 acres of land in Eddington for his next airport. According to a handwritten note, recorded when he was quite elderly, Buehl purchased the Eddington property in 1941. This date seems surprisingly early, but he penned that date more than once.

Although the lease at Somerton was good until 1952, it had a sale clause that could force him to vacate with only 60 days' notice. Buehl was aware that there was pressure to sell the land at Somerton for home sites, and after the War ended, the real estate market ticked up. A newspaper announcement titled "Flying Dutchman Moves Airport" confirmed that the move from Somerton to Eddington occurred because the site of the old airport was going to be divided to make lots for new homes.

The announcement stated that the formal opening of the airport at Eddington was going to take place on 1 March. Officially called "Buehl Field," the Eddington airport opened in 1947. For a time, Buehl operated both Somerton and Buehl Field. Until the entire operation was moved to Eddington in February 1952, George Townson supervised the new field while Buehl continued at Somerton.

The airport at Eddington looking across the runway, toward the intersection of Street and Hulmeville Roads, with T-hangars in the mid-ground and the airport buildings above them. PHOTO/SKYPHOTOS

Buehl Field as it appeared on 8 December 1954, looking across Street Road at the hangars. The gray hangar with the plain peaked roof is hangar #3. Above it, with the checkerboard roof, is hangar #2. It includes the shop. Just above and to the right is the landing direction indicator with its circle. Next is the hangar with the rounded roof. The office is located there, as are the barber shop and the Airport Grill. The gas station is at the intersection of Street and Hulmeville Roads, just above the middle and to the left. PHOTO/SKYPHOTOS

An article published in 1947 talked about how establishing a new airport allowed Buehl to apply what he had learned at Somerton. Buehl realized that flying did not appeal to many people as a hobby because it was expensive, time-consuming, and even inconvenient. At Eddington, Buehl attempted to address each of these issues.

Trying to keep it all affordable for those who did not live at the airport, Buehl Field was "hands off," letting people do as much as they wanted to do by themselves. For example, Buehl built T-hangars so that people could easily store their own airplanes, rolling them by themselves into storage in the same way they might store their trailered fishing boats.

Almost as though they were cooperating with Buehl's vision, following World War II, manufacturers produced civilian aircraft designed to be affordable to middle-class families. An interested person in Philadelphia could even go downtown to the John Wanamaker Department Store, one of the first deparment stores in the US, and buy an inexpensive airplane there. Training was readily available.

Buehl planned to eliminate the time it took to commute to the airport. He imagined that people would like to live in moderately priced homes located at the airport. Each home would have its own hangar that would open onto an apron and connect to the airport's runway. This would save time, and the flier would not need to monopolize the family car (in 1947, most families had only one car).

The runway at Eddington was a nice, flat grass strip 2,100 feet long. At the time Buehl purchased the land for the Eddington location, airplanes were relatively slow-moving, and the wings were designed to provide a lot of lift. When taking off in Buehl's Challenger biplane, for example, the pilot would taxi slowly, and within a short distance, the plane would become airborne. The monoplanes available in 1941 had similar handling characteristics. A 2,100-foot runway seemed like plenty.

Buehl's vision slowly began to fray: airplane design changed within the decade. By the late 1940s, it was known that airplanes could be

Part of Buehl Field at Eddington, the gas station, along with the barber shop and the grill, was a part of a comprehensive plan to make flying more convenient. PHOTO/EBC

Tri-Pacers ready for students at Eddington. PHOTO/EBC

made to be safer if the wings were designed with less lift. The problem with the older planes was that, with their greater lift, winds would toss them around. A wing is designed so that when air moves rapidly over its top, a vacuum is created, lifting the wing and anything attached to it. An unexpected gust could hit the wing and carry off an airplane in a direction unintended by the pilot. In breezy weather it took quite a bit of skill and experience to keep an airplane in the air.

To compensate for the wing having less lift, however, the newer planes had to move faster to create the vacuum needed to lift the plane. More speed, of course, meant that the airplane needed a longer distance to take off and to land. Suddenly, a 2,100-foot runway was too short.

As airplane design continued to change, grass strips became less and less suitable. The older airplanes were "tail draggers," with their noses sticking up a little when all three wheels were on the ground. Newer airplanes, like the Tri-Pacer, lacked this characteristic. When a Tri-Pacer is parked, its cabin sits parallel to the ground. This feature meant that there was less clearance for the propeller on take-off and landing. Like most of the newer aircraft, the Tri-Pacer had smaller tires, which gave less drag when flying, and therefore more speed. Unfortunately, the small irregularities of a grass strip were felt more strongly in an airplane with smaller tires, possibly even compromising the safety of a landing. New aircraft could be operated from a grass strip but had less margin for error. Over time and to this day, some insurance companies prohibit the use of grass strips, and little training is done on grass now, so pilots tend to be uncomfortable using them.[††]

Buehl's vision really began to unravel when people figured out that airplanes are not very useful as a family vehicles. They can only be used during good weather, they cannot carry much luggage, and once arriving at the destination, what does one do for ground transportation? Airplanes made sense for business, not as transportation for

---

[††]   My thanks to Bill Lokes, a pilot who used to work at Buehl Field, for this explanation.

families. This sort of thing has been a problem for many industries, from package delivery to linking homes to the internet. It is referred to as the "last mile problem." The problems were solved for many industries but have never been solved for personal aviation.

As time went on, Buehl's vision for aviation faded. Individuals were not buying airplanes to serve their family's transportation needs, and there were not enough hobbyists to allow Buehl to make a living serving their needs. To stay in operation, he increasingly sought to attract business fliers.

Businesses wanted to fly faster, more powerful aircraft, including twin-engine airplanes. These required even more space to land. By 1960,

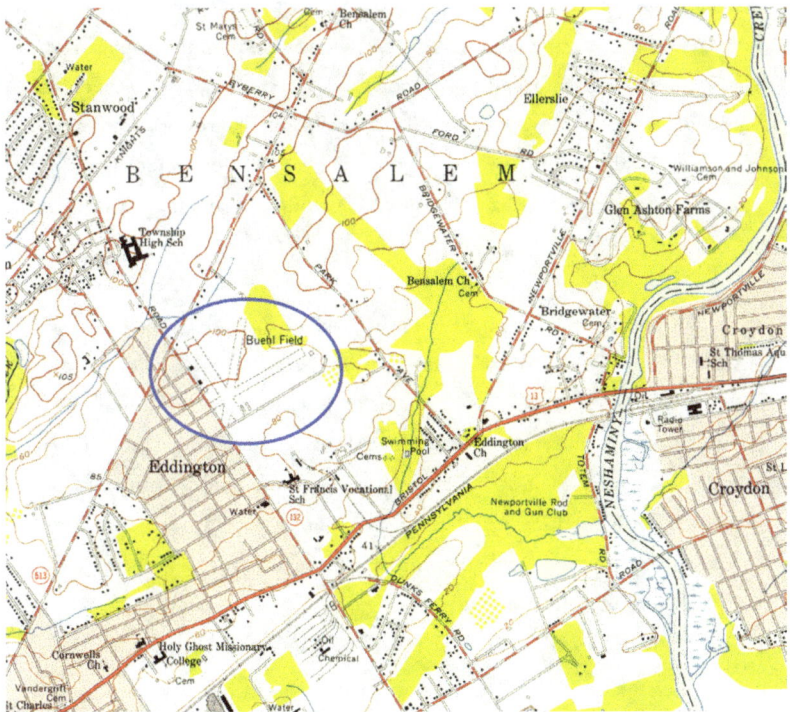

Buehl Field at Eddington (circled) is seen a little left of the midline at about the middle of the image. PHOTO/PUBLIC DOMAIN

Tail Draggers

Tail dragger aircraft enjoy a near cult-like following. There are many pilots who learned how to fly in a tail dragger who love them. It is possible to take off and land in more places in a tail dragger than in a tricycle geared airplane, and there is a romance associated with the old-fashioned stick-and-rudder skills needed to fly tail draggers. This book is staying out of the debate, but in fairness it is important to point out why tricycle landing gear has become dominant.

Aircraft having a steerable nose wheel, tricycle landing gear, are much easier to control on the ground. More than anything, the issue with tail draggers is that during landing, take off, or even taxiing, they can go into a horizontal rotation called a "ground loop." The front end of the airplane suddenly wants to switch places with the tail end. The result can be catastrophic. To give an intuitive analogy of what happens, one pilot suggested we picture trying to steer a child's tricycle while pushing it backward. It is very difficult to control.

Another problem is that a tail dragger cannot even taxi in a straight line. The pilot has to constantly turn the airplane through S-shaped curves in order to be able to see what is ahead. An airplane with tricycle gear can just steer straight to where ever the pilot wants it to go. Colonel (ret.) Roosevelt Lewis once mentioned this in the course of telling a funny story about his own first flying lesson with Chief Anderson. His first lesson took place at Moton Field before it was paved. It was just several acres of mowed grass. Lewis described taxiing from the hangar to where he would start his take-off. He said that watching from a distance the way he moved the airplane that day would have been like watching an anaconda slowly moving through the grass.

the grass runway was clearly insufficient. Moreover, the Eddington airfield had no room for expansion and could not offer the longer, hard-surfaced runway needed to accommodate expensive airplanes used by businesses. Buehl needed more room to be able to serve the needs of more modern aircraft, such as the twin-engine Piper Apache he wanted to sell.

In addition to the inadequacy of Buehl Field's runway, Buehl had other reasons to sell. Although the land around the airport had been largely empty when Buehl opened Eddington, the population in the area grew fast, and the land filled up with houses occupied by people who were not interested in owning an airplane and who, in fact, did not want their homes filled with the sounds of aviation. By 1960, residential areas entirely surrounded the airport.

With the increased population, the township planned to build a sewer system and pay for it with taxes based on road frontage. This

(above) An orphanage was located adjacent to the airfield. Pilots used to orient themselves on take-off by placing the orphanage tower in the middle of their windscreens. PHOTO/EBC (left) PHOTO/EBC, SKYPHOTOS

would be done in conjunction with widening Street Road (PA 132) to become a major highway. The highway would further crowd the airport, leaving it with a margin of only 200 yards between the Street Road highway and the runway. The airport also had 3,300 feet of road frontage, so the tax burden was going to be large in comparison to possible revenue.

Also, over the airport's fifteen years of operation, three large schools had been built nearby. By the time the school district opened a high school near the airport, the Buehl family was receiving serious threats related to the continuing operation of the airport. On at least one occasion, someone left a bomb in their mailbox. With the schools came houses and other developments.

Finally, there was less demand for air services at Eddington. North Philadelphia Airport was large enough and near enough to offer business aircraft proper facilities, and competition with the publicly funded facility was impossible.

Buehl Field at Eddington was sold in 1960 to a developer named Hyman Korman. The *Bristol Daily Courier* announced the sale as its lead story on page one. It was said that Buehl had been operating the airport at Eddington since 1942 [sic] and that he would "continue to operate the field for two years." Korman did not announce his plans for the land at the time of the sale, but he was known for developing both residential and commercial properties.

In the end, the money Buehl was offered for the land seemed quite good. It was clear that the "highest and best use" of the land had changed.

Langhorne

At Langhorne, Buehl's vision was to build an airport serving light industry. He thought that if every home should not include its own hangar, then at least every business should have an airplane parked at a nearby airport. He wanted to construct a modern, hard-surfaced airstrip that could focus on the needs of businesses. To this end, he located a good amount of land that was bounded on two sides by busy railroad lines and had only a few residents within a mile of the center of the property. It would have room for a mile-long runway, all modern services, and an industrial park nearby. He purchased the land for about $250,000 in December 1960 and took full possession in December 1961.

This was the beginning of Buehl's last big adventure: a major fight that included a scandal implicating local government officials. It was

An early view of the airport in Langhorne, Pennsylvania. The airport's runway is about half the way down on the left side of the picture. Wood Lane and the railroad are visible along the left. The industrial park, in the area of the trees above the cleared area, would have easy access to the airport and nearby rail transportation. PHOTO/SKYPHOTOS

Buehl Field is located between Bucktoe and Woodbourne, near the intersection of the Penn Central and Reading railroads on this 1966 map. It was accessed from Wood Lane. The highway passing to the east of the airport and leading to a cloverleaf was added after Buehl had established the airport. PHOTO/ USGS, PUBLIC DOMAIN

a fight that lasted beyond Buehl's retirement in 1969, when he turned over the airport to his son, Ernie, Jr. Even after retiring, Buehl continued to defend general aviation in numerous articles in local newspapers.

We have very few pictures of the airport or activity at Langhorne. What we have is a collection of plans, clippings, and legal papers. This imbalance, as compared to our data on Somerton and Eddington, results from the fact that for as long as the Langhorne airport was in operation, Buehl was tied down in legal fights to keep it from being closed. Langhorne was never built to completion, and its plans were never realized.

In 1961, it would have been impossible to predict how events finally unfolded. Before Buehl purchased the land, all the township supervisors assured him that they would do everything to help him get started, "short of giving him money," as the vice chairman of the Board expressed it. Part of the land was purchased from the senior supervisor on the Board of Supervisors of Middletown Township.

Early discussion of land use for the area the Langhorne airport would occupy was reported in August 1961. *The Philadelphia Inquirer* covered the unveiling of a "master plan" for Middletown Township, a plan that called for industrial development to take place in the Woodbourne area (specifically where the airport was located, near Langhorne). Factors favoring the plan included the flat, easily developed land there, the availability of a plentiful supply of labor, and proximity to transportation facilities. This was to be a 50-year master plan based on three years of study in cooperation with the Lower Bucks County Planning Commission.††

In October 1961, Buehl asked Middletown Township to change the zoning classification on a 183-acre tract in the middle of the 2300-acre industrial park from "light industrial" to a classification that would permit construction of an airport. The township's manager, Charles Melchior, supported the change, saying "such an airport is a necessity to service an industrial park in this air age."

Plans were submitted, and on 17 April 1962 the zoning was changed to "industrial." Buehl bore the expense of the zoning change and received approval to use the site for an airport, pending an inspection by the Pennsylvania Aeronautics Commission. The Federal Aviation Agency (FAA) approved the site on 7 June 1962.

Buehl quickly began developing the runway. A strip of ground 3,250 feet long by 200 feet wide was leveled off, and subsurface infrastructure was installed. This work cost over $28,000.§§

The Grand Opening for Buehl Field at Langhorne was planned for 15 June 1962. This would have allowed the existing client base to transfer their aircraft to Langhorne from Eddington and continue working with Buehl without interruption.

Now two months after receiving the zoning change to accommodate

---

†† Nearby Lower Makefield Township announced a similar, overlapping, plan at the same time.

§§ Sixty years later, this sum is roughly equivalent to $258,492 in 2022 dollars.

an airfield, Buehl still did not have final written permission from local authorities to build an airport. Needing to move ahead, Buehl asked for a variance to finish his runway and operate his airport. By this time, the senior supervisor who had supported him had died, and the vice-chairman, who was also friendly to his cause, had moved out of state. The new chairman of the Board of Supervisors now stated that the previous board had acted too hastily. He noted the fact that the local zoning code itself did not mention airports as an allowable industrial use.

Buehl spent June, July, August, and September 1962 working to inform the Board of Supervisors about the benefits of general aviation. He supplied testimonials, magazine articles, and other materials. The Aircraft Owners and Pilots Association (AOPA) provided a letter on 27 August 1962 outlining the essential importance of general aviation to business. The letter pointed out that many large corporations would not consider locating "a site for research or [a] manufacturing facility that is more than two miles from a general aviation type airport." Anticipating objections, he also addressed the "good neighbor" issue of having an airport nearby. AOPA supported Buehl, writing, "Those airports designed to accommodate aircraft up to 12,500 pounds gross weight generate less noise than any state or Federal public road (FAA has provided the evidence). If Bucks County communities can live with the motor vehicle traffic and stop-go noises of US Highways 1 and 611, or state roads 413, 263, and 232, a general aviation airport will offer no good neighbor problems."

On 28 August, Buehl asked for an official meeting with the Board of Supervisors. It was scheduled for 11 October 1962. For this meeting, Buehl arranged to have in attendance aviation experts, government aviation officials, state aviation officials, business pilots, and manufacturers to help make his case. Among those attending to support Buehl's application were the Chief of the FAA, Eastern Division Chief of Airports; the District FAA engineer from Harrisburg; the Director of the Pennsylvania State Aviation Commission; the President of the Aviation Council of Pennsylvania; a representative of the Civil Air Patrol; and a member of the Middletown Township Commercial and Industrial Development Commission. The result: when these men arrived at the Township Building, they were informed that there would be no action taken because the chairman of the board, James Cahill, was not going to attend the meeting. No explanation was given for the chairman's nonattendance.

Discussion of the issues went forward that evening anyway. Several residents were present to object to Buehl's request to the Board of Supervisors. One said he doubted the evidence that an airport in Middletown would attract industry. Furthermore, he mentioned there already was an airport in the area, "apparently referring to Mercer Airport in New Jersey." Others objected that an airport was a "safety hazard, would be noisy, and would interfere with TV reception." (The FAA engineer present conceded that an airplane might cause minor fuzzing of a TV signal for the moment it was overhead).

One man shouted that the board had "already decided in favor of Buehl." Another man challenged the legitimacy of the expert witnesses Buehl had invited, threatening that "he was going to check on their statement that they were appearing in their official FAA capacities."

Arguing in favor of Buehl, the FAA district engineer stated that "studies showed Bucks county needs three such airports, and the one proposed in Lower Bucks was most attractive, since it did not require Federal aid" because Buehl was funding the entire cost. He contrasted Buehl's airport with another planned airport near Quakertown that was going to require a Federal grant and substantial local government investment.

After the meeting, Buehl took out a paid advertisement, dated 21 October 1962, saying, "In the endeavor to create a new runway 3,250 ft on our new property near Langhorne we encountered zoning problems which delayed our expected Grand Opening June 15, 1962."

Following this fiasco, the Township manager advised Buehl to obtain the services of an attorney, who could draft a proposal that would allow a private airport in the township. Buehl and his attorney requested the Supervisors consider this proposal on 21 December 1962. However, the senior supervisor was on vacation and the vote on the proposal was deadlocked in a 2-2 vote.

Ten days later, on 18 January 1963, Buehl re-submitted to the supervisors the proposed ordinance that would have allowed a private airport in the township. The senior supervisor gave a lengthy speech supporting approval of the airport, but the chairman of the board spoke against the ordinance, saying that an airport would be too dangerous: aircraft might fall out of the sky in residential areas. Buehl lost his bid on a 3-2 vote. By this time, Buehl has been trying to obtain permission to open his airport for two years. From this point forward, the story becomes even more convoluted, its twists being told in front-page above-the-fold articles in the regional newspapers.

By that Spring, it became clear to nearly everyone that Lower Bucks County needed an airport for general aviation. On 4 April 1963, the Bucks County Airport Authority announced plans for building one. Buehl's existing airport became one of several sites under consideration. One site was near Maple Point, only about a mile from Buehl Field, where the tentative plans called for a new airport to be built at public expense.

To defend his existing investment, Buehl talked to nearly anyone who would listen if he thought they could help him. He was represented up to this point by John Wood, Esq., but Wood asked to be relieved of the case because he saw he had a conflict of interest. Buehl then talked with a friend, William Engle, who recommended he hire attorney Paul Beckert. The arrangement was made early in May 1963.

Beckert recommended Buehl wait until after the Primary Election before approaching the Township supervisors again. Since it was one more delay and he felt he needed action sooner, this was frustrating to Buehl. When he and Engle talked again, Engle gave him the phone number of another attorney, William B. Allen. Immediately on first contact, Allen stated he was familiar with the issues of the case and seemed insistent that Buehl hire him. Suggesting he could influence a vote, Allen mentioned that he was a close friend of Supervisor Thomas Thompson. Buehl quoted Allen as saying, "Beckert won't do a damn thing for you because I would know it if he did." He went on to say, "This is going to cost you some money." Buehl asked how much. Allen would not say. Buehl said he would think about it.

When Buehl did not get back to him, Allen called Buehl to check on his thinking. Again, Buehl asked what his charge would be. Allen assured him, "It won't be too much. We can talk about it when we get together." Buehl was hesitant. Allen demanded, "What the hell's wrong with you—do you want this airport or don't you?" Again, Buehl asked what the charge would be and invited him to "Come up with a figure." Allen replied, "It won't be much—you can afford it." Buehl did not contact Allen again. The entire interaction left Buehl with a bad feeling about Allen's ethics as an attorney.

At this point, Walter Farley, a supervisor of Middletown Township, called Buehl on business unrelated to the airport. Farley was in charge of fundraising for the Democratic Party's Campaign Fund, and he was himself running for Bucks County Commissioner. Buehl was a man who contributed money to both Democrats and Republicans but remained largely nonpartisan. On 19 May 1963, Buehl made out a check to the Fund and took it to Farley's house. While there, Buehl mentioned the conversation with William Allen. Farley interpreted Allen's actions as an outright attempt to solicit a bribe.

Farley urged Buehl to help set up a "sting" to trap Allen. Buehl wanted nothing to do with it, but on 5 July, Farley persuaded him that they should go together to Beckert's home and report the concern. Buehl had already visited with Beckert about this so he did not see the point, but it was on this day that he learned Beckert was not only his attorney but also the Chairman of the County Republicans and the District Attorney.

When nothing much happened following the meeting with Beckert, Farley publicly accused Beckert of conflict of interest. He said the DA's duty to investigate the bribery charges and his duty as Chairman of the county GOP were "incompatible." He accused Beckert of a "whitewash." To defend himself against Farley, Paul Beckert, Buehl's own attorney, said the bribery charges were not worth investigating because "the information supplied by Buehl was not 'reliable.'"

It is hard to know what Farley's purpose may have been. Not only was what Farley doing bringing unwelcome attention to Buehl, the whole thing became painfully reminiscent of the scandal in which Buehl had been mired 40 years earlier. Once again, he had become a football for people whose interests had little to do with him. In the press, Buehl faced public scrutiny in every article as being the businessman approached to pay a bribe, but it was not until much later that the names of those accused of soliciting a bribe were named in the press. For example, Supervisor Thomas Thompson's name only became publicly associated with this case on 2 October, when he filed a libel suit against Walter Farley.

In September, Buehl was questioned by the police in conjunction with the official inquiry into the scandal. In a sworn statement, Buehl was asked directly if he felt that the attorney who was accused of soliciting a bribe, William B. Allen, had done something that "amounted to a criminal act." Buehl replied that he had no proof but that he did feel that the attorney's actions "were unethical." Privately, among family and close friends, Buehl admitted that he felt he was being pressured to pay a bribe to one of the township planning commissioners, but he did not discuss this any further in public. For that matter, he never wanted to discuss the matter in public, and he was not the one who had taken the matter to the public in the first place.

Scandal or no scandal, with the closure of the Eddington airport and with his assets now locked up in the land he had purchased for his new airport, Buehl had no real choice but to proceed—either that or go out of business. Buehl proceeded to develop the airport without the approval of the township authorities. By early 1964, he had spent $300,000 acquiring the field and putting in a 3,200-foot runway. He wanted to spend another $38,000 to finish the runway, but in this he was blocked. *The Philadelphia Inquirer* stated bluntly, "The hesitant mincing of county and township officials and red tape are both the curse of Buehl's existence and the reason he says official recognition of his airfield has been blocked."

Characteristically, Buehl fought back with humor. On 23 April 1964, he placed an advertisement in the *Bristol Courier and Levittown Times*, saying:

Free Country & Opportunity? [...] In Middletown Twp., Buck's County. Available 180 acres of virgin land with no improvements, only restrictions.[...] For information write owner and taxpayer Ernest H. Buehl or Flying Dutchman Air Service, 3103 Hulmeville Rd., Cornwells Heights, Pa."

The conflict dragged on. Three years later, *The Bucks County Courier Times* published a concept drawing of the industrial installation proposed to be built south of the airport. Buehl also ran an advertisement offering an industrial building for rent, which would be convenient to airport services.

The township zoning board again moved to close him down, this time contending that Buehl had failed to live up to a clause in an agreement that said he had to begin construction of the industrial park within a six-month period from the issuance of the permit. In

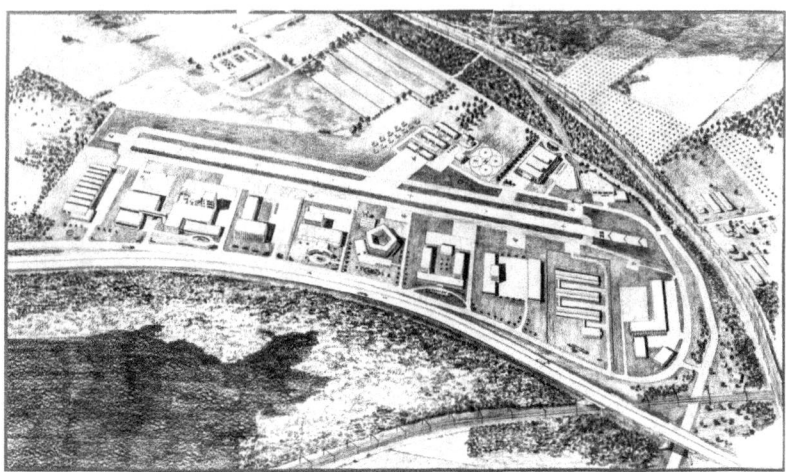

WOODBOURNE   INDUSTRIAL   COMPLEX
buehl field   wood lane,   langhorne
middletown   township   pennsylvania

franklyn b spiezle   architects   a i a

Concept drawing for the Woodbourne Industrial Complex that was part of Buehl's vision.
PHOTO/EBC

response, Buehl pointed out that he had posted $30,000 in escrow to provide for a road into the complex and had built a new hangar. He was also installing lighting to allow after-dark landings. The fact that an industrial park had not yet appeared was at least partially the fault of the Township. The fact that the fate of the airport was not settled prevented Buehl from closing the deal with businesses that were otherwise attracted to what he had to offer.

Finally, late in 1967, the township agreed to a plan under which Buehl would promote and develop an industrial park to be associated with the airport. Approval was granted to operate the airport "only as an adjunct to an industrial park." No one seemed to know just what this meant. In January 1968, *The Bucks County Courier Times* reported that attorneys for Buehl and for Charles Wildman (who had opposed the airport from the beginning simply because he did not want an airport anywhere near his home) agreed that the matter might have to go to court:

The fact that Buehl has actually been operating the airport for years seems to complicate matters. Several years ago the township went to court with a petition calling for Buehl to cease operations at the airport. Buehl promptly appealed and a decision was never handed down. [...] The meeting results would appear to place Buehl in a similar spot to the one he found himself on Jan. 25, 1962 when he first petitioned the supervisors.

By September 1969 the issue still had not been resolved. *The Bucks County Courier Times* reported that the case was still under appeal. Buehl told the newspaper that local officials had been very happy with his plans in 1960, when he started construction on the airport: "When I first bought the place [...] they said it was the best thing that ever happened." Over time, he had built the airport into a thriving business. Buehl Field was the "biggest privately-built airport in Bucks County." It was used by many Bucks County residents and businesses, including customers of Reedman Motors and students from George School, nearby. Recalling the objection that had been raised years before, that airplanes might fall out of the sky, endangering residences near the airport, the newspaper asked if there had been any fatalities associated with the airport. There had not been. Following the 1965 cease and desist order, Buehl continued to operate the airport "with a private license from the Federal government."

A hearing was held to consider the new cease and desist order. A newspaper article that Buehl clipped says that finally, by December 1969,

It is expected that Ernest Buehl's six-year battle with Middletown Township might be over and he will be allowed to operate his airport in peace. Tonight the township zoning board will reconsider Buehl's situation. The zoners hit the airport with a cease and desist order

last month and will probably rescind it tonight. Township Manager Frank Girard, who is also township zoning officer, feels Buehl has met his commitment to begin the industrial park.[…] The township solicitor and the board of supervisors agree.

෨෴

The conflict obviously took its toll on Buehl. When he was planning his airport at Langhorne, he was 63 years of age and at the peak of his experience. He had been flying for 46 years and had worked and socialized with some of the top aviators of his age: Fokker, Stinson, Rickenbacker, and many others. He had been behind the success of the first flight into the stratosphere, when a pilot flew so high that his airplane left a vapor trail. He had participated in key events in opening the continent of North America to aviation. He had already owned two airports, and he had trained many, many pilots. He had dedicated his life to promoting general aviation, and he had achieved nearly universal respect among his peers. With Langhorne, though, his final vision had been blocked by township supervisors who would not approve the development of the airport.

Why did he not just pay the bribe and get on with his business? After all, he was told at the start that the remaining issues would not be difficult to fix and that paying the bribe would even be relatively inexpensive. Buehl never talked about any of this outside his family, and even in that context he never gave a clear answer to the question. The reasons were complex and layered, rooted deeply in the experiences that shaped his character. Some reasons mentioned in newspaper accounts were undoubtedly pragmatic. Other reasons were probably hidden even from himself, having arisen from painful experiences of which he was ashamed.

The taproot of Buehl's character in this situation, I believe, was his experience in 1922 when he participated in the arson at Larsen's airfield on Long Island. Buehl was ashamed of what he had done. He had gone along once with a criminal activity. He knew he would not want to live with himself if he went along with another illegal scheme.

Another important consideration for Buehl was that he had received a second chance from legal authorities in the United States. Through this, as well as his long residence in his adopted country, he had acquired a profound respect for what it meant to be a citizen. His citizenship had been earned, and he valued it deeply, especially the concepts that all citizens are equal under the law and that one cannot be ordered by someone in authority to do something morally wrong. Being an American citizen also included the ideal of living in a society free of official corruption. He was not going to go along with something that violated the laws or even the ideals of the nation that welcomed him.

In the end, Buehl was not bitter. Instead, he wrote of his dedication to his adopted country and of his gratitude for the opportunities he found here. One would have hoped this sense of dedication would be rewarded. Buehl finally retired in 1969, when he was 72, passing the management of the airport to his son, Ernie Junior. In the end, Buehl's vision for the airport was never realized.

In a hand-written document, undated but penned in 1969, when he was 72, Buehl wrote on the problems he faced at Langhorne (there is editing for brevity and clarity):

I can not emphasize enough the great opportunity my country has offered me and still does, and I write this document with a thought of gratitude.

For years, Bucks County Airport Authority has been looking in vain for an airport site in Lower Bucks County. If they had built the airport at public expense, it would have cost the taxpayers several million dollars. Here I am willing to pay taxes and supply the county with an adequate airport.

From a money-making standpoint, an airport operation is not a paying proposition. It requires a large piece of land; if you want to serve people, you must locate nearby, not in the boondocks where land is less expensive. Dedicating my services in aviation to the problems, I feel money spent on improvements and safety at the airport are a better investment than paying for political privileges, as this would only benefit a few.

Following our government's call for more airports, I show my gratitude to my country by dedicating my aviation career to the American people.

Over the years, from the time Buehl retired, housing and small businesses moved closer and closer to the airport, replacing the open farmland that had been there when the airport was first built. Finally, by 1990, when Buehl died, the land had become too valuable, and within a few years his last airport was sold to developers.

The final irony is that in 1996, when Ryland Homes offered to purchase the airport in order to develop the land for homes, township supervisors opposed the plan. Chairman of the supervisors, Kevin Hastings, is quoted as saying, "I hope the county would buy the property so we can leave it an airport."

❧

Selected Sources

88th Birthday—Bavarian Club. AAC, MPEG-4 Video. Bavarian Club, Philadelphia, Pennsylvania, 1985.

Afro-American. "Fliers Stage Air Circus at Flying Dutchman Airport." June 8, 1935.

"Albert Einstein: The Negro Question (1946)," *On Being*, accessed April 11, 2012.

Anderson, C. Alfred. U.S. Air Force Oral History Interview Series, AFHRA. Interview by James C. Hasdorff. Transcript, June 8, 1981. U.S. Air Force Academy. The segment discussing Buehl begins 11 minutes 26 seconds into the recording and ends at 15 minutes 24 seconds.

Baxter, Gordon. "The Biplane." *Flying Magazine*, June 1975.

Breeze Newspapers. "Farewell to Somerton Airport as Veteran Plane Leaves for Buehl Field," February 1952.

Bristol Daily Courier. "Flying Dutchman Airport Sold to Development Co. Korman Pays $625,169 for Bensalem Site." August 10, 1960.

Brock, Pope. "Chief Anderson." *People Magazine*, November 28, 1988.

Buck, Olga. "Eddington's Buehl Airfield Home to Oldtime Flying Dutchman." *Bucks County Sunday Press.* December 13, 1953.

Bucks County Courier Times. "Airport Operator Marks Anniversary with Application," January 18, 1968.

Bucks County Courier Times. "Buehl May Get OK for Airport," December 3, 1969.

Bucks County Courier Times. "Future Site (Plans for Industrial Park)," June 28, 1967.

Buehl, Ernest H. "An Airport vs. a Community." Unpublished typed sheet, 1963. Ernest H. Buehl collection.

Buehl, Ernest H. "Buehl Lists His Accomplishments." Manuscript on yellow tablet paper, 1969. EBC.

Buehl, Ernest H. "Free Country & Opportunity?" *Bristol Courier and Levittown Times*, April 23, 1964.

C. Alfred Anderson Legacy Foundation. "Father of Black Aviation." (web page)

C. Alfred Anderson Legacy Foundation. "First Lady Eleanor Roosevelt's Flight." (web page)

"Charles Anderson—the Father of African-American Aviation - Tuskegee Airmen Inc.—The Legacy of The Tuskegee Airmen." (web page)

Chicago Defender. "Lincoln Payne, 'Flying Mail Carrier' Dead," October 31, 1936.

"Congressional Gold Medal to Tuskegee Airmen Public Law 109-213," April 11, 2006.

Daily Intelligencer. "Libel Suit Is Filed on Bribe Charge." October 2, 1963.

Daily Intelligencer. "Middletown Board Will Call in D.A." August 29, 1963.

Daily Times. "Strictly Personal He's 'The Flying Dutchman.'" May 1, 1953.

Davis, David Brion. "The Central Fact of American History." *American Heritage*, March 2005.

Davis, Jr., Benjamin O. *Benjamin O. Davis, Jr.: American: An Autobiography.* First. Smithsonian Institution Press, 2000.

Encyclopedia.com. "The 1930s Education: Chronology | U*X*L American Decades."

Ernie Buehl Talks to the Experimental Aircraft Association, Pennsylvania Chapter 76. Videotape, 1986.

Evening Bulletin. "Deaf Dog Flies to Aid Ears." n.d.

"Frankford Quadrangle Pennsylvania-New Jersey." Topographic, 1:24,000. 7.5 Minute Series. Reston, Virginia: U.S. Geological Survey, 1950.

Glenshaw, Paul. "For a Few Magical Years, It Looked like Every Family Would Own an Airplane. Buy Your Airplane at Penney's." Air & Space Magazine, November 2013.

Haulman, Daniel L. "Nine Myths About the Tuskegee Airmen," October 21, 2011, 30.

Haulman, Daniel L. "Tuskegee Airfields During World War II." Air Force Historical Research Agency, February 4, 2015.

Haulman, Daniel L. Eleven Myths about the Tuskegee Airmen. Montgomery, AL: NewSouth Books, 2012.

Informal Interview with Chief Anderson. HBCU Tours Black College Tours. Moton Field, Tuskegee, Alabama, 1994. YouTube.

Interview with Roosevelt J. Lewis, Jr. at Moton Field, Tuskegee, Alabama. Interview by Mark Taylor. Digital audio, February 15, 2014. YouTube.

Interview with Roosevelt J. Lewis, Jr. at Moton Field, Tuskegee, Alabama. Interview by Mark Taylor. Digital audio, February 15, 2014. YouTube.

Johnson, Carol Ferguson. Interview by Mark Taylor. 15 February 2019.

Lokes, Bill. "Cloud Story," November 17, 2014. Captain Lokes retired after a career as a pilot for American Airlines.

Miller, Alyssa J. "Don't Let the Ground Loop Get You: Tailwheel Training Provides Challenges, Boosts Stick-and-Rudder Skills." Text. AOPA website, January 17, 2013.

Moye, J. Todd. Freedom Flyers: The Tuskegee Airmen of World War II. Kindle. New York: Oxford University Press, USA, 2010.

National Park Service. "Stories—Tuskegee Airmen National Historic Site Freeman Field Mutiny," February 25, 2016. (web page)

New-York Tribune. "Negro Classes in Aviation," September 18, 1910, sec. 1.

Payne, Lincoln. "Aviation and the Negro." Philadelphia Tribune, February 9, 1928.

"Petition for Naturalization—Ernest Buehl." United States Department of Labor, September 26, 1928.

Philadelphia Convention. "Constitution of the United States," June 21, 1788. National Archives.

Philadelphia Inquirer. "'Flying Dutchman' Wants Recognition of Middletown Airport." February 9, 1964.

Philadelphia Inquirer. "Airport Plans Are Studied by Middletown." October 9, 1962.

Philadelphia Inquirer. "Forced Landing (Advertisement)." October 21, 1962.

Philadelphia Inquirer. "Master Plan to Be Unveiled at Middletown," August 2, 1961.

Philadelphia Inquirer. "Proposed Airport for Middletown Ignites Hot Debate," October 11, 1962.

Philadelphia Tribune. "Aviation Club Is Organized Here," April 28, 1932.

Philadelphia Tribune. "Flying Activities at Patco Airport," May 25, 1933.

Richards, Ryan. "Preserving Legacy of Lower Merion's 'Chief' Anderson: Father of Black Aviation." Main Line Media News. February 13, 2013.

Robie, William and National Aeronautic Association (U.S.). For the Greatest Achievement: A History of the Aero Club *of America and the National Aeronau-tic Association.* First Edition edition. Washington: Smithsonian, 1993.

Sabatini, Richard. "OK Expected on Air-port-Industry Complex." *Philadelphia Inquirer*, October 24, 1968.

Sawyer, Miriam. "Forsythe, Albert Ed-ward." In *American National Biogra-phy*, Supplement 2:177. Oxford Uni-versity Press, May 12, 2005.

Slater, Robert. "Buehl: I Should Get a Cigar, Not Criticism." *Bucks County Courier Times*, September 16, 1969.

Smith, Monica Renee. "Free Skies: The Ascent of Black Aviation." Master's thesis, Goucher College, 2017.

"Statement of Ernest Herman Buehl Re. Bribery." Penna. State Police sub station, Trevose, September 3, 1963.

Studebaker, Dan. "400 Learn of Plans for County's Future." *Levittown Times*. April 5, 1963.

Studebaker, Dan. "Residents Up in the Air on Airport Proposal." *Bristol Dai-ly Courier*, October 11, 1962.

Thompson, CC. "Letter of Support from AOPA," August 27, 1963. EBC.

"Tony Brown's Journal." Transcript. ep-isode 802. *The Chief*, 1985.

United States Post Office—About. "Father of Black Aviation Immortalized on Stamp," March 13, 2014. (web page)

unknown newspaper. "50-Year Master Plan for Lower Makefield to Be Unveiled Today," September 25, 1961.

unknown. "E.H. Buehl Opens Somer-ton Airport: Returns from Lancaster, Pa., as Flying Restrictions Are Lifted Here," n.d.

unknown. "Flying Dutchman Moves Air-port. Growth of Building Develop-ment Makes Site a Center for New Homes," n.d.

unknown. "New Airport to Feature Han-gars in Private Homes," May 7, 1947.

Ward, J.I. "Over Middletown's Buehl Airfield, Town and Developer Wage a Dogfight Local Officials Want to Keep the Planes. A N.J. Builder Sees Houses." *Philadelphia Inquirer*, June 2, 1996.

CHAPTER **6**

Last Flight and Epilogue

The Challenger lovingly restored and on display in front of its hangar at Langhorne, about 1981. PHOTO/EBC

After Buehl completed the restoration of the Challenger but before he sold it to Fairchild in late 1981, he decided he would fly it one more time. He was 84 years of age.

Of course, he should not have flown that day. He was not even allowed to drive a car. He had the diminished reflexes of old age, and he was blind. Because of macular degeneration, he could not see anything in front of him; he had only peripheral vision.

Buehl went to the airport office that afternoon, retrieved his flying helmet, and strapped it on. He got a little help wheeling Challenger out onto the tarmac, got in and started its World War I-era ox-5 engine. A small crowd at the airport gathered to see what he was going to do.

Buehl asked those nearby if the runway was clear. He treated the affirmative answer as though he had been given permission for take off. He waved, goosed the engine, and rolled down the runway.

It is different watching an old bi-plane take off. With so much lift from its two pairs of large wings, the Challenger did not so much zoom into the air as it would just start floating. The slow speed at which this happened can be disorienting to those who have never watched it. Before he was one-third of the way down the runway, his Challenger took off and Buehl's muscle memory took over. He flew the airplane on a short pattern around the airport, then landed safely.

No one took pictures.

Epilogue

Pull a thread of Buehl's career, and it leads to a significant scene in the tapestry of the history of aviation. Follow the thread and we see the tapestry.

Buehl appeared at a time when we were just inventing civilian uses for airplanes. He got his start in Europe before World War I, at a time when aviation there was progressing more rapidly than in the US. The technology advanced quickly during the War as airplanes proved their worth as machines of war, as airplanes first replaced horse-mounted cavalry and then took other uses. After the War, people began experimenting with civilian uses. Buehl worked with some of the most advanced manufacturers in Europe—BMW, Junkers, Fokker—contributing his world-class skills to their efforts to bring airplanes to the public.

Airplanes had to be safer, more economical, and more comfortable. There needed to be better training for pilots. There needed to be a stable industry to create and maintain the infrastructure needed to operate airplanes across continental distances. Buehl's work contributed to all of that. His skills made the airplanes work in cases when no one else could do the job.

In the US, at a time when advances in aviation were stalled, Buehl's work allowed the demonstration of some of the world's most advanced aviation technology. His work made it possible for us to see new uses for airplanes. It got people here to think about aviation as a commercially important segment of the transportation industry. His work took us out of an era symbolized by slow cloth-covered biplanes, the wings held out with struts and wires, and into a new era of fast, powerful metal monoplanes with cantilevered wings. With his contribution, airplanes were increasingly used for global exploration. His work directly helped to push back major frontiers, both physical and social.

It might be objected that Buehl was not the leader in many of the adventures for which he became known. This is true. Step back from most of the stories that circulated about Buehl during his lifetime and we see they involved team efforts, breaking records and notching "firsts." In all of these, he worked with the team leaders. But isn't that really the nature of most achievement in a complex field like aviation? At this level, it can be seen that Buehl's contributions are much like those of most other famous aviators and especially astronauts. We could raise the same question about them as we might when evaluating the significance of Buehl's work.

The stories about Buehl that were widely circulated during his lifetime were dazzling, but they nearly eclipsed the really big story.

Early in aviation, we asked ourselves as a society, who had the right to use airplanes? According to Buehl, the answer was "everyone." He lived by the American ideal of equality of opportunity for all citizens. Everyone who possessed the skills, abilities, and interest should have a shot.

Anderson

In Buehl's entire career, training C. Alfred Anderson was his singular contribution. Someone else would have done the other things. Of course, someone was going to put an airplane into the stratosphere. In fact, a us team did just that only months after Buehl's German team. Of course, someone would fly across North America. Plans were already being made before Buehl's team arrived to do it.

However, when Buehl taught Anderson and then insisted he be examined for his Air Transport License, there was no one else who *would* do what Buehl did. This was an act that required more than a skilled pilot and trainer; it required a man with the vision and courage to deliberately ignore the prejudices of his day and place. One might say that many could have done what Buehl did, because there were many trainers who had the skills necessary to have helped Anderson, but at that moment, only Ernest Buehl showed the particular combination of skills and moral courage to make it happen.

In consequence, Buehl helped to open a door to racial integration in the United States. Granted, it was a door with many locks, but Buehl turns out to have had one of the keys as well as the willingness to use it. Many people, including Anderson's family, and others at Tuskegee University who are familiar with this story, flatly state that if Buehl had not agreed to help Anderson, the Tuskegee Airmen would never have existed. Anderson had the intelligence and personality to bring the Airmen into being, but it took Buehl to force open the door for him.

Summary of Accomplishmenta

What did Buehl accomplish? His contributions, though small at the time he made them, came so early to his field that they can be seen to have had a nonlinear effect, changing our relation to space, time, nature itself, and with one another. Thanks to Buehl and the people with whom he worked, many frontiers have disappeared. We now can visit every place on the planet's surface. We routinely cross continents in hours instead of days. A mile of pavement in Montana can allow an airplane to take off to visit anywhere in the world. Even social frontiers are slowly dissolving, as aviation became a leader in advancing the ideal of social equality.

Selected Sources

Goldstone, Lawrence. *Birdmen: The Wright Brothers, Glenn Curtiss, and the Battle to Control the Skies.* New York: Ballantine Books, 2015.

Harris, Vascar G. Impromptu interview with Vascar G. Harris, Ph.D., Department of Aerospace Science Engineering, Tuskegee University. Interview by Mark Taylor. Digital audio, February 15, 2014.

APPENDIX 1

Bukovina

When Buehl first entered the military in World War I, he was sent to fight in Bukovina. Since Bukovina no longer exists as a nation, a reader might ask where it had been and what happened to it. The map shows the location of Bukovina in the context of greater Romania and surrounding countries.

Bukovina was carved up in World War II. At that time, Germany agreed not to protect Bukovina from Russian invasion, as a part of a larger pact of non-aggression between the two countries: the notorious Ribbentrop-Molotov Pact. The Soviet Union took the northern part of Bukovina in 1940, and this area is now part of Ukraine. The southern part of Bukovina is now part of Romania.

When first looking at Buehl's photographs of this region, it is puzzling that the civilians shown seemed to be smiling in such a friendly manner when a German occupier was taking their pictures.

Map of Bukovina ("Bucovina" in Romanian) and surrounding countries. Tiny Bukovina is located at the top, in the middle. MAP/ WIKIMEDIA COMMONS, PUBLIC DOMAIN

However, the explanation becomes clear when one realizes that many people of Bukovina regarded the German troops as protectors, soldiers who were defending them against invasion by Russian troops.

(right) Friendly Bukovinian woman poses with her child.

(above) Woman in front of her home.

(below) Local houses in Bukovina in 1916.
PHOTOS/EBC

Exploration of the Stratosphere

Diemer's 1919 flight was accomplished with hardly any of the drama that would highlight the challenges he faced. By contrast, the story of the first balloonists ever to enter the stratosphere illustrates well the dangers of early high-altitude flying, as does the story of an American pilot, Rudolph Schroeder, who made a similar flight shortly after Diemer. Both narratives put the challenge in perspective.

Today it is routine for commercial aircraft to fly in the stratosphere, which has less turbulence than the troposphere. Also, the stratosphere is very cold, which helps aircraft to conserve fuel. Continent-hopping flights would be less economical, less safe, and less comfortable if we were not able to fly in the stratosphere.

Stratospheric vapor trails are a part of our everyday life. They are now so common that they have become significant modifiers of Earth's climate. Vapor trails prevent heat from the sun from hitting Earth during the day and then prevent the loss of heat from Earth into outer space at night, dampening the range of temperatures we experience between night and day. From 11 September to 14 September 2001, when aircraft were grounded in the United States following the attack against the World Trade Center in New York, the

A vapor trail over Montana.
PHOTO/AUTHOR

sudden lack of vapor trails over the entire nation reinforced the sense of the gravity of our situation. At the same time, meteorologists observed that the lack of vapor trails resulted in a sudden increase in the range of temperatures from day to night during that period.

Coxwell and Glaisher

The first time humans entered the stratosphere, they were not flying an airplane. On 5 September 1862, Henry Coxwell and meteorologist James Glaisher reached about 36,000 feet in the open basket of a hydrogen-filled balloon. Glaisher was associated with the Royal Observatory at Greenwich, and Coxwell was, we might say, a professional adventurer. He was selected as the person to operate the balloon. The British Association for the Advancement of Science initiated the study because they wanted to know more about the upper atmosphere.

Coxwell and Glaisher took off from the University of Wolverhampton's Science Park in their balloon, the Mammoth. The balloon was overfilled with very high-quality hydrogen, so when they were untethered the two men were carried into the sky with unexpected speed. Ears popping, they very quickly reached the stratosphere. In the thin air at that altitude, Glaisher lost consciousness, and

James Glaisher.
PHOTO/PUBLIC DOMAIN

Henry T Coxwell.
PHOTO/PUBLIC DOMAIN

Coxwell was unable to use his hands when they became frostbitten in the high wind and low temperature.

In 2003, some of the dangers of this expedition were reviewed in the journal *Neurology* In a surprisingly moving story presented in a scientific journal not known for stories of human interest, Glaisher's own account includes personal descriptions of sensations and symptoms of what, in fact, were the "marked neurological compromises" that he suffered. Besides altitude sickness, the ascent was so rapid he suffered decompression injury. His arms and legs became paralyzed, the paralysis spread to his torso, and he temporarily became blind before he passed out.

Although this is a complication not reported, many who have experienced such frigid temperatures as a child will know that tongue and lips stick to any metal they touch, and freeing them from the metal is very painful. It is likely that Coxwell lost pieces of his tongue and lips as he was forced to use his teeth to operate the controls in his desperate efforts to get the balloon to descend.

Schroeder

Like Glaisher and Coxwell, American Rudolph Schroeder was among the first to test the physical limits of life in the cold reaches of the atmosphere. Only eight months after Diemer's flight in Munich and only sixteen years and two months from the day the Wright brothers made their first flight at Kitty Hawk, American Army Major Rudolph Schroeder flew an open-cockpit LePere biplane into the stratosphere, beginning his flight at Dayton, Ohio, on 27 February 1920. As with Diemer's flight, a vapor trail was observed behind Schroeder's airplane.

Until that day, no one in the world outside of the few in Munich who had observed Diemer's flight had ever seen a vapor trail follow an airplane. Since Schroder's airplane was so high that observers on the

From Le Voyage dans la Lune, *1902 French silent film directed by George Méliès, inspired by Jules Verne's writing.* PHOTO/WIKIMEDIA COMMONS

ground could not see it, the appearance of the vapor trail was unexplained, leaving people to speculate about what it might be. Some thought a comet had appeared, and some may have thought space aliens from Mars were visiting Earth.

There is every reason to ask why people in 1920 would think of Martians when they saw this unfamiliar phenomenon in the sky? Clearly, they were primed to make that connection. Indeed, people had been imagining intelligent extra-terrestrial life for decades.

The day after Major Schroeder set his record, the headline in *The New York Times* said, "Climbs 36,020 Feet in Plane and Lands After 5-Mile Drop." He was trying to reach 40,000 feet.[*]

Entering the stratosphere, Schroeder ran out of oxygen and passed out. He had taken off with what he believed would be a three-hour supply of oxygen, knowing that he would not need it to breathe below 18,000 feet. At that time, oxygen was not generally delivered by means of a mask strapped to the face; usually a pilot would just breathe from a rubber tube held in his mouth. In his open cockpit, Schroeder was exposed to exhaust fumes and carbon monoxide, which he was breathing along with his oxygen.

As he approached his peak altitude, Schroeder said that he knew he was flying higher than anyone had ever flown in an airplane, and he noted that he had enough fuel to keep flying for another hour and a half. He had to change from his original oxygen tank, though, to his

---

[*] The U.S. news coverage of Schroeder's flight compares his achievement to those of a few others but does not mention Diemer.

reserve tank because the original stopped working. Unfortunately, he found that his reserve was empty. When he tried to turn back to his original oxygen tank, it still did not function properly, so he had to repair it while sitting in the open, in the prop wash of his 400-horsepower supercharged v-12 Liberty engine, the air temperature already an extremely dangerous minus 67°F.

Running out of oxygen is one of only two true medical emergencies, defined as events so serious that the response cannot wait even briefly (the other emergency being cessation of heartbeat). He urgently had to fix his oxygen supply, but the conditions under which he had to work were impossible.

Scientists agree Martians are a super race. The press promoted the idea that Martians might be observing us. It would not be a stretch to believe that they might come to visit.
NEW YORK TRIBUNE *8 FEBRUARY 1920/PUBLIC DOMAIN*

Schroeder was protected in a flight suit "lined with the fur of Chinese Nuchwang dogs," and the whole suit, including his headgear, moccasins, and gloves, was electrically heated. His airplane, though, was covered with ice an inch thick. His goggles, too, were covered with crystallized motor exhaust and ice, so the goggles themselves interfered with his vision. Because he was fumbling with his oxygen supply and because his goggles were nearly opaque, he lifted them briefly to see what he was doing. As soon as he did, his eyelids froze

Timeline: Extra-Terrestrial Life

1584 Giordano Bruno published his opinion that civilized populations are common on planets throughout the universe.

1865 Jules Verne's *From Earth to the Moon* was published.

1877 There was strong speculation about life on Mars following the discovery of what appeared to be "canals" on the surface of that planet.

1895 Astronomer Percival Lowell popularized the idea that these were signs of intelligent life on Mars.

1897 H.G. Wells published *War of the Worlds*, in which Martians attack Earth.

1902 A movie by George Méliès, *A Trip to the Moon*, depicts humans encountering extra-terrestrial creatures.

1920 Just weeks before Schroeder's flight, on 8 February, *The New York Tribune* ran a front-page story headlined, "Scientists, Agreeing Martians Are Super-Race, Believe That Planet May Be Signaling to Us."

to his eyeballs. At nearly that moment, he lost consciousness and his aircraft nose-dived. He fell against the ignition switch in his cockpit and the impact turned off the motor. Fallen, his head was hanging over the edge of the cockpit.

When he passed out, he lost control of his aircraft and fell more than five miles before recovering consciousness at an altitude of about 2,000 feet. The sudden change in air pressure during his fall, from about three pounds per square inch at his peak altitude to about thirteen pounds per square inch as he passed 2,500 feet, crushed the gasoline tanks on his airplane, and the implosion jolted him awake. Recovering a bit, he was able to straighten out the plane. Schroeder said, "I guess I just became an automaton and came down all right." He was able to see well enough to land his plane at McCook Field. Although it is not reported, it would be surprising if his ears had not imploded, too.

When he landed, he was numb from the cold and in shock. He collapsed and required immediate medical treatment. The 28 February *New York Times* article says that ground attendants who first got to the plane when it landed "found Major Schroeder sitting erect in the machine, apparently lifeless."

On 12 March 1920, Schroeder, by now medically recovered, told more of his story. He explained that the purpose of his flight had been to study "trade winds" that were believed to exist above 30,000 feet. Schroeder said that he did encounter a wind at the peak of his climb that was blowing west to east at a rate of 220 miles per hour. In that environment, although he was attempting to fly westward and had been flying at a speed of 120 miles per hour, when he entered the stratosphere he "was literally traveling backward 120 miles per hour."

In 1920, Schroeder explained the current thinking among scientists of his time. Although he believed that he might be able to fly as high as 48,000 feet in an aircraft having a closed cockpit, he did not think it would be possible to go much higher. He said, "scientists believe" that 48,000 feet "is the ultimate ceiling of the world." It was Schroeder's dream to "figure out exactly just what the roof of the world really is."

As spectacular as Schroeder's story was, Diemer was there first, and he carried his feat off without the death-defying drama. Buehl was on the team that made that first, flawless flight into the stratosphere possible. It was a big accomplishment, and it still carries significance for us.

Selected Sources

Doherty, Michael J. "James Glaisher's 1862 Account of Balloon Sickness: Altitude, Decompression Injury, and Hypoxemia." *Neurology* 60, no. 6 (March 25, 2003): 1016–18.

New York Times. "Climbs 36,020 Feet in Plane and Lands after 5-Mile Drop. Major Schroeder, Oxygen Exhausted, Loses Consciousness at Record Height over Dayton. Thousands Watch His Fall. Streak in Sky Made by Exhaust Mistaken for Comet—Rights Plane at 2,000 Feet.," February 28, 1920.

New York Times. "Gale Hurled Back Schroeder's Plane." March 12, 1920.

Pain, Stephanie. "Balloon Ride into the Stratosphere." New Scientist 195, no. 2622 (September 22, 2007): 54–55.

Roderick, Michael L., and Graham D. Farquhar. "The Cause of Decreased Pan Evaporation over the Past 50 Years." Science 298, no. 5597 (November 15, 2002): 14-10–1411.

USAF. "Fact Sheet: Flights to High Altitude." National Museum of the USAF. Accessed January 3, 2010.

APPENDIX 3

The JL-6

Technical Specifications

The following are the "preliminary specifications"
given for the JL-6 in a typed source that was in Buehl's possession:

* *Overall length*—31 feet 6 inches
* *Wing span*—48 feet 6 inches
* *Height to top of cabin*—
  ten feet two inches
* *Motor*—six cylinders, 185 h.p.,
  1,400 revolutions per minute
* *Weight of machine empty*, includ-
  ing cooling water—2,245 lbs.

*Cockpit of JL-6. This
photo shows single
controls; others
had dual controls..*
PHOTO/PUBLIC
DOMAIN

* *Gross weight*—3,895 lbs.
* *Fuel capacity, at full speed*, fully load-
  ed—six to seven hours
* *Fuel capacity at most economical speed*,
  fully loaded—ten hours
* *Landing speed*, fully loaded—50 miles per hour
* *Average speed*—112 miles per hour at
  12,000 feet altitude, fully loaded
* *Climbing speed*—12,000 feet in 35 minutes, fully loaded

The typed specifications continue:

"As the J.L.6 airplane has been especially designed for passenger traffic

unusual attention has been given to the construction and arrangement of the passenger and pilot's cabins. The pilot's compartment is
arranged for two people and is fitted with dual control mechanism
so either person can act as pilot.

The passenger cabin is entirely enclosed with suitable windows in the
sides and in front, and is fitted with two large comfortable bucket
type front seats, and an especially wide rear seat, which holds three
persons, making the normal cabin capacity five persons. The cabin
has large doors on either side affording easy entry and exit for the
passengers.

The cabin's interior is luxuriously upholstered with very comfortable
cushions and arm rests and all modern accessories, such as those
found in high-class limousine cars. All seats are fitted with safety
belts, and the floor is so arranged as to provide comfortable foot rests.
The windows in the sides of the cabin are arranged so they can be
lowered to admit fresh air, if desired. There is also a large space provided for baggage, access to which is by means of a hinged rear seat
cushion. By means of a suitable window in the front of [the] cabin
the passenger can observe the principal instruments on the pilot's
dash, such as revolution, height and speed indicators.

Owing to the construction of the wings they are easily and quickly
removed and replaced (can easily be done in 20 minutes) and as no
truing up is required this can safely be done by any mechanic, thus
making storage easy.

The landing chassis is especially designed for commercial airplanes
and is made with shock absorbing devices in all four load carrying
struts, thus making landings as free from harm to the machine as
possible, and as the wheels are located well forward there is little
danger of the machine nosing over, if landing on soft ground."

Use of Aluminum

One of the most distinctive features of the F-13/JL-6 was its corrugated metal skin made of an aluminum alloy. Junkers first used aluminum in 1916, well before anyone else understood how to use aluminum in production aircraft.

Aluminum was still considered in those days to be a new material for any purpose. Although it is the third most common element on Earth, it was exceptionally difficult to extract from its main ore, bauxite, and only became available in commercial quantities after 1886. By 1916, aluminum was a high-tech material, requiring significant expertise to use. Pure aluminum has only about a third the stiffness of steel, it is soft, and it has such a low melting point (660°C) that a ten-year-old can turn a piece of it into a puddle using tools commonly available in most homes.

It has to be alloyed to improve its strength, and careful management of the way it is cooled is crucial to ensure that it forms properly. The alloy Junkers used was known as "duralumin." It was aluminum mixed with about 4% copper. First created in a laboratory in Germany, duralumin was not commercially available until 1909.

Today the duralumin alloy would be specified under the International Alloy Designation System (IADS) as belonging to the "2000" series. These alloys are still used in the aviation industry today. The disadvantage of them is that they corrode whenever they are exposed to air. This is among the reasons why so few original F-13s exist today. These alloys are replaced in many applications by 6000 and 7000 alloys.

Because even aluminum alloys are more easily bent than steel, forming the aircraft's skin with corrugations was an elegant way to improve the stiffness and strength of the body of the F-13 while taking advantage of the element's light weight.

The lightness of aluminum, as compared to other metals, was an advantage that overcame the difficulties associated with its use. Besides the lightness, in his American patent for the all-metal construction used on the F-13, Junkers discussed some other important advantages. Pointing out an obvious issue, the fabric normally used in airplane construction is delicate, easily torn or dented. Aluminum is less vulnerable to these problems. This meant the wings of the JL-6 were not as vulnerable to rough bush landings. The aircraft could land on an unimproved field, and the wings would not be damaged if scratched by shrubs. Even a small stick could tear the fabric making up a conventional wing, but a metal wing would be safe.

Describing a less obvious issue solved by using aluminum, Junkers pointed out that over time, a fabric covering gets pulled out of shape by the forces acting on the wing, affecting the airplane's performance. An all-metal wing is not affected in this way.

Also, given the way the wings were attached, there was less drag through the air because there were no struts or exposed control wires. It was estimated that these wires reduced the speed of conventional airplanes of the day by as much as 25 miles per hour.

It was possible to leave a JL-6 outdoors without worrying about damage from the weather. This was a huge advantage when making long trips because it was not necessary to construct a hangar for every stop. Some canvas was used to cover the cockpit and to protect the engine when the plane was on the ground, but the fuselage and wings were safe without protection. It was estimated that the necessity of building a hangar added between $4,000 and $6,000 to the cost of acquiring other airplanes, money saved when owning a JL-6.

Replacing the wood and fabric of a conventional airplane with all-metal construction meant that the JL-6 was not only strong but, it was thought, "fireproof." Eddie Rickenbacker, America's top ace during World War I, endorsed the JL-6 for its safety, mentioning this exact reason. He is quoted in the *Salt Lake City Tribune* as saying: "This monoplane is about what the people have been waiting for. The dangers attendant on riding on a plane of any kind have kept people away from it. They are waiting for something safe. This machine is fireproof and seems to be proof against most everything."

Buehl's documents include a copy of a letter from Larsen's insurance agency, The Home Insurance Company, dated 24 October 1921, in which E. Stockton Martin, Manager of the Aircraft Department, compliments Larsen

> "on your exceptional record of operation of JL planes. [...] We appreciate the fact that you have made numerous cross continental trips from New York to San Francisco and return, and others into Mexico and Canada nearing the Arctic Circle, some of which were made under very trying conditions."

Speaking for the agency, Martin states

> "that the right machines, properly flown are a pretty safe risk both for the public and for the insurance companies. An experience such as you have had for the past two years is a tribute not only to yourself but to aviation as a whole."

A newspaper reporter in 1920 summed up what people were thinking: before seeing the JL-6, airplanes made of wood and linen had seemed sturdy enough. "Only a cyclone or a crash" could damage a fabric-covered airplane, but such an airplane "appears as fragile and delicate as a china vase beside the JL-6."

Buehl posing beside JL-6 *with the hood open.* PHOTO/EBC

View of the engine from the cockpit with the cowling removed. PHOTO/EBC

(above, top) View of a JL-6 with the wings removed. The wings were fastened to the body in a way that allowed them to be easily removed and then reattached in the field.

(above, bottom) View of a section of wing with the covering removed, revealing the internal bracing.
PHOTOS/EBC

Performance

Fuel economy was excellent, the engine using one-half or even a third as much fuel as other engines of the day. With their BMW-III engines, even traveling at an average speed of 100 miles per hour, a JL-6 would consume an average of only eight gallons of benzol an hour (12.5 miles per gallon).

We are not familiar today with benzol, so an explanation is needed. When asked about this once during the course of a demonstration of the JL-6, ace pilot Eddie Rickenbacker explained that "benzol is a lower grade of oil than gasoline and costs less." German engines used synthetic fuels because Germany had little access to natural deposits of oil, limiting its ability to make gasoline. On the other hand, she had plenty of coal. The story of how Germany developed a variety of processes for turning coal into liquid fuels during World War II is fairly well-known, but Germany actually began developing these techniques as early as the 1910s. Benzol was a synthetic fuel available in the US.

Not only was the JL-6 economical with respect to fuel consumption, it was capable of operating on a small field. According to the *Salt Lake City Tribune*, the JL-6 could land in a short distance. From its point of touch-down, a JL-6 would take only about 200 yards to slow enough to begin to safely steer it to the hangar.

What Does "JL" Mean?

The design work for the F-13 was initiated in 1915 with the factory type designation given the letter "J," which stood for Junkers. These J numbers were used for internal designations. The first in this line was the J-1. By the time the series reached J-13, the decision was made to release it to the market. For its external designation, Junkers used the names of Nordic deities, so in 1919, the public designation for this aircraft was given the letter "F," for the goddess Freya.

When the airplane was brought to North America, the name was changed to JL-6. As much as the meaning of the number six was clear, the meaning of the initials, "JL," was obscure. It is likely that the initials were deliberately selected because they were ambiguous. In 1977 Buehl himself was asked about this point, but even he was unsure. He listed a few possibilities.

- Junkers-Larsen (this was the most widely-believed alternative and is the version given in Junkers official histories. A web search of records at the Smithsonian finds only this version).
- Junkers Limousine (the aircraft were very luxurious)
- John Larsen (this is most likely)

On 13 September 1919, a Junkers F-13 equipped with a BMW-IIIa engine, the same plane as a JL-6, achieved a world record for altitude in a transport aircraft. The chief test pilot for Junkers in Germany, Emil Monz, took an F-13 with seven passengers on board to an altitude of 22,146 feet. This achievement led to some lovely advertising copy comparing the altitude reached in the F-13 with the elevation of the highest peak in the Alps, Mont Blanc, at 15,776 feet.

As of August 1920, the JL-6 claimed the following records:

+ *Speed*: flying six passengers from Atlantic City to Philadelphia and back, a distance of 130 miles, in 59 minutes. *Altitude*: climbing to 20,600 feet in 97 minutes carrying six passengers, then flew a distance of 140 miles.
+ *Non-Stop Flying*: starting with 970 pounds of fuel (about 158 US gallons)[*] and 45 pounds of oil, traveling from Omaha to Philadelphia, a distance of 1,200 miles, in 10 hours and 58 minutes. Flying weight was 4,184 pounds.
+ *Economy*: flying eight passengers 130 miles in 88 minutes, using 12½ gallons of gas, costing $3.00.[†]

Over the next two years, the JL-6 proved itself in many environments and in a wide variety of conditions. It was the airplane that opened a number of major air routes in North America, changing the way we think about time and distance. Its versatility enabled it to fly from New York City to San Francisco, taking passengers and cargo for continental distances, and functioning well in all types of weather, including the scalding heat of August in the Southwest and the bitter cold of the sub-arctic in January.

୫

---

[*] At 77°F, a U.S. gallon of gasoline weights 6.15 pounds.

[†] 10.4 miles per gallon. Average speed 89 miles per hour.

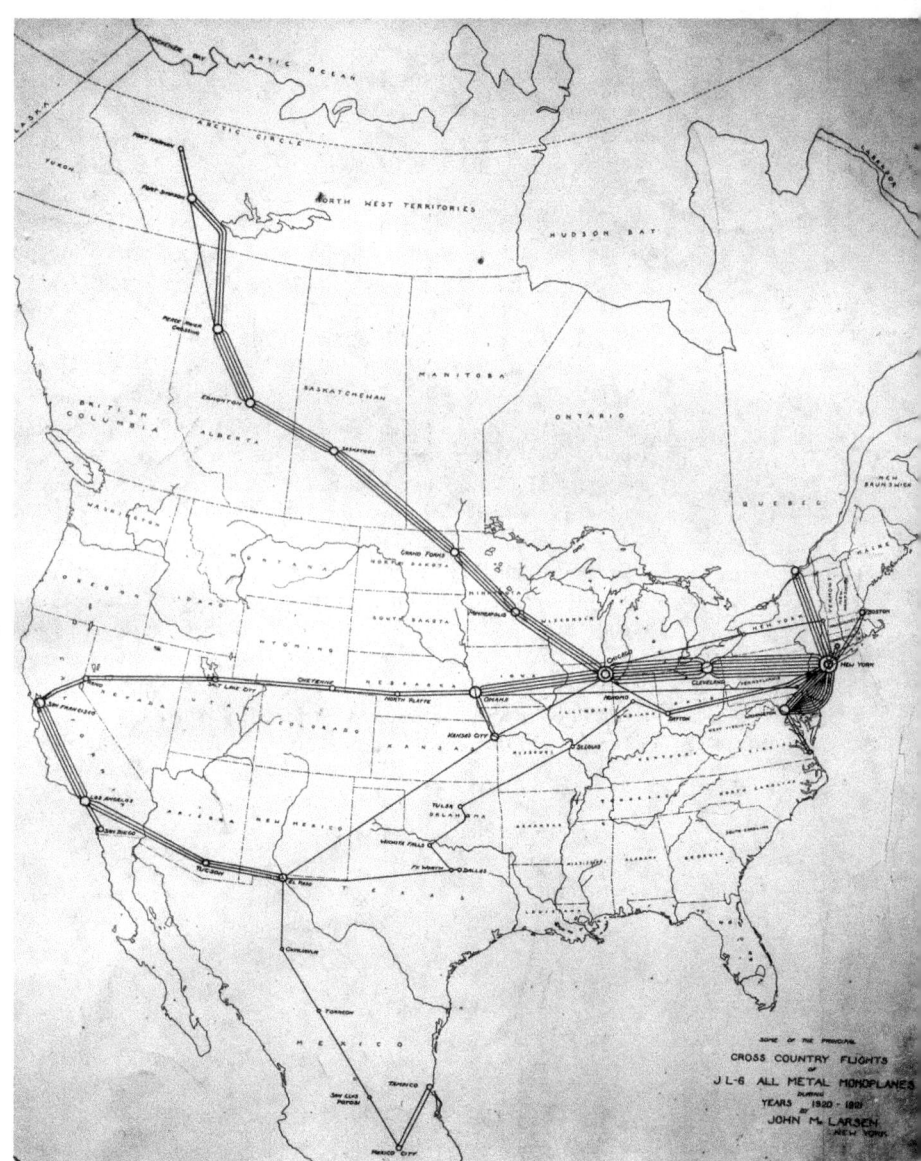

Map of routes opened by the JL-6. PHOTO/EBC

Sources

Becker, Peter W. "The Role of Synthetic Fuel in World War II Germany." Air University Review, July 1981.

BMW-Group Archives. "Höhenflugrekord Franz Zeno Diemers," June 17, 1919. lang. German. (web page)

Fleischman, John. "Where Did Max Miller Die?: One Man's Search for the Place Where the U.S. Air Mail Service Lost a Star." Air & Space Magazine, August 2015. Amazingly, this source reports the JL-6 aircraft were "dangerously slow."

Jasper News. "Marks New Era in U.S. Flying: All Metal Plane Will Revolutionize Aircraft Design and Construction." July 29, 1920.

JL Corp. "Preliminary Specifications of J.L.6 Airplane." Unpublished typed sheet, n.d.

JL-6 (Advertisement)." Aircraft Journal 7, no. 2 (July 12, 1920): 16. The ad does not specify if these are world records or US records but most are US records.

Junkers, Hugo. Flying-machine covering. US1553695 A, filed June 26, 1920, and issued September 15, 1925.

Junkers, Hugo. Shock-absorbing means. US1661182 A, filed May 6, 1922, and issued March 6, 1928.

Martin, E. Stockton. Copy of typed leter. "Letter to J.M. Larsen from E. Stockton Martin, Manager, The Home Insurance Company." Copy of typed leter, October 24, 1921.

Morning World-Herald. "Benzol Fuel for Metal Monoplane Product of Coal." August 3, 1920.

New York Times. "All-Metal Plane Back from Pacific." August 23, 1920.

New York Times. "All-Metal Plane Economy: No Hangars Needed, as They Are Not Affected by Sun or Rain," June 27, 1920.

Salt Lake City Tribune. "Pioneer Airplane Carrying U.S. Mail Arrives in City from Cheyenne in Four and One-Half Hours." August 5, 1920.

Stranges, Anthony N. "Germany's Synthetic Fuel Industry 1927-1945." Energeia, 2001. Center for Applied Energy Research, University of Kentucky.

The Aluminum Association. "Aluminum Alloys 101." Trade association, 2016. (web page)

Brief Biographies

S ome names documented here do not figure prominently in the story, but they all flew with Buehl at one time or another. They were directly involved in the stories told in this book. Gould Dietz is an example—an exceptionally prominent citizen who briefly accompanied the airmail flight in 1920. They are mentioned because their inclusion gives a much broader sense of the perceived importance of the enterprise in which Buehl became involved.

Bertrand Blanchard "Bert" Acosta

Like Buehl, Bert Acosta taught himself how to fly. Born in 1895, he was two years older than Buehl. He got an earlier start in flying,

Burnelli's RB-1. *Buehl was present for its demonstration flight on Long Island.* PHOTO/EBC

too, beginning to fly in 1910. A natural aviator, he quickly became one of the best. He worked for Glenn Curtiss beginning in 1912, and he became the test pilot for many aircraft, including Burnelli's RB-I and the "batwing" airplane designed by William Stout.

During World War I, he worked out of Mineola, training Army pilots how to fly. He was, at that time, Chief Pilot Instructor and Director of Flying and Engineering for the Army Air Service. By all accounts, he was an excellent trainer.

Acosta worked with Larsen for less than a year, beginning in May 1920 and ending that same year in August. While with Larsen, he set numerous American and world records.

Shortly after separating from Larsen, he won the Pulitzer Trophy race in 1921, the first civilian to do so. (H.E. Hartney also flew this race but was injured when his plane crashed). Within weeks after the Pulitzer Race, he became the first American pilot to fly 200 miles per hour. Acosta was inducted into the National Aviation Hall of Fame in 2014.

There are many stories of Acosta's personal difficulties. Unlike Buehl, Acosta was a notorious womanizer. Acosta was so distracted by some women that his job performance sometimes suffered.

His drinking was a worse problem. Acosta had his license suspended in 1928 for trying to fly under a bridge in Connecticut, and his license was revoked in 1929 for flying too low and stunting. He was arrested in 1930 for flying without a license. From then on, he was in and out of jail: flying without a license, drunkness, and other charges.

Edmund Edward Allyne

E.E. Allyne was an industrialist, the president of Aluminum Castings Company of Cleveland. His name is variously given as Edward or Edmund. His appearance anywhere was typically news in itself, but over the course of the 1920 airmail flight, he was eclipsed by Rickenbacker's star power (as was everyone).

Allyne was both a businessman and an inventor. In 1916, for instance, he filed for a patent on a "composite piston" for use in internal combustion engines. It was made up of a composite of several metals (iron, steel, bronze), fastened to components made of an aluminum alloy. With the right application of rapid chilling during the casting of the aluminum, a fine-grained metal structure could be obtained that would be suitable to resist the stresses found during the operation of an internal combustion engine.

The same month in which he flew with Larsen, Allyne's name was appearing in a national advertising campaign endorsing Marmon automobiles. One ad states that Allyne's company was the world's largest manufacturer of aluminum castings. Another lists his name along with many industrial heavyweights, such as Herman Hollerith.[*]

In 1920, he was elected to the Motor and Accessory Manufacturers Association.

Allyne and his wife were socially connected. There are lovely Society Page descriptions of parties at the Allynes' home, and it made social news whenever the couple wintered in Florida. The Allynes had three children: Vernon, Edmund Jr., and Rollin. He had a brother, Alfred H. Allyne, and two sisters, Mrs. E.A. Spencer and Mrs. Ward C. Bell.

President of one of the world's premier aluminum manufacturing companies, Allyne was included in the trip because Larsen and Rickenbacker wanted

Marmon automobiles are not widely remembered today, but it was an exciting brand. In 1911, a Marmon won the first Indianapolis 500. By 1920, Marmon was using a lot of aluminum in their automobiles. They were among the earliest companies to develop the knowledge and skill to control heat flow in an aluminum engine. They also used a good deal of the same element in their coachwork. Allyne supplied Marmon with aluminum castings, and it is likely that the company licensed his patent for making composite pistons. His name first appeared in endorsements for the Marmon automobile in February 1920.

---

[*] Hollerith is today remembered as the father of modern automatic computation, having invented the punched-card tabulating machine. The Tabulating Machine Company, founded by Hollerith, was later renamed IBM.

his help to supply materials for the manufacture of the JL-6. The fact that Larsen, Allyne, and Rickenbacker almost always rode together on the same aircraft indicates that they were interested in exploring these possibilities.

Allyne kept a daily logbook that provides a good, first-hand account of the trip's details. He was generally present for all of the events, flying in the same airplane as Larsen and Rickenbacker. His account is much more reliable than any found in newspaper reports. But perhaps the log's main strength is that it gives us the perspective of someone who made the entire trip, and it was considered an important document at the time. When Allyne presented a copy to the mayor of Cheyenne, it made the news. It made the news again when the mayor presented the same logbook to the Wyoming State Historical Society.

The limitation of this source is that Allyne expressed little interest in what the Post Office was doing. As much as Larsen and Rickenbacker

Caricature of E.E. Allyne that appeared in a book called Cleveland Club Men in Caricature *(1910).* PHOTO/EBC

were courting him to join them in a major manufacturing enterprise, he writes of the experience as though it were a purely social event. The model of a discrete businessman, he discusses almost nothing of the trip's behind-the-scenes but nevertheless obvious purposes. The perspective he presents is restricted to what was happening on the airplane in which he was a passenger.

Although much more personal than Lent's account, there are several times when his discretion is almost too much. There were many occasions in which events had participants on the edge of panic, but Allyne's narrative exudes calm. It seems to me that Allyne actually was more emotionally stable than most, but it also seems that he deliberately omitted details that would undermine a reader's willingness to fly. After all, he was considering entering a partnership to manufacture airplanes.

Franz Zeno Diemer

Franz Zeno Diemer was born in Oberammergau, a well-known Bavarian city located south of Munich and about 174 miles from where Buehl was born in Neustadt im Schwartz-wald. Whether the Diemers and the Buehls ever met is unknown, but it is possible that the Buehl brothers knew Diemer before 1919. There were places between Neustadt and Oberammergau to which Diemer and the Buehl brothers all traveled.

One location they all had in common was Friedrichshafen, a hub of aviation interests and the home of the Zeppelin and the Dornier companies. Another location was Mittelwald, a tourist destination known for its spectacular alpine scenery. Franz Zeno Diemer's father was Michael Zeno Diemer, a famous Bavarian artist who loved to paint in Mittelwald. We know that the Buehls spent time there, too, because Buehl's scrapbook contains numerous photographs from the area.

Mittelwald.
PHOTO/EBC

Gould Dietz

One of the prominent industrialists involved in the trip, Gould Dietz, based in Omaha, made his fortune in lumber and coal. It was said that he was a key leader in building Omaha's city airport.

His interests in the airmail flight encompassed several levels. First and most basic, he had been interested in aviation since 1903. Second, he was a community leader who wanted to encourage the airmail route to come to his city. A third and deeper interest may have related to his investments in Wyoming coal. He thought it possible that the introduction of German aircraft engines would broaden the demand for synthetic fuels made from his product.

Samuel Custer Eaton, Jr.

S.C. Eaton, Jr. was an airmail pilot on the New York-Washington, D.C. run. At the time of the airmail flight we discuss, Eaton was employed by Larsen.

Anthony Herman Gerard Fokker

Fokker began manufacturing aircraft in Germany years before World War I. When the War came, he guided the design of a number of German military aircraft. He is notorious, though, for perfecting a synchronized machine gun that could be fired from an airplane.

It should be clarified that while Fokker had great intuitive engineering skills, he was self-taught and had gaps in his knowledge. He did not personally create some of the things for which he is credited. For example, in the invention of the synchronized machine gun, the key designer on the Fokker team was Heinrich Lübbe, and there is clear evidence that Fokker's design borrowed ideas from at least two already patented designs. In another example, it was Reinhold Platz who principally created the design of Fokker's best airplane of the World War, the D.VII.

What Fokker really did was guide the engineering and perfect innovations to the point that they could be brought to market. Even if his role in these inventions was limited, the

> **Fokker's Lead Designer**
>
> Reinhold Platz was Fokker's lead designer but he did not have formal training as an engineer, either. The two of them, Platz and Fokker, would move quickly from inspiration to prototype, test-fly it, and then refine the design based on seat-of-the-pants experience. Given the state of the art in the 1910s, this produced airplanes that were outstanding for their day. It is clear that by the late-1920s, neither Platz nor Fokker had the knowledge and skills needed to create the larger, more sophisticated airplanes that were being developed then.

importance of Fokker's visionary leadership should not be underestimated. He introduced a number of important innovations that put Germany far ahead of the rest of the world.

Fokker aircraft dominated aerial warfare in World War I. The first aircraft used in aerial warfare were sent up simply to observe enemy positions and movement. Until the middle of 1915, military airplanes were unarmed. As a platform from which to observe the enemy, airplanes quickly replaced the major role of horse-mounted cavalry. The advantage an airplane-mounted observer had was so significant that both sides realized that if they saw an enemy airplane armed only with a camera, they had to do all they could to shoot it down before it could return home with its film. In the next step of escalation, the fighter airplane was invented, and before too long, airplanes were outfitted with machine guns.

The first fighter airplane was a Fokker invention, the Fokker E.I. The E.I. was a monoplane that depended on bracing wires to support the wings. Unlike most other airplanes of the day, it was covered with sheet-metal instead of fabric. With their mounted synchronized machine guns, Fokker aircraft were unchallengeable until early 1916, when the Allies were able to match the German weapons. Up to that time, Allied pilots referred to their own airplanes as "Fokker fodder."

As the War progressed, Fokker moved away from his monoplane design. Near the end of the War, he favored a triplane construction, his famous Fokker Dr.I (Dreidecker). Even though the Dr.I was slower than Allied airplanes, it was astonishingly maneuverable in a dogfight, able to maneuver a sort of sliding 180° turn, making it possible to come into attack position against an enemy fighter that only seconds before had been on its tail.

Near the end of the War, Fokker came out with his D.VIIf. When equipped with the BMW-IIIa engine, the D.VIIf was so capable that it could seem to "hang on its propeller," allowing its pilot to position it behind and underneath Allied aircraft, bring its nose up at full power, and then in a nearly stalled condition, fire into the unprotected belly of the opponent aircraft. The effect was terrifying. It is speculated that if the Fokker D.VIIf had become more widely available earlier, it could have changed the outcome of the War.

After the War, as Fokker moved into manufacturing for the civilian market, he created the first airliner used by KLM on its route to England in 1920. Later, Fokker's sturdy Trimotor entered the record books as the first airplane to fly over the North Pole. He moved to the United States in 1924, where he established the Fokker Aircraft Corporation. Fokker Technologies continues to operate, designing and manufacturing a range of aerospace products.

Anthony Fokker died in New York City at age 49, on 23 December 1939. In 1980, he was posthumously enshrined in the United States National Aviation Hall of Fame.

Harold Evans Hartney

Like Rickenbacker, H. E. Hartney was a World War I ace. Born in Canada and trained as a barrister, he flew for the Royal Flying Corps in 1915. He transferred to the U.S. Air Service in 1918 and was given command of the 1st Pursuit Group, becoming Rickenbacker's commanding officer.

Hartney became a U.S. citizen in 1919, and after the War he lived in the US. He became Chief of the Air Service School of the U.S. Army. After leaving the Army in 1921, he worked as a technical advisor and consulting aeronautical counsel to numerous aviation companies.

Hartney and Larsen developed a personal relationship over time. Shortly after this expedition, Larsen called on Hartney to affirm his identity so that he could renew his US passport. Hartney also helped Larsen in other capacities, endorsing his judgment and character.

Paul Henderson

Photos of Paul Henderson appear in Buehl's scrapbooks. Henderson became the Second Assistant Postmaster General in 1922, a very high-ranking appointment, big enough to hit the newspapers around the country. In this, he was in position to influence the development of transcontinental mail service. This, of course, was well after Buehl had anything to do with the airmail, Larsen, or the JL-6.

A little background on Henderson: he served in World War I, rising to the rank of major in the ordnance department. During this time in France, he began to learn about the military use of airmail. Returning after the war, he rose to lieutenant colonel in the Army Reserve Corps. During this time, he worked to establish municipal airports.

Working in the office of the Postmaster General, Henderson did three things that caught my attention.

First, he defended the promotion of a black railway clerk in Virginia to "clerk in charge." The two Senators from Virginia, several Congressmen, and other prominent citizens objected, but Henderson directed the clerk to continue in the job, and he even threatened that he would send in the Army to enforce his decision.

Second, Henderson worked out how to establish nighttime airmail flights. It was he who installed the system of navigational arrows and beacons across the country. Under Henderson's leadership, mail was delivered across the continent in 28 hours. A flight leaving New York in the morning would arrive in Chicago by that evening. The leg from Chicago to Cheyenne was the first to be lighted, so that mail could continue all night. Some consider this to have been Henderson's greatest achievement.[†]

Third, under Henderson's leadership, the Post Office operated airmail for an entire year without an accident. For this achievement,

---

† The Collier Trophy for 1923 was awarded for these improvements in navigation. The Collier Trophy is considered to be the highest honor awarded in aviation in the United States.

the Post Office was awarded the 1922 Collier Trophy.

So why did Ernie collect pictures of Paul Henderson? I have no notes or written documentation at all related to this trip, and none of the photos we have include Buehl. Furthermore, Henderson is never mentioned by name, either by Buehl or in anything written about Buehl.

The images we have of Henderson relate to a trip taken in 1920 in the southwest. These pictures were taken before Henderson's high-ranking appointment with the Post Office, and before his appearance was particularly newsworthy.

Confusingly, pictures of the trip are spread across several pages in Buehl's photo album. His picture is glued onto pages among images of the airmail flight taken in the summer of 1920, but also with images of Canada. My guess is that Buehl met Henderson in 1920, when they both had some association with Larsen, and then he continued to follow news of Henderson after moving to Philadelphia and Henderson became more prominent.

Henderson's trip took place sometime around November 2, 1920.

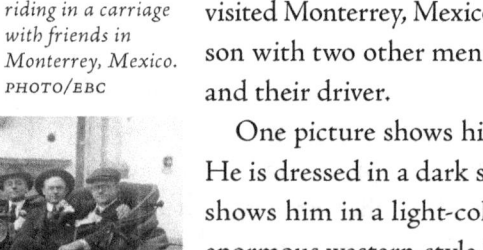

Henderson (right) riding in a carriage with friends in Monterrey, Mexico. PHOTO/EBC

One place he landed was Fort Bliss, Texas. Also, he visited Monterrey, Mexico. One shot shows Henderson with two other men in a horse-drawn carriage and their driver.

One picture shows him standing next to a JL-6. He is dressed in a dark suit and overcoat. Another shows him in a light-colored suit and wearing an enormous western-style hat with a flat brim and an uncreased crown. Yet another shows Henderson, seated, wearing a medium-dark jacket and vest, with no hat. He is young and has a lot of hair on his head. His glasses are distinctive, and he is wearing them in all but one of the photos.

MONTERREY, MEXICO.
1920

Images of Paul Henderson. PHOTOS/EBC

Henderson's trip covered territory visited in August 1920, during the return flight of Larsen, Rickenbacker, and the others, following the survey flight for the first transcontinental airmail.

There is no indication that would tell us why, in what capacity, Henderson was traveling. It is likely that it was not in an official government capacity. One suggestive bit of evidence is that among the pictures taken at Ft. Bliss, there are no news pictures of General Howze or any other high-ranking officer greeting him.

In the August 1920 flight through the area, the party did not fly into Mexico, but on Henderson's trip, he did enter Mexico. We know that the Mexican government purchased two JL-6 aircraft, so it is possible that Henderson was actually working for Larsen on this trip, traveling there to negotiate the sale of airplanes.

Charles B. Kirkham

Charles B. Kirkham was born in 1882 and died in 1969. He was a gifted designer of gasoline engines. Kirkham began building motor-cycle engines in 1903 and building aircraft engines in 1910. His career from 1900 to 1920 was impressive, and his numerous accomplishments in that period are reviewed in the Smithsonian Annals of Flight.

He is best known for his work with Glenn Curtiss. He worked with

Curtiss for four years, first as motor engineer, then as chief engineer. In his position there, he helped to design and build the popular ox-5 engine. For several reasons, including the fact the market for airplanes slumped at the end of World War I, he left Curtiss in the spring of 1919. When he left Curtiss he formed his own company, Kirkham Products.

Larsen met Kirkham in 1919 on Long Island, then hired him in early March 1920. Larsen was beginning to import F-13s and BMW engines and needed an expert who could help him. Kirkham's first duty was as a salesman of BMW airplane engines. By the end of that March, Kirkham was assigned to handling the airplanes in their entirety.

He traveled to Germany in April and early May 1920 to consult with representatives of Junkers. Kirkham and Larsen were there together for about four or five days, then they returned together, arriving in New York again on either the 16th or 17th of May.

When they returned, Kirkham oversaw the modifications made on the airplanes they sold as JL-6s. In general, these were minor modifications, but they included putting new unions on the gas lines, replacing the celluloid windows used on the F-13 with fireproof safety glass, and installing better shock absorbers on the landing gear. No structural changes were made to the airplanes.

The earlier airplanes, including those sold to the Post Office, were sold with high-compression BMW engines, but later airplanes, including those sold in 1921 in Canada, were more modified. These had more modifications to the fuel lines, and the high-compression pistons were replaced with low-compression pistons. After this modification was made, the BMW engines could be run using gasoline, benzol no longer being needed.

It was Kirkham who designed the engine mounting modifications to be made to the JL-6 to make it into the JL-12. In 1921, he made the installation drawings to mount the Liberty engine into its nose, submitting them to Larsen in May or June of that year. Larsen was in

Canada during the time this work was done. Kirkham was unaware of the overall plans for the JL-12 and did not otherwise contribute to the design of the airplane.

Kirkham left Larsen's employ in July 1921, but while still working for Larsen, in June 1921, the U.S. representative of the Junkers company, Carl Seitz, approached Kirkham and L.B. Lent, informing them that the rights to sell the F-13 in the United States were on the market, the arrangement with Larsen having been canceled. Kirkham and Lent were considering forming a company to handle the import of F-13s directly from Junkers but were unable to work out the details to represent Junkers in the U.S. The two of them went into business together in February 1923, purchasing three of the Post Office's unused JL-6s to recondition and resell.

John Miller Larsen

John M. Larsen was born on the far northern tip of Jutland in Hjorring, Denmark, on 10 November 1874, but whether in the county or small city of that name is unknown. His formal education was at ordinary public schools in Denmark. He learned the creamery business there, so after he came to the United States in 1893, he continued in that line of work, first establishing himself as an independent businessman in Fond du Lac, Wisconsin, near Green Bay, in 1899.

Larsen married Jennie Annette Klitgaard in 1894, when he was just 19 years old. Jennie, two years older than John, was also Danish. She was the daughter of a fish seller in the small city of Nørresundby, in the county of Aalborg. The Larsens had three children, Harry, Esther, and Dorothy Jane.

Eight and a half months after the Larsens married, Harry was born in Concord, Wisconsin, a tiny unincorporated community just west of Milwaukee. The young family then moved to Fond du Lac, where Esther was born in 1898. Larsen eventually left Wisconsin, moving his operation to Omaha. Dorothy Jane was born in Chicago in 1911. Later the family moved to New York City. Larsen applied for US citizenship in 1916.

From a modest start, he developed business and manufacturing interests in both the United States and Europe. By 1919, Larsen had made a fortune manufacturing refrigeration equipment. He was said to be a millionaire. By the time Buehl met him in late 1919, John Miller Larsen was an impressive man, a tycoon. He lived mainly in New York City, his address being a luxurious apartment at Ninety-first Street and Riverside Drive, a tony address in Manhattan overlooking the Hudson River, about five blocks west of Central Park. He also maintained a large country home in Park Ridge, New Jersey, as a ref-

John M. Larsen in 1920 PHOTO/EBC

uge for his wife when she wanted to get away from the City. Larsen had a factory in Omaha where he built refrigeration equipment, but he also operated substantial manufacturing facilities in New York City itself. His business office was located in the Equitable Trust Building at 347 Madison Avenue, close to Grand Central Terminal. His airfield was located on Long Island near the hamlet of Plainedge. A number of important airfields of the time were located nearby.

When Buehl knew him, Larsen was five feet six inches tall, and, as some people would politely describe him, "prosperous-looking." He had a full face, a medium forehead, a straight nose, and a double chin. He had blue eyes, and by 1920, when he was in his mid 30s, his blond hair had darkened to brown.

John Larsen's son, Harry, was about two years older than Buehl. It appears that the elder Larsen took an avuncular interest in Buehl in much the same way a man might take some interest in the talented son of a less-prosperous brother. Larsen seemed to like and trust Buehl and they got along well. The rest of the Larsens knew Buehl, but their relationship with him was no more than one would expect. To them, Buehl was the hired help.

Leon B. Lent

L.B. Lent was the Superintendent of Engineering of the United States Post Office Air Mail Service.

Prior to Lent's installation as the Post Office's chief engineer, all technical problems related to the organization and operation of the Air Mail Service were managed by the department head, an advisory board, and a consulting engineer. As the service grew, a full-time, dedicated manager was needed to take charge of understanding the problems of the increasingly complex organization, of solving those problems, and then of reducing what was learned to a concrete form that could be shared with the aviation public. The Air Mail Service, in its pioneering efforts to maintain daily schedules in all kinds of weather, was in a unique position to hammer out solutions to the problems that eventually would face all commercial transport aviation.

Lent's duties included designing and improving all airplanes, equipment, and facilities used by the airmail service. His mission was to improve its safety, reliability, and economy. Lent had everything to do with the selection of the JL-6 for use by the Post Office, but, although a major organizer of the trip, he was pushed out of the spotlight by the other personalities involved. It was the Post Office that triggered the interest on Larsen's part, but by the time the expedition was organized, there were so many people and purposes in play that Lent did not make much news.

As the official Post Office representative, Lent was responsible for the mailbag. Upon delivering it to the postmaster in Oakland,

California, Lent returned to Washington, D.C., and prepared his written report in which he describes how the trip came about and what he observed that would be relevant to the business of delivering the mail. It is a detailed and business-like report with a focus on the time it took to fly from point to point, the supplies consumed, navigational issues, the conditions of the landing fields, and so on. Lent had little to nothing to say about whom they met, what anyone talked about, or the other sights they saw.

Harold Turner "Slim" Lewis

Slim Lewis is included in this list because he joined the expedition as a pilot later in the trip. He was born on 3 October 1894 in Woodville, California. He soloed in 1916 in a Curtiss Pusher. Lewis went on to fly for United and became their chief pilot in 1934. He retired abruptly in 1947, moving to a ranch he had purchased in Wyoming eight years earlier. He died in Cheyenne on 25 July 1965.

Lewis said that he retired because, as far as he was concerned, the fun had gone out of flying. He did not particularly enjoy flying in an enclosed cockpit. Also, he did not like all of the dials and gauges that, over time, began to crowd the instrument panel.

Lewis was one of the first four inductees to the Wyoming Aviation Hall of Fame (1995).

Emil Monz

In 1920, Emil Monz ranked among the Junkers company's best test pilots. To put it another way, he was one of the best test pilots in the world.

Monz was born in Stuttgart, a large and very old city in the German state of Württemburg. When he was born, Stuttgart was a hub of world-class technology. The city is about 95 miles north of Neustadt, where Buehl was born.

In the First World War, Monz was a reconnaissance pilot. After the War, in 1919, he was hired by Junkers. He was the first test pilot of the F-13. During 1919, he developed more experience with the F-13 than anybody. He also set an altitude world record for a passenger airplane on 13 September 1919, taking an F-13 to an altitude of 22,301 feet, which is more than 6,900 feet higher than the highest peak in the Alps.

After his successes as a test pilot, Monz was advanced in the company and given the job of airfield manager. He was bored with this desk job and badly wanted to return to being a test pilot. When he had the chance, Monz implored Larsen to hire him.

Of the pilots working for Junkers, there were two candidates: Hugo G. Schafer and Emil Monz. Monz was very well-known and highly qualified. He had been the first test pilot of the F-13. During 1919, he acquired more experience with the F-13 than anybody else. However, Larsen selected Schaefer to be his demonstration pilot, largely because Schaefer spoke fluent English and, with his English-sounding name, seemed likely to pass for English.

Bored with his desk-bound duties at Junkers, Monz badly wanted to be flying again. Soon after winning a good deal of fame for his achievements as a pilot, he had been promoted to a management position that he did not like. Since he believed Larsen would give him a better opportunity to demonstrate his skills to the world, Monz directly asked Larsen to hire him in addition to Schafer.

Larsen agreed, but knowing the harsh prejudice Monz would face as a German, Larsen insisted that he must never indicate that he was a pilot. Instead, he should present himself as an engineer. He was to say that his role was to be a manufacturing consultant, and he was to declare that he intended to become an American citizen.

After he arrived, Monz became a permanent resident of the US. His address was given as 242 W. 72nd Street, New York. His occupation was given as "aeroplane engineer." His wife, Melene Monz, remained in Dessau. She did not travel to the US with him.

Tragically, Schaefer was killed on 3 February 1920 in a test flight of an F-13 in Dessau. From that point, Monz would be Larsen's only pilot for introducing the F-13, but it proved impossible to soften the impact of Monz's German origin.

After the relationship of Monz with Larsen broke down, he returned to Dessau in September 1920. Junkers tried to assign him to be a pilot with an airline, Lloyd Ostflug, but Monz remained deeply unhappy. By 7 January 1921, Junkers officials were beginning to question Monz's stability. He was not flying "with the former calm and caution." Junkers manager, Carl Seitz, remarked that Monz's recent bad experiences and the "current uncertainty of his situation" left him damaged and insecure.

On 18 February 1921, Monz was assigned to fly the technical manager of the Lloyd Ostflug company from Konigsberg to Berlin. Near Lauenburg, Prussia,[‡] Monz encountered very bad weather. It was foggy and there was snow, but Monz had proven himself capable of flying in worse weather. Even so, at about 10 AM, people in the area reported hearing an airplane and then hearing a blast. It was two hours before the fog cleared enough to locate the crashed F-13, but the evidence recovered indicated that Monz had flown the airplane directly into the ground at full speed. This was not hilly country so there was not a problem related to challenging terrain. There was not enough of the airplane left to discover if there had been a technical problem. No one has ever been able to rule out the possibility that he committed suicide. Junkers records attribute the cause to having had inadequate instrumentation to fly in those conditions.

Harry S. Myhres

H. S. Myhres needs a comment because he appears often and is

‡ Now Lębork, Pomerania, Poland, west of Gdańsk

not well known. Sources vary on the spelling of Myhres' name. Many give his name as "Dick Myers" or "H.S. Myers." Others give his last name as "Meyers," and a number of articles mentioning him only give his first initial, "H," rather than his whole first name (Harry). In all cases, they are talking about the same person, H.S. Myhres. A photo of Myhres appeared in the QB club newsletter for the Los Angeles Hangar. Myhres was one of the "first year men," in other words, a founding member of that chapter of the club.

Myhres' name is listed in the 20 September 1917 Air Service Journal among aviators whose qualifications were to be evaluated for rating as junior military aviators. He is also listed by the Society of Air Racing Historians among the "pre-World War II pilots" He placed fifth in the 1929 Thompson Cup race.

Edward V. "Eddie" Rickenbacker

Rickenbacker was America's Ace of Aces in World War I.
PHOTO/PUBLIC DOMAIN

The flight's most famous participant was Captain Eddie Rickenbacker. Until Lindbergh's solo flight across the Atlantic, Rickenbacker had been America's premier aviator, largely due to his reputation as the nation's most successful fighter pilot during World War I. To become an "ace," a pilot had to shoot down five enemy aircraft. Rickenbacker had 26 victories, by far the most of any American pilot until World War II. After initially receiving the Distinguished Service Cross (nine times), his medals were upgraded in 1931 to the Congressional Medal of Honor. Rickenbacker continued a distinguished career of service until his death in 1973.

There is a good deal of confusion with respect to what Rickenbacker was doing on this expedition. Some books and articles indicate that he helped pilot one of the airplanes. Many also believe that Rickenbacker had a key role in organizing the flight. David W. Lewis, Rickenbacker's definitive biographer, in particular, states these positions. Contrary to Lewis, it is clear in Allyne's account that Rickenbacker flew the plane once, taking it for a short ride, perhaps in Cleveland, but that he never was at the controls for an entire leg of the journey. He was never the pilot; he was always a passenger.

Rickenbacker's motivation to join the flight was that he and his partner in the enterprise, Larsen, could see mutual benefits from collaboration. Rickenbacker's endorsement certainly could mean a lot to Larsen, and his fame guaranteed lots of publicity for the enterprise. Rickenbacker, for his part, impressed with the capabilities of the JL-6, appeared to be looking at forming a lucrative partnership with

Woman sitting on the prop of a JL-6. This trip attracted what we would today refer to as groupies. PHOTO/EBC

Larsen. Several sources indicate that Rickenbacker had business in mind. In answer to a direct question, he was reported to have "admitted his future activities might be linked with the future of the Larsen monoplane, but declined to state any of his plans."

Rickenbacker did play a notable role in organizing the expedition. In his autobiography, he states that he "helped Larsen to arrange a cross-country tour." He said that he had two things in mind: first, he wanted to promote air transportation; second, he wanted to demonstrate the use of duralumin alloy in aircraft construction. It was Rickenbacker who connected Larsen with aluminum manufacturer E.E. Allyne.

Rickenbacker was present on this flight because he intended to work closely with Larsen to sell the JL-6. Rickenbacker was invaluable to the enterprise because he was guaranteed to attract a crowd of celebrity-followers everywhere they landed. Indeed, Buehl recalled that his attraction was so powerful that women would come out to the airplane and want to kiss the seat that Rickenbacker had sat in. According to Buehl, having "Rickenbacker in the back seat was a promotional idea." From the Post Office's perspective, the most important feature of Rickenbacker's involvement was the fact that, with the considerable respect he commanded, he was able to lecture civic leaders in cities where they landed about the duty of communities to build good municipal airports.

In the background, Rickenbacker was talking with H.E. Hartney, too. More than one source says that the entire adventure was quickly organized by these two, following the 31 May 1920 demonstration of the JL-6 to the Army Air Service and the Navy, in Washington, D.C. Hartney was then head of training and operations for the Army Air Service, but he was thinking of leaving the Army and going into business with Rickenbacker. The two of them, impressed with what they saw, approached Larsen, and then all three began developing a marketing promotion for the JL-6.

Edward Anderson "Eddie" Stinson, Jr.

Eddie Stinson, jr. came from a family of well-known fliers. In fact, he had two sisters and a brother who were also famous, Katherine, Margery, and Jack. The four of them gave flying demonstrations at carnivals and state fairs, billing themselves as the "Flying Stinsons."

The story of his sisters is arguably more interesting than the story of Eddie. His older sister in particular, Katherine, was the first woman to perform a "loop." Also, she was the first pilot to carry airmail in Montana. According to Montana Department of Transportation historian Jon Axline, while Stinson was doing some demonstration flying in Helena, Montana, at the Montana State Fair on 23 September 1913, she took off from the fairgrounds with a pouch of mail, flew a few miles to downtown Helena, and dropped it on the Post Office. Katherine Stinson is a 2019 inductee into the National Aviation Hall of Fame. Eddie Stinson, though, was the one with whom Buehl directly connected.

Born in Alabama on 11 July 1893, Eddie's first powered flight was made in 1911, at age 17. He had been building gliders since he was 15. During World War I, Stinson served in Texas as a flight instructor.

Stinson's name is remembered today for the company he started and for the aircraft he designed and built. There were many aircraft companies started in the 1920s, but most disappeared. Stinson's was a rare success story. He formed his aircraft company much earlier than many people realize. He began the Stinson Airplane Company, located in Dayton, in 1920. He did not do much with it for several years, though. In the meantime, he worked other jobs.

He began working for Larsen at some point after the War, and in October 1921, he raced the JL-6 as a part of the Larsen team in Kansas City. By October 1921, Stinson was one of only five people remaining on Larsen's payroll. Given that two of those remaining employees at Larsen's aerodrome on Long Island were laborers, it suggests how hollowed-out Larsen's company had become. In contrast to the number of stars Larsen attracted in the summer of 1920, by the fall of 1921 Stinson was the only remaining star.

On 29 December 1921, along with Lloyd Bertaud, flying a JL-6, set a world record for non-refueling, sustained flight: 26 hours 19 minutes. This story broke as very big news, and this was the achievement that attracted Roald Amundsen to the JL-6. The clear implication was that economical flight over very long distances, even in dreadful weather, was possible in this airplane.

In February 1922, at the time of the fire at Larsen Field, Stinson was still working for Larsen. When Buehl gave his statement immediately after the fire at Larsen Field, Stinson happened to be in

Larsen's Madison Avenue office and signed the affidavit as a witness. In this statement, Buehl admitted he caused the fire but said it was an accident.

Later in 1922, Stinson worked as a test pilot for William B. Stout, testing the Stout ST-1. Also in 1922, Stinson purchased four surplus JL-6 aircraft from the U.S. Airmail Service, and in June of that year set off with Rickenbacker on a three-month national tour demonstration flight. The demonstration flight did not go well; by the end, Rickenbacker dropped out of the project. By that time, of course, Buehl had nothing more to do with the JL-6.

In 1925, offered financial backing from the Detroit Board of Commerce, Stinson moved his Stinson Airplane Company from Dayton to the Detroit area. His first product was the SB-1 Detroiter. The Detroiter incorporated the advanced feature of having brakes on the landing wheels. The company had good backing from investors and was able to produce several successful designs. In 1926, the Detroiter made a footnote in the history of the FAA because on 7 December that year, the first airworthiness inspection of an American aircraft was of a Detroiter before its delivery to Canadian Air Express.

In the 1920s, endurance records did not stand for long, so the record Stinson and Bertaud held late in 1921 was soon enough broken. Seven years later, though, Stinson retook the endurance record, with George Haldeman as his co-pilot: 53 hours 30 minutes, flying a Stinson airplane.

A Detroiter SM-1, a single-engine, six-seat airplane, was Stinson's first production aircraft. One of these was used in 1927 in a planned around-the-world trip that was to start in Detroit. It was flown to Europe, then across Asia, finally stopping in Japan, not wanting to risk crossing the Pacific Ocean. Unfortunately, this flight inspired a number of other aviators to attempt flying across oceans in Stinson aircraft. All of them were lost at sea. As much as Stinson needed to sell airplanes, he quickly stated that he would refuse to sell aircraft for transoceanic flying.

Although his aircraft company eventually emerged as a success, it was a major struggle. During his lifetime, Stinson earned more as a stunt pilot than he did as a manufacturer.

In 1926, Stinson sold 10 Detroiters, which does not seem like a lot, but it was enough to keep the company going. In 1929, majority interest in Stinson's company was purchased by E.L. Cord, whose name is better remembered now as an automobile manufacturer. Cord's company, Aviation Corporation (AVCO), eventually combined Stinson and Vultee aircraft, retaining both names. In 1948, Piper purchased the Stinson Division of Vultee. The last use of the Stinson nameplate was in 1950, with the Stinson Voyager. By the time the last Voyager was delivered and after 24 years of manufacturing, Stinson's name had been imprinted on 12,320 aircraft. (In another intersection of people and events, it was Lewis E. Reisner, a designer of the Challenger that was Buehl's first airplane, who designed the airplane that became the Stinson Voyager).

Stinson died in January 1932. By that time, he had 16,000 flying hours, which was more than anyone else. At only age 38, he was hailed in his *New York Times* obituary as the "Dean of American Fliers."

His death was an accident. He took off from Chicago, planning to fly back to Detroit. Over Lake Michigan, he found that he was nearly out of fuel, so he turned back. He was forced to attempt a landing on a golf course, but by that time it was dark. He made a good touch down, but his right wing clipped a flag pole, causing the airplane to spin out of control and then crash.

William Bushnell Stout

Another industrialist who briefly accompanied the expedition was William Bushnell Stout, a versatile engineer who designed innovative automobiles for Packard in the 1910s and then began designing aircraft in the 1920s.

Stout studied the F-13 and immediately saw the benefits of the cantilevered wing design and all-metal construction. He wanted to experience flying in the most advanced aircraft of its day, so he asked to be invited.

Stout's most successful airplane was his Stout 3-AT, a three-engine transport aircraft. In 1924, his company, the Stout Metal Airplane Company, was purchased by Ford, and his 3-AT became the basis for the Ford Trimotor. Stout clearly understood the advantages of the JL-6's distinctive corrugated aluminum skin because he copied it for the Trimotor.

Selected Sources

Allyne, Edmund E. *First Round Trip Transcontinental Passenger Flight: July 29th to August 22nd 1920.* self published, 1921.

Andersson, Lennart, Gunter G. Endres, Rob J. M. Mulder, and Gunther Ott. *Junkers F13: The World's First All-Metal Airliner.* EAM Books EEIG, 2012.

Birdseye, Claude H. "Stereoscopic Phototopographic Mapping." *Annals of the Association of American Geographers* 30, no. 1 (March 1940): 1–24.

Bisbee Daily Review. "All-Metal Plane Breaks Propeller." August 14, 1920.

Boyer, Diane, and Robert Webb. "Damming Grand Canyon: The 1923 USGS Colorado River Expedition." All USU Press Publications, January 1, 2007.

"Cheyenne Airfield, Fountain: Photographs, Written Historical and Descriptive Data, Field Records." Historic American Engineering Record Intermountain Regional Office, National Park Service, U.S. Department of the Interior, 12795 West Alameda Parkway, Denver, CO 80228., n.d.

Cleveland Plain Dealer. "Woman, Children Fall In Airplane Mrs. E. E. Allyne and Family Then Go Up With Rickenbacker." July 31, 1920.

Davie, John L. His Honor, the Buckaroo: The Autobiography of John L. Davie. Reno, NV: Jack Herzberg, 1988.

Ernie Buehl Talks to the Experimental Aircraft Association, Pennsylvania Chapter 76. Videotape, 1986.

Eytinge, Bruce. Field Guide and Pilot's Log Book. Eytinge & Uden, NYC, 1920.

Grand Forks Daily Herald. "John M. Larsen Made Defendant in Damage Suit at Omaha, Neb." November 8, 1921.

Hugo Junkers—Ein Leben für die Technik. "18 Februar 1921: Junkerspilot Emil Monz tödlich verunglückt," March 18, 2014.

Lent, Leon B. "United States Air Mail Survey Flight New York - San Francisco." U.S. Postal Service, n.d. RG 18 Stack area 190, row 39, compartment 16, shelf 1. National Archives.

Maurer, Maurer. "Aviation in the U.S. Army, 1919-1939." General histories. Office of Air Force History, United States Air Force, 1987.

Montana.gov Official State Website. "Airway Beacons," January 7, 2021.

National Aviation Hall of Fame. "Acosta, Bertrand 'Bert' B."

Nevada State Journal. "Mail Airplanes Leave Today on Flight to Coast. Local Field Too Small." August 7, 1920.

New York Times. "Air Mail to Span Continent." March 14, 1920.

New York Times. "Phone to Pacific from the Atlantic." January 26, 1915.

Omaha Daily News. "Lost over Lake Erie with Dwindling Gas Supply Has No Appeal to Gould Dietz," August 2, 1920.

Omaha World Herald. "From Pony Express to Swift Air Mail," October 31, 1920.

Omaha World Herald. "Larsen Ill, Halt Trip of All Metal Planes." August 2, 1920.

Rickenbacker, Edward V. Rickenbacker: An Autobiography. First. Englewood Cliffs, NJ: Prentice-Hall, 1967.

Salt Lake City Tribune. "Pioneer Airplane Carrying U.S. Mail Arrives in City from Cheyenne in Four and One-Half Hours." August 5, 1920.

Smithsonian National Postal Museum. "Pilot Stories: Lewis, Harold T. 'Slim,'" 2004.

Airmail

Putting the Airmail in Perspective

These days, about 100 years later, when it is routine to transmit complex documents via email and when long-distance voice communication over the Internet is basically free, transcontinental airmail delivery might not seem terribly impressive.

In 1920, though, the options for same-day communication between coasts were expensive and very limited. Telegraph was an option for sending short, urgent messages, but one paid for every word transmitted. To open a long-distance telephone connection, one paid by the second while the line was open.

Transcontinental telephony was inaugurated on 25 January 1915. At that time, the *New York Times* reported that the charge would be $20.70 for the first minute and $6.75 for each subsequent minute. It was estimated that it would take about ten minutes to put a call through from New York to San Francisco, and during the time the two people were talking, the entire apparatus between these two cities, valued in 1915 at over $2,000,000, could not be used by anyone else.

Using the Post Office, one could send business documents and other complex messages by mail for a reasonable cost. It just took a long time. By rail, under the best of conditions, a letter leaving New York on Monday just before 9:00 PM could be delivered in San Francisco just after noon on Thursday. Results as quick as this depended on the mail train making an on-time connection in Chicago, but, on average, in two of every five days of operation this connection was missed. In January 1920, it was missed every day, which added another 24 hours to delivery time. On the other hand, mail leaving New York at daybreak on Monday could be reliably received on Wednesday if sent by air. Since many messages for business are time-sensitive, airmail became crucial.

Neither telephone nor telegraph would transmit a physical document, and telegraph or telephone, the mail was private. Many people would see the contents of a telegram, and it was routine for people to eavesdrop on telephone conversations, but the message contained in a piece of mail was sealed in its envelope.

A feature mentioned by Otto Praeger, then the Assistant Postmaster General in charge of Air Mail Service, was that sending mail by air was cheaper than by rail. Praeger stated that when airmail service between New York and Chicago started, it cost $365,000 to maintain the route, but even so, that much plus another $121,000 in delivery costs was saved by using airmail. It took fewer mail clerks, and no shipping costs needed to be paid to railroads. Similar savings were noted upon the establishment of an airmail route between New York and Washington, D.C. Maintaining the transcontinental airmail route for a year would cost $1,100,000, but Praeger estimated savings of $1,200,000. Furthermore, Praeger gave reliability figures: airmail had a 92% on-time delivery rate, while railroads averaged only 72%.

Navigation

In 1920 as today, pilots often followed highways or railroads, but a route that makes sense on land may not be the most efficient by air. Airmail pilots needed to unlink from the older modes of transportation. The problem immediately presented itself: in the nearly featureless landscapes of the largely unsettled west, it was hard to figure out where you were by just looking out the window at the ground.

The first accurate US maps based on aerial photography were not produced until years later. The first standard USGS 15-minute quadrangle based on data from aerial photography was produced in 1922. Before that, topographic maps were produced with laborious, ground-based methods, and accurate coverage was spotty. In 1920, basic Rand-McNally highway maps were the most useful maps available, and they were obviously inadequate. Clear maps useful to pilots would not be available for the foreseeable future, so an alternative was needed.

The Post Office eventually responded to the need by selecting a route that more-or-less followed the lower elevations across the country to connect New York and San Francisco. Along this route, they installed a system of big lighthouse-type beacons that were powered by on-site generators. These beacons, together with great navigational arrows made of concrete, allowed airmail to move 24 hours per day. Spaced every ten miles, the arrows and associated beacons made reliable landmarks. Erected in 1924, the arrows defined the map of the transcontinental airway.

A 1926 airway beacon concrete arrow, indicating a slight change in heading and pointing generally north-northeast. This 50-foot concrete arrow is one of four that can still be found in the vicinity of St. George, Utah. PHOTO/GREATER SOUTHWESTERN EXPLORATION COMPANY

While beacon towers have mostly been removed and their materials recycled, they are not entirely obsolete. In the state where I live, Montana, seventeen of the electric beacons were still operating into the twenty-first century, guiding pilots safely through mountainous areas. The navigational arrows are now almost all that remains of the ambitious effort predating the radio beacons used today to guide airplanes. As such, the arrows are a matter of archeological interest, sometimes surprising people who stumble across them in remote regions.

The obvious question we would ask today is, why not use radios? Radios were not carried on airplanes until years later, though in 1920 some military experiments with radiotelegraphy put them on airplanes, enabling fliers to send and receive messages tapped out in Morse Code. However, radio communication between airplanes and ground stations was found to be excessively unreliable. At about the same time the Army was experimenting with them, the Forest Service also tried radios on fire-spotting airplanes. They soon found that if an aerial observer discovered a fire, it was better just to drop a message from the plane asking whoever found it to inform the agency.

Ground-based radios proved to be very useful, though. In only two months, by late October 1920, radios linking aerodromes along the route signaled when a pilot took off, so that the receiving airfield could expect his arrival. Information transmitted included the pilot's name, the plane's tail number, how much he was carrying, and any other data needed to prepare for his arrival.

Buehl's 1920 flight entirely predates the installation of any ground-based navigation equipment for airplanes. In fact, his was the survey flight that allowed planners to create these systems. With the basic survey work done, the route developed quickly.

Summary of Allyne's log

In the following, Allyne's log will serve as the framework for a day-to-day summary of events during the expedition. Most of what is presented here is from Allyne. Some other information is added where a reliable source can be found.

There is a lot of misinformation circulating about this first transcontinental airmail flight. Much of the misinformation revolves around Rickenbacker's role. When this trip is remembered at all, the writers tend to pick out Rickenbacker and maybe one or two others, and then ignore everyone else who was along. For example, one source focusing on Bert Acosta's career mentions this trip but nearly implies that the trip was principally the work of Acosta and Rickenbacker.

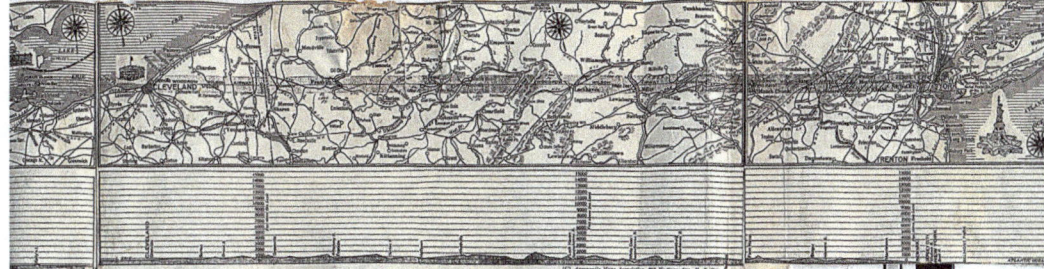

Woodrow Wilson Airway, New York to Cleveland PHOTO/EBC

Outbound: New York to Cleveland

The expedition took off from Long Island, New York, on 29 July 1920, heading for Cleveland. Within minutes Larsen's plane—with Emil Monz as pilot, Buehl co-pilot—lost its way. Acosta was piloting the "camera plane," while Hartney had the controls of the Army plane. All three aircraft took off at about 9:15 AM, joining their escort of nine other planes in the sky over the airfield. All twelve circled the field, and then the expedition planes were supposed to break away and fly to Cleveland, their first stop. Monz, however, did not see the other two go and became disoriented. Cross-footed in this little aerial ballet, he had to return to Long Island to recover his bearings. They took off again at 11:40 AM.

By 2:30 PM, Monz was lost again. They flew for about an hour and were over Lake Erie before they recognized where they were—near Westfield, New York. While they were over the water, they discovered their fuel supply was low and they would have to land before they got to Cleveland. When they put down at 4:20 PM in little North East, Pennsylvania, Allyne commented that they had gone "much too far South," concluding that they "might better have followed railroad tracks via Albany."

In Monz's defense, it has to be said that the maps supplied for navigation were not very good. There was a crude Army Air Service transcontinental map that had been prepared in 1919, and there was a Post Office map. To get more detail, Rand McNally road maps of every state they crossed were carried. As Lent said, "It was impossible to get one good cross-country flying map showing in detail everything a cross-country flier needed and yet not showing unnecessary and confusing detail."

In North East, everyone in the community seemed to come out to see the airplane. According to Dietz, it must have been the first time an airplane had ever been there because, he said, "The population nearly mobbed us." Finally, they were able to get some gasoline and proceed to Cleveland, taking off at 5:20 PM. Of course, both of the other planes were already there. Larsen's plane did not get to Cleveland until dusk, at 7:15 PM, so the runway at Martin Field had to be lighted with flares.

During the flight between New York and Cleveland, Monz and Larsen got into "a heated argument." According to a letter Larsen wrote to Junkers, Monz had made himself "politically impossible," and he seemed to be arguing that Junkers should break its contract with Larsen. According to Larsen's letter, Monz argued that it would be no loss to Junkers, as Junkers would still be competitive in South America even if the company lost the opportunity in North America with Larsen. He was furious that Larsen took credit for inventing the JL-6, and he was fed-up with the abuse given Germans. Larsen described Monz as "ungrateful" and a "schemer."

The relationship between Larsen and Monz had broken down by the time the party reached Cleveland. Upon arriving there, Larsen transferred Monz to the camera plane and replaced him with Acosta. Monz then flew the camera plane to Chicago, leaving Cleveland at 3:00 PM. On the way to Chicago, again Monz found he did not have enough fuel and was forced to land about five miles from the airfield.

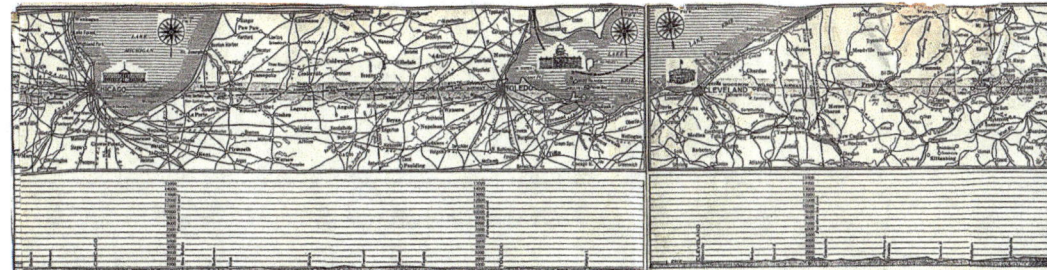

Woodrow Wilson Airway, Cleveland to Chicago PHOTO/EBC

Outbound: Cleveland to Chicago

While in Cleveland, which was Allyne's hometown, it was arranged for Hartney to take Allyne's wife and three children for a flight over the city on 30 July at 10:30 AM. On take-off, he hit a telegraph pole, went through some wires, and came down in a vacant lot. The airplane was wrecked, but there were no injuries. Mr. Allyne witnessed the crash and began running toward the wreck, but before he got there he saw his wife and children climb out and begin walking toward him. They were laughing and evidently enjoying themselves. His ten-year-old son, Rollin, had been carrying a camera, so he took pictures of the wreck. As far as they were concerned, the crash just added an unexpected thrill to the events of the day.

Given their happy mood, Larsen asked Mrs. Allyne if they would like to try it again. More adventurous than most of us might be, the Allynes all stated that they would love to go again as soon as possible. Mrs. Allyne and the three children transferred to another plane and had a successful flight. (It is possible that this was the time that Rickenbacker was at the controls). Later that day, Allyne's children all agreed that flying was "great."

Hartney's airplane had to be replaced with a new one to be delivered from New York, so he had to wait in Cleveland while the remaining two airplanes flew on to Chicago. Gould Dietz dropped out of the party, although he followed them by train to Omaha. He admitted that he became anxious about flying after his airplane ran low on fuel over Lake Erie, and after witnessing the crash of Hartney's plane.

The camera plane flew to Chicago on 30 July, taking off at 3:00 PM. This put them into Chicago a little after dusk, as it took more than six hours of flying to cover the distance. They ran out of fuel directly over the city but were able to land safely only five miles from their destination. From Cleveland on the previous day, Larsen telephoned to New York for S.C. Eaton to meet Monz in Chicago. Monz was dismissed upon landing in Chicago, his duties taken over by Eaton.

According to Lent, "They found it inadvisable to carry the German Pilot." It does not appear that the reason he was fired had to do with his nationality—after all, they continued to employ Buehl on the trip—but more a result of Larsen's and Monz's deteriorating opinions of one another.

(left) Checkboard Field, the official field used for airmail in 1920, was little south of West Roosevelt Road and east of First Avenue, in what is now Miller Meadows Forest Preserve. By 1922, operations were transferred to Maywood Air Mail Field, which was larger and immediately next to Checkerboard Field. MAP/UNIV. OF CHICAGO
(right) The 1963 Berwyn Quandrangle, shows no trace of any airport. MAP/PUBLIC DOMAIN

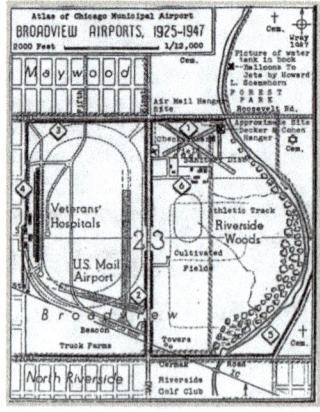 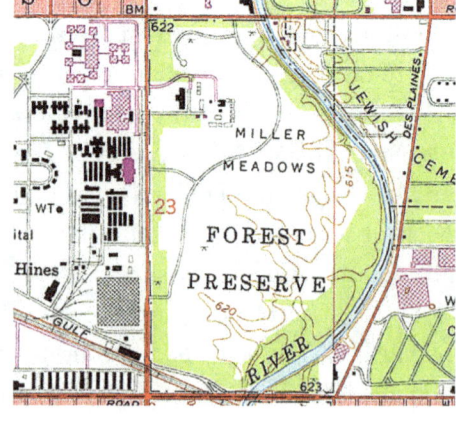

Larsen's plane stayed in Cleveland until 31 July. Their flight to Chicago was uneventful. Acosta took over as the pilot and Buehl remained on the airplane as co-pilot. Just before noon, the passengers had lunch and enjoyed the views. They landed at Checkerboard Field at 3:50 PM.

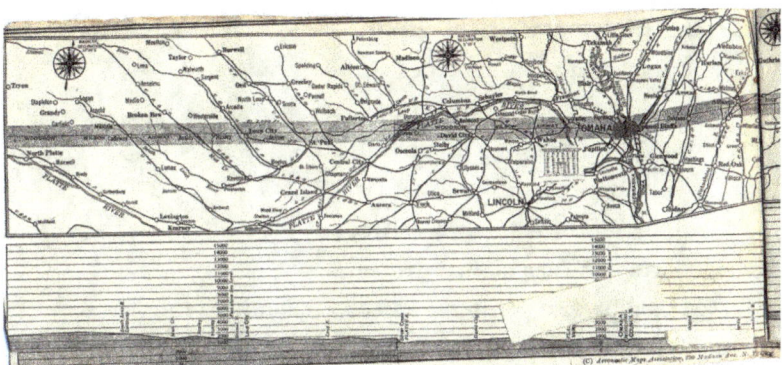

Woodrow Wilson Airway, Omaha PHOTO/EBC

Outbound: Chicago to Omaha

Both planes left Chicago on 1 August at 8:00 AM and arrived at Omaha's Ak-Sar-Ben* field at 11:35. The flight was so uneventful that Allyne could only comment on how comfortable it was. The passengers drank coffee and read magazines. Allyne even took a mid-morning nap.

As they approached their destination, there was a good crowd waiting for them at the airfield. Larsen told Acosta "to do some maneuvering over Omaha before landing." Allyne recorded that they were "in for a thrill as Acosta's maneuvers are not tame ones." Five minutes before landing, the acrobatics were still so aggressive that Buehl's cap blew off and, as Allyne said, fell "in beautiful spirals, which brought forth applause from the crowd gathered to receive us."

Eaton's plane arrived in Omaha shortly after, and Hartney caught up with the group late that evening.

---

* "Nebraska" spelled backward.

Outbound: Omaha one more day

They all stayed in Omaha the following day, 2 August. Larsen had been
feeling ill when they left Chicago, and
he saw a physician when they arrived
in Omaha. He had lived in the city and
had manufacturing facilities there, so
he stayed with friends, the O'Briens,
to recover. While he was recuperat-
ing, Larsen surprised them by inviting them to join the expedition. They
agreed to go, and that night, Mr. and

JL-6 taking off. PHOTO/EBC

Mrs. O'Brien packed a suitcase apiece. Rickenbacker had traveled in
Acosta's plane with Larsen to Omaha, but as they were preparing to
leave, Mrs. O'Brien took his place in the plane piloted by Acosta. Mr.
O'Brien and Rickenbacker took a seat in Hartney's plane.

Outbound: Omaha to Cheyenne

Take-off was at 10:15 AM. Eaton left first, then Acosta. As they
watched from the air, they saw that Hartney did not make the take-off
and crashed into a house. Allyne reported that the crash destroyed
the house, "collapsing it completely with little damage to the machine
other than crumpling" the leading edge of the wing. But Allyne was
minimizing the effect on the airplane. Photos of the wreck show a
significant bend in the right wing and a broken propeller. The airplane
was unrepairable at the time.

Observers were impressed that the crash site did not look like other
airplane wrecks: the all-metal construction meant that the body of
the airplane had not broken into splintered wood. Also, they noted
that the triplex glass of the cabin windows had not broken.

Acosta returned to the field to check on everyone and to reunite

Mrs. O'Brien with her husband, who had been riding in Hartney's plane. No one was injured in either the house or the airplane, but the O'Briens decided not to go on. This was the end of the trip for Hartney, also. In late 1921, Larsen and Hartney were sued by the owner of the house.

In later interviews, Rickenbacker said that this was the first airplane crash he had ever been in. Asked if he had been hurt, he admitted that he had "suffered a severe fracture of the straw hat." I find it remarkable that after Hartney's involvement in one crash after another, years later Rickenbacker still identified him as the "best pilot" of those flying this expedition.

When asked why he had crashed, Hartney explained that his plane was not as powerful as the others and that it was heavily loaded. He also commented that "the field is very heavy" and that he could not get up enough speed to make sufficient altitude. At the time of the crash, the plane was going 70 miles per hour.

Outbound: North Platte

Rickenbacker rejoined the group on Acosta's plane, and they took off again at 12:35 PM, with Eaton following. Allyne was uncharacteristically nervous, almost certainly because he was not calmed down after witnessing the crash of Hartney's plane—and because he was hungry. He complained that Eaton was flying too close to them and was dismayed that "someone ate our sandwiches at Omaha." According to him, they decided to land at North Platte because everyone wanted lunch. However, Lent explained that the Post Office intended to build an emergency landing field at North Platte and he needed to see what was there. He said that he was choosing favorable places for fields in case of forced landings, as well as looking at places for hangars.

At 3:55, they landed in North Platte, stopping for 50 minutes. They ate a lunch provided by the local citizens, and Lent examined the field, which was described very favorably. One of the nice features of the cabin of the JL-6 was that it was equipped with bud vases; Allyne notes with approval that flower vases were filled by ladies of North Platte who had come out to greet them.

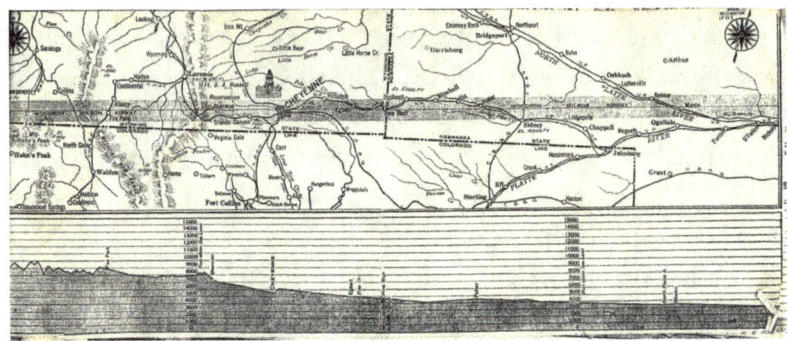

Woodrow Wilson Airway, Cheyenne PHOTO/EBC

Outbound: Cheyenne

Leaving North Platte, they flew at 12,000 feet and made good speed. Just outside of Cheyenne, Wyoming, they met a storm. The wind-driven rain pelted those sitting in the exposed cockpit. Allyne wrote that "rain cuts pilot's face." He said that Buehl was "making signs—Indian scalping him. He has quite a sense of humor." To their relief, they were able to land at Wales Field, in Cheyenne, only about ten minutes later.

Both Allyne and Rickenbacker expressed their gratitude that among the dignitaries was a woman, Mrs. Samuel Ohenstein, who offered them two dozen bottles of "real beer" upon their landing. Rickenbacker responded to her offer, saying, "Lady, you have lost all sense of proportion. Give us half of that and we will be truly thankful."

In an incidental comment, Allyne explains that Wales Field was named for Lt. Edward V. Wales, an Army pilot who had crashed a DeHavilland DH-4 into Elk Mountain while flying during a snowstorm the previous year. Although Lent was pleased with what he saw at

Wales Field, it was next to Fort D.A. Russell and was a military airport.[†] The War Department refused to share it for civilian purposes,
so the Post Office had to find another field. This meant that Cheyenne
had to scramble to create a civilian airport for use by the Post Office.
They completed the work on 1 September, having built the landing
field and a concrete and steel hangar large enough for four airplanes.
Upon leaving Cheyenne, Rickenbacker joked, "We do not want any
fields named after us."

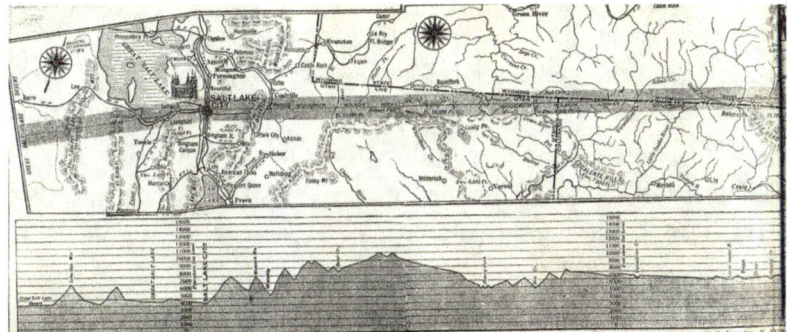

Woodrow Wilson Airway, Salt Lake City PHOTO/EBC

Outbound: Cheyenne to Salt Lake City

From Cheyenne, the next stop was Salt Lake City. Take-off was at
7:35 AM. Flying at 22,000 feet over mountainous terrain, the fliers were
very cold. In a gesture that would not be tolerated today, the passengers
passed some whiskey to Acosta "for warmth," and at mid-morning,
they decided to open a bottle of Mrs. Ohenstein's beer.

By 11:30, they were expecting to see Salt Lake City just below, but
then they realized that they had mistaken Utah Lake for the Great
Salt Lake, meaning they were 40 miles too far south. Correcting their
course, they soon could see Salt Lake City. They landed at 12:05 and
were greeted by Governor Simon Bamberger and other dignitaries.

† In 1949, Fort D.A. Russell was renamed Francis E. Warren Air Force Base.

Bamberger was remarkable in many ways. In the first place, he was not a Mormon. In fact, he was Jewish and had been born in Germany. These factors should have worked against his political career, but he won people to his side with his wit and good humor. At one point, when he was campaigning for office, he was labeled a "gentile" by his political opponent, which he found exceptionally amusing.

Outbound: Salt Lake City

In Salt Lake City, the fliers found that Buena Vista Airfield was excessively rough, and there were hazardous telegraph wires nearby. It was one of the two worst fields on which they had to land. Rickenbacker, able to gather a crowd and command respectful attention, spoke firmly to community leaders about their "civic obligation" to establish and maintain suitable airfields. As Rickenbacker saw it, an airfield is a public good that benefits everyone, so the municipality should create it and control it for the public benefit.

Rickenbacker told members of the Salt Lake City Commission:

The establishment of a suitable landing field for planes is without a doubt a civic obligation. You must bear in mind that aviation represents our most pronounced public utility. There can be no restrictions in the way of franchises; rail privileges or rights of way may not be encountered in the air; it will mean the realization of a genuine public utility, and, at the same time, nothing ever progressed so rapidly from a commercial standpoint as aviation.

Because of the fact that landing fields will be for the general public service, under municipal regulation of community regulation they should be created by our municipalities and leave abandoned the thought that some private corporation or other institution will be in control. We cannot control the air any more than we would presume to control the sea.

If you have examined your agreement with the postal service relative to the establishment of a landing field here, you will observe that the postal authorities stipulate that the fields shall be for general use and under the direction of democratic rules.

I would advise that in developing the landing field for Salt Lake that you make it big enough, say 3000 feet by 2000 feet, and have it high and dry and free of telephone or high tension wires. Attention to such details now would save you a great deal of trouble.

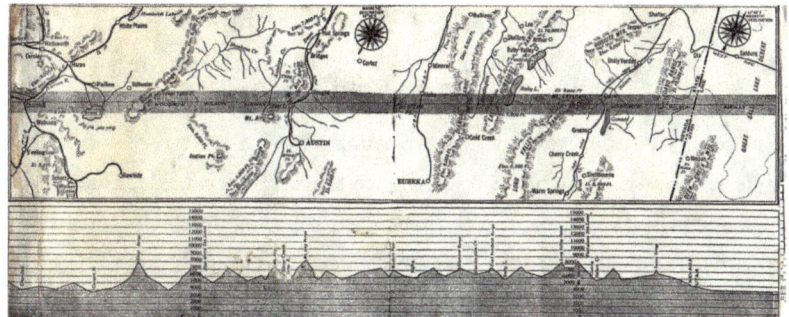

Woodrow Wilson Airway, part of the route across Nevada PHOTO/EBC

Outbound: Salt Lake City to Elko

A little less than an hour after their 7:35 AM take-off from Salt Lake City the next morning, Allyne reported that the motor "falters for first time." They had filled the gas tanks the night before, so he guessed the trouble was due to condensation. The engine was still sputtering a half hour later and nearly stopped while they were flying at 14,000 feet. A few minutes after that, it was running well again.

Buehl later mentioned this event in a speech to the Experimental Aircraft Association. As Buehl said, everyone in the passenger cabin became alarmed because the engine started sputtering. The issue, he explained, was that Acosta was adjusting the carburetor to the altitude but not operating the controls smoothly. The correct procedure at high altitude was to push in the adjustment lever until the "engine sneezes" and then back off a bit. Acosta operated the control too quickly, and it caused the passengers a moment of panic. Buehl told Acosta how to solve the problem, and it did not occur again.

A few minutes later, Larsen thought that they were passing through rain, but it turned out that Buehl had opened a bottle of the homemade beer they received in Cheyenne. From his open cockpit at their altitude of 15,000 feet, the beer "pours forth an unending fountain of foam, which blows past our window."

They found Elko and descended for a landing. Allyne wrote that they "will be first machine to dedicate field here." Touching down at 9:35 AM, they were not expected so soon, and the town dignitaries had to rush out to meet them. Everyone was in a festive mood. The civic leaders had decided to dedicate the airport as "Rickenbacker Field," so they were excited to meet their guest of honor. Allyne dryly commented that at lunch "everybody has to make a speech."

Outbound: Elko to Reno

The planes did not have far to go to get to Reno, so they took off again at 3:00 PM. Flying into "terrific headwinds," the flight was rough, the air extremely hot. They followed the railroad for 45 minutes, then struck out across the dry, gray, sterile-looking mountains. The view lacked interest for the passengers, with only the sight of the numerous mines to attract their attention. A smelter came into view, giving them something different to look at. With so little to guide them, Allyne was impressed with Acosta's "uncanny sense of direction."

At 5:00, Larsen passed a note to Acosta, saying, "there are 3,000 peppy women in Reno looking for entertainment, therefore give them 10 to 15 minutes' nice maneuvers." They landed fifty minutes later.

After dinner with a local family, the Brullatours, the party checked in to the Riverside Hotel.

Outbound: Reno delay

Although the condition of the field at Reno was described in a 1920 field guide as "good," the airmail expedition was found to be tiny, rough, and surrounded by telephone wires. In fact, it was almost the worst they saw, exceeded only by Salt Lake City's Buena Vista Airfield. It was agreed that it would be unsafe to attempt to take off from Reno with a loaded aircraft, so the planes were unloaded in Reno. Acosta and Eaton would fly alone the next morning to a nearby dry lakebed and reload the airplane. They would take off from there to proceed to San Francisco. While the crew made arrangements to leave, the passengers took a quick motor trip to Lake Tahoe and enjoyed "hot sulphur" baths.

Outbound: Reno delay, again

Unfortunately, due to the condition of the field, the landing at Reno the day before had been so rough that the landing gear on Acosta's airplane had cracked. They did not discover the damage until Acosta tried to take off to transfer the airplane to the dry lake bed. Allyne described the issue they encountered:

> *Acosta takes off and as he goes over wires one main strut of landing gear, which had been cracked when we landed rather roughly at Reno, broke and protruded forward. [...] Eaton takes off after him and by signaling indicates to Acosta that something is wrong with his machine. Acosta maneuvers his machine close to a hillside so that he can see from his shadow the nature of the trouble. He makes a beautiful landing on one wheel,*

Acosta, facing away from his airplane, while technicians repair the landing gear. Buehl is in the white shirt, just behind Acosta. PHOTO/EBC

holding the damaged side well up until the machine slowed down, gradually letting the weight rest on the damaged side of gear until wing touched the ground, slewing the machine around with no further damage.

Certainly, the party learned something very important about the route from this experience, and civic officials in Reno had some work to do before the routine use of their field could begin. As the local newspaper related, Rickenbacker addressed the issue with civic leaders:

"The Reno landing field will necessarily be enlarged if it is to be used for planes of the JL-6 type," according to Captain Rickenbacker, who stated that it would be impossible to "take off" from the field with a load of any weight. "The fact that the air in this altitude is light," said Rickenbacker, "makes a larger field imperative. A plane leaves the ground slowly in light altitude, whereas in a lower altitude a field of this size might be satisfactory." It is possible to lengthen the local field considerably, and this will probably be done according to the flyers' recommendations.

While the landing gear was being repaired, Eaton showed up with the rest of the crew and passengers, some spectators, and a movie camera. Rather than stand around and curse, they improvised a melodramatic movie that they called Aerial Bandit's Defeat. Larsen took the part of "the father," Acosta was the villain, Rickenbacker was the hero, and Allyne was the minister who prayed with the villain just before he was lynched. Yvonne Brullatour, the daughter of the family with whom they had dinner the day before, played the heroine.

The landing gear was repaired by 4:45 PM, and they could still have flown to San Francisco that evening, but a crowd had been waiting for their arrival in Oakland since noon, so it was decided to fly the next day in order to arrive at a more convenient time for the spectators. That afternoon, they took both planes flying over Lake Tahoe and made some movies of the flight. The Brullatour offspring accompanied the fliers on this excursion. The family hosted another dinner, and the party stayed in Reno one more night.

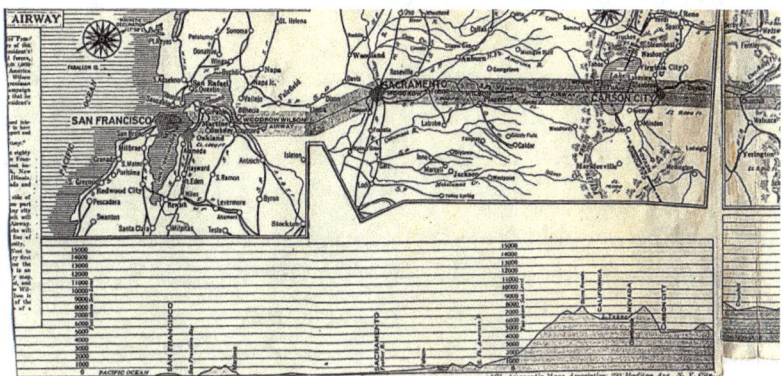

Woodrow Wilson Airway, San Francisco. PHOTO/EBC

Outbound: Oakland to San Francisco

On 8 August, they took-off at 11:35 AM, planning to get to their destination, San Francisco, by 3:30 PM. The surface of the lake bed was already extremely hot, so they had some trouble getting enough lift at ground level. Adding to their difficulty, they also had to fight a strong current of cold air draining from the mountains. With this cold air falling on them and pushing them down, it was hard to gain altitude.

Eaton was finally able to get some altitude, but when he turned west, he found himself stuck in the sky, unable to make any progress against the wind. Flying into the wind, he could only hover in place. Finally, he turned to go with the wind, and he was carried away at high speed. In this direction, he was finally able to make enough altitude to escape the wind that held him over Reno. It was rough, dangerous flying, with no chance of being able to land.

For the next hour, they had a very rough ride. A little after noon, Donner Lake came into view, and Larsen's passengers and crew got a good view of Lake Tahoe. The winds were very bad, and the plane was lurching. At 16,000 feet, it got very cold in the cabin and everyone put on their coats. Given the pounding they were taking, Allyne's engineering mind started to wonder about the factor of safety engineered into the wing fastenings.

By 12:30 PM, Acosta had caught up with Eaton, and by 12:45 they could see the Sacramento Valley open up ahead of them. Rickenbacker was asleep. They woke him up and had coffee and a little lunch at about 1:00 PM. By 1:20, they were passing Baker Army Aviation Field, and the army sent out a Fokker to escort them. The three planes—Acosta's, Eaton's, and the Army Fokker—performed spirals and chandelles together. "Thrills aplenty," as Allyne commented.

Unexpectedly, Eaton landed his plane at Baker Field at 1:35 PM. Furious, Larsen ordered Acosta to go back to find out why. Evidently, Eaton wanted to show the machine. Larsen gave him five minutes to get back in the air or be fired. At 1:57, they took-off again, with the Fokker leading the way and a DeHavilland joining the escort.

All of the airplanes continued to play in the sky, alternating up and down, leapfrogging one another, spiraling. At 2:25 PM, Eaton flew very close to Acosta so that they could take pictures from the camera plane. Rickenbacker opened the door and waved.

By 2:40 PM, the ocean came into view. Skies over San Francisco and Oakland were clear, and Allyne described the sight as one of the most beautiful of their entire journey. However, a wall of fog was entering the Bay via the Golden Gate, and they were briefly concerned that it might beat them into the Bay (to picture this, one has to imagine the Golden Gate without its iconic bridge, which was constructed in the mid-1930s). Once they got closer, though, they realized they had time, so they flew back and forth over Oakland and San Francisco. They put on maneuvers for the benefit of the people waiting for them in Oakland. About 20 minutes later, San Francisco was mostly enclosed by the fog.

At 2:25, as they were above over the Sacramento Valley, Eaton flew very close to Acosta so that they could take pictures from the camera plane. Rickenbacker opened the door and waved. PHOTO/EBC

By 3:16 PM, they were getting ready to land. Acosta put on a show of spectacular maneuvers, including roll-overs and flying the plane on its edge, with the wings vertical. From Allyne's viewpoint in the plane, he commented humorously, the "Earth performs great antics." As they approached for landing, Acosta performed one more "hair-raising" chandelle and then zoomed down to the field. They landed in Oakland at 3:25 PM. They were received by dignitaries, were interviewed by the newspapers, and welcomed many callers.

A crowd greeted them upon landing in Oakland. PHOTO/EBC

Among those greeting the party was Mr. Davie, who was the Mayor of Oakland, and one of the most colorful characters encountered on the entire trip. They were also met by Mr. F.E. Moskovics, who was vice president of the Nordyke & Marmon Company and a business associate of Allyne's. The party had dinner that

The mayor of Oakland greets Larsen. Left to right: Mayor John L. Davie, E.E. Allyne, Eddie Rickenbacker, John M. Larsen, Ernie Buehl, Bert Acosta, Postmaster J.J. Rosborough. PHOTO/EBC

night with Mr. and Mrs. Moskovics in their apartment at the St. Francis Hotel. Chief of Police White and Mrs. White joined them.

They remained one more day in San Francisco.

Return Trip: Oakland to Los Angeles

The transcontinental flight participants remained for two days in San Francisco until 10 August. Acosta was detained in Oakland, so Eaton took over as pilot, with Buehl continuing as mechanic in his plane. Myhres piloted the camera plane. They took off at 11:30 AM.

Although the scenery had much to recommend it, Allyne was especially impressed by the number of oil wells they saw and duly counted them: 196 in one cluster and more than 500 in another.

By 3:03 PM, they were crossing a rough stretch of mountains and were experiencing rough winds. Allyne said he "did not previously appreciate size of mountains in Southern California." Six planes came up to escort them as they approached Los Angeles, and on the ground there was a great string of cars. They landed at 3:35 PM. Eaton's plane was "maneuvering nicely, but nothing like Acosta's."

They were greeted at Mercury Field by Mayor Snyder and Cecil B. DeMille, and were "showered with flowers by movie queens." There were a lot of movie cameras, and a colorful Hollywood parade formed that included a Rocky Mountain Stage Coach and a turn-of-the-century Ford rear-entrance tonneau. They had dinner that evening at DeMille's home. Evidently, they were able to take advantage of his film-processing facilities because that evening they watched some of the movies that they had been taking en route.

In addition to his interest in film, DeMille owned Mercury Aviation, one of the world's first passenger airlines to fly regularly scheduled routes. It has been claimed that Mercury predated Dutch KLM by almost half a year. It is true that KLM started in late 1919, but their first regularly scheduled flights started in 1921. DeMille founded Mercury in early 1919 and announced regular service from Los Angeles to other cities in California that same year, using military biplanes, not JL-6

(below, left)Acrobat hanging by his teeth from an airplane during a barnstorming demonstration in Los Angeles
(below, right) In Los Angeles, they were entertained with some barnstorming demonstrations. This was never something that Ernie would do when he became a pilot, but he was impressed enough to keep these pictures. Note that Los Angeles hosted a lot of oil derricks at that time. PHOTOS/EBC

Welcome at Mercury Field. Left to right are: Rickenbacker, Allyne, deMille, and Larsen. PHOTO/EBC (FROM ALLYNE'S LOG)

aircraft. In the end, Mercury was never actually able to establish regularly scheduled air service, whereas KLM continues to fly to this day.

Larsen, Buehl, and the rest of the party spent the next days socializing and meeting the "leading people of Los Angeles." Fatty Arbuckle, a prominent comedy star, had his picture taken with Larsen, two large men side by side.

Return Trip: Los Angeles to Tucson

After a couple of days in Los Angeles, the planes left early on 13 August. Take-off was at 5:15 AM for a planned non-stop flight to El Paso. Four five-gallon cans of benzol carried in the cabin would provide sufficient fuel, but they also represented quite a bit more weight: the total load would now be 2,000 pounds. The crew and passengers were aware that this added some risk. Allyne noted that there were "many oil derricks" near the field that they would have to clear while hauling the extra benzol.

Acosta was still in San Francisco, so Eaton was the pilot. Taking off at dawn, their rate of climb was slow. They made it to 6,000 feet after about 40 minutes.

After an hour or so in the air, they tried to feed some extra fuel to the main tank, "but tube was either kinked or plugged and gas did not flow." The cabin filled with the odor of benzol, and it became clear that they would have to stop en route to El Paso to fill the gas tanks with the extra fuel they were carrying in the five-gallon cans.

Flying east so early in the morning, the glare in their eyes was terrific, particularly as they were flying over dazzling white clouds. The fog would open up occasionally, but they were not able to see much below except rocks. As far as they could tell, there would be no place to land if the motor quit. The glare became so bad for Eaton that he asked to borrow Rickenbacker's cap to shield his eyes. The prevailing winds in that region generally flow from west to east, but this morning the wind was blowing from the east, slowing their progress. They passed over the Salton Sea at 7:05 AM. Twenty minutes later, they were over Arizona and had left the fog behind.

They crossed the Colorado River at 8:00 AM and the Gila River at 9:00 AM. The smell of fuel in the cabin was still bothersome, but the sky was clearer, and the conditions were less rough. They had a bite to eat, and everyone cheered up.

However, high mountains lay ahead, and Eaton had to gain altitude. The opposing wind was fierce and was tossing them violently. At 10:25, the motor stopped suddenly, "but Eaton noses down, keeping propeller going until he switches to other fuel tank." They landed in Tucson in order to take on more fuel. As long as they were there, they got some lunch.

There was concern that they would not be able to take off again in the heat of the day. Even so, they attempted a 2:45 PM take-off, but Eaton "erred in turning the wrong fuel valve, using gasoline when he intended to use benzol. We had not gone half the length of the field before we realized that motor was heating badly and just managed to clear telegraph wires at far end of field. Plane will not rise further and motor spurts hot water in the faces of the pilots."[‡]

[‡] It is likely that something similar happened in the two plane crashes involving Hartney. The first in Cleveland, when trying to take Allyne's family for a flight over the city before going

They continued to fly but could not gain altitude for three or four minutes. At that point, the motor quit and they crashed in a field of mesquite, breaking their propeller. People saw what had happened and went into the desert in their autos to pick up the fliers. The party was forced to remain in Tucson, staying at the Congress Hotel. The hotel was very new, having been established in 1919. The proprietor refused any compensation.

Amusingly, the *Bisbee* (Arizona) *Daily Review* listed "E.E. Allyon of Cleveland, O." as the pilot during this take-off. Larsen and Rickenbacker were listed as passengers. No one else was mentioned. The article said, "Allyon made a spectacular descent from several hundred feet in the air. The propeller was twisted off when it became entangled in the mesquite."

Also amusing, when Rickenbacker, in his autobiography, recalled this crash, he got the reason exactly wrong. He wrote that "our regular procedure was to use gasoline on the take-off, then switch to benzol when aloft." In his log, Allyne (not a pilot) got it right, and ace pilot Rickenbacker was the one who got it wrong.

Because the airplane did not land at an airport, they had to arrange some way to get it out of the desert. This involved taking off the wings and landing gear and carrying it back to the airfield in a wagon. Once back at the field, the propeller had to be replaced, and the landing gear, which had suffered some damage in the crash, had to be repaired. They telegraphed to DeMille in Los Angeles, asking to borrow the propeller from the machine they had just delivered to Mercury Aviation. He sent it.

Return Trip: Tucson for another day

While Buehl and Rickenbacker were working on the airplane, Allyne, Larsen, and the hotel proprietor drove to Mexico for some

---

on to Chicago. The second as they were taking off from Omaha to fly to Cheyenne.

Although showing a different airplane, this photo illustrates how Eaton's airplane was removed from the field where it crashed. Eaton's plane did not have this much damage. Buehl is standing on the right. PHOTO/EBC

sightseeing. During this time, Buehl and Rickenbacker connected in a friendly way.

Two factors explained their connection. First, Buehl said the two of them connected because Rickenbacker was also a mechanic and "he loved all that stuff." The second factor might have been that they had a similar heritage. Rickenbacker was born into a German-speaking family that had come from Switzerland, so he may have shared a cultural understanding with Buehl, who grew up just north of the Swiss border. Language was no barrier for them. Although Buehl barely spoke any English, Rickenbacker was fluent in German. They simply were comfortable with one another.

To the end of his life, Buehl was surprised at how well he and Rickenbacker got along. The two of them seemed to bond that day in Tucson. As Buehl stated years later, "you wouldn't have thought there had just been a war on."

Return Trip: Tucson to Roswell

The following day, Acosta arrived from San Francisco at 1:30 AM. He brought another 40 gallons of benzol, which they sent ahead to El Paso by train. They realized that their next supply of benzol would not be forthcoming until they reached Kansas City.

They took off in the just-repaired plane at 9:45 AM on 15 August,

Acosta resuming his duties as pilot. It was a rough, slow flight against hot headwinds. An hour later, they were flying at 7,500 feet and it was so hot the passengers were in their shirtsleeves (this signals how uncomfortable it must have been, because in those days gentlemen generally did not take off their jackets under any circumstances). At 11:15, they opened lunch and tried to eat, but they were being knocked around by such strong headwinds that they had trouble serving their food and beverages.

They followed the railroad, although they knew they could take a more direct route to their destination. The issue was not one of navigation, however; it was safety. The country was so sparsely settled that if they were forced to land in the desert they would be in serious trouble, severely isolated and cut off from rescue. At least near the tracks they could be more confident that someone would eventually come by and find them.

At 12:20, they were flying near the Mexican border. Rickenbacker wrote that someone began shooting at them. He said, "I saw orange flashes and little puffs of smoke beneath us. Mexican border guards must have thought we were the forefront of a gringo air invasion." Allyne never mentioned any of this, but commented about seeing soldiers below, saying he waved his handkerchief to them.

As they flew over Columbus, New Mexico, Allyne recalled news of the recent incursions of Pancho Villa along the border, the revolutionary having attacked Columbus only four years earlier. In retaliation, General Pershing was sent across the border into Mexico and was there until 7 February 1917, chasing Villa. Villa was still in the news in 1920.

The fliers landed near El Paso at Fort Bliss at 2:00 PM, where they were met by Major General Robert L. Howze (Allyne identified him as "General Howard"), who hoped they would stay for lunch.

Allyne described the general as charming and jovial. Born 22 August 1864 in Overton, Texas, Robert Lee Howze was a son of an Army captain. A second lieutenant at the time, Howze received the Medal of Honor for action while serving in the Sixth Cavalry in South Dakota in 1891. Howze's Company K, under the command of Captain John Brown Kerr, was attacked by about 300 warriors from the Brulé band of the Lakota nation seeking revenge for the Seventh Cavalry's massacre of women and children at Wounded Knee a few days earlier. The presidential citation does not say specifically why the medal was awarded to Howze. He achieved the rank of major general in 1910.

The Larsen party was very behind schedule, though, and could stay only long enough to refuel. They took off again at 2:45 PM, hoping to reach Amarillo before dark. The flight was very rough, and they could not reach a good altitude. They were forced to fly at 6,000 feet over some extremely rugged terrain. If there were an emergency, they realized, there would be no place to land. At 4:40 PM, the motor stopped suddenly, evidently due to the failure of a pump. They dropped 1,000 feet. Using an emergency hand pump, they were able to get the motor

General Howze and staff welcome the party at Fort Bliss, Texas. The general is second from the right and is wearing his Medal of Honor. Buehl is seen in the background, leaning over the engine of the JL-6. One of his children thoughtfully drew a little arrow on the picture to point him out since all we can see is his backside. PHOTO/EBC

started again. At 5:00 PM, they were approaching Roswell and quickly decided to land to repair the pump.

Acosta was desperate to find a safe place to put down. As Allyne calmly put it, "Acosta treats us to a new sensation, flying over fields very close to the ground at 80 miles an hour, hunting for a landing place." Skimming trees and fences and circling the place a couple of times, he landed the plane at 5:15.

Examining the fuel pump, they discovered that a small square shaft had sheared off. Allyne noted parenthetically that this turned out to be the only mechanical trouble on the entire trip. To their amazement, they found a good machinist in Roswell (on a Sunday night) who was able to turn a new shaft for them.

The fliers noted that the movie theaters in Roswell had posters announcing that the newsreels of their landings in San Francisco and Los Angeles were to be shown on Monday.

Return Trip: Roswell to Kansas City

Allyne said that everyone got up early on 16 August to fix the fuel pump, but it is more likely that Buehl got up early to fix the pump. In any case, they were able to take off from Roswell by 6:50 AM.

Traveling for a bit less than three hours, the party enjoyed a much more comfortable ride than they had the previous day. The weather was overcast, and there was even some rain in the area. Acosta skirted the storm. The morning remained cool and comfortable. Also, from this point forward, they were relieved to have left the mountains behind. Landing in Amarillo to take on gasoline at 9:25, they particularly wanted to conserve their small supply of benzol.

Taking off again at 11:05 AM, they were in flight when the motor stopped, started, and sputtered suddenly only fifteen minutes later. Acosta nosed down to keep the propeller turning, and they started the hand pumps. He climbed to a safer altitude of 10,000 feet and decided to follow the railroad rather than make a bee-line for their destination across the desert badlands. The country below was rough, and the passengers wondered what they would do if they had to make a forced landing.

As they passed from Texas to Oklahoma, the land flattened, and survival seemed more likely if a forced landing became necessary. They served lunch at 12:45 PM.

Less than 100 miles from Wichita, at 2:00 PM, the motor stopped again. They switched to the other fuel tank and got it going again. At 2:10, the motor stopped and they went back to the hand pumps.

Not all of Buehl's ideas were good ones. At 2:15 PM, Allyne wrote: *Motor acting badly and fuel tank almost empty. Critical emergency for surface below is very bad. Buhl conceives idea of improvising means of pumping benzol from reserve can (we are still carrying four five gallon cans benzol in the cabin) into main tank and calls for a can and rubber hose which we pass to him thru bulkhead. He then disconnects air line attaching hose and tries to suck fuel with hand pump from open can, thru line into tanks without success. Open exhaust spitting flame and sparks into cockpit during this operation. Experience my first real fright, expecting every instant that machine will be blown to pieces, and it is a miracle that we did not burst into flames. I forcibly demand giving up the attempt and the return of the can, preferring to take my chance on a crash.*

By 2:30 PM, the gauge indicated that they were out of gasoline. Flying with the nose down, they were able to continue flying for a little longer.

By 2:40 PM, they found a small spot, Medicine Lodge, Kansas, where they could land and refuel. They realized that from then on they would have to stop frequently to refuel because they could use only half of their fuel-carrying capacity. In one tank they were carrying only a small quantity of benzol, which they did not want to dilute since it would be needed when they were taking off. They could fill only the other tank to capacity.

When they examined the engine to see why they were having so much trouble, it turned out that during reinstallation of the fuel pump a union in the gas line had not been tightened properly and this allowed air to be sucked into the line. It is not clear who installed the pump, whether it was a machinist in Roswell or Buehl, but it would have been a surprising error for Buehl.

They took off from Medicine Lodge at 4:40 PM with 240 miles to go to Kansas City. They did not experience any more trouble and made good time. It was getting dark and hazy. Flying at about 9,000 feet, Acosta realized that although they still had plenty of sunlight at their altitude, it would be much darker on the ground. He did not want to be tricked into staying in the air for too long and then running out of enough light to land safely. With another half hour of daylight they could have made it to their destination, but they had to land before actually reaching Kansas City, so they touched down at Lawrence at 7:15 PM.

Larsen, Allyne, and Rickenbacker drove to Kansas City, arranging for the plane to meet them at Swope Field early the next morning. The major guide to airports published in 1920 listed Swope Park as an emergency landing field of only 1,500 feet by 500 feet.

Return Trip: Kansas City to Chicago

Arriving at Swope Field in Kansas City before daylight, the passengers had a longer wait than anticipated. Acosta had duly taken off from Lawrence and flown to Kansas City. However, the airport was so fogged-in that he could not even find it, much less land there.

While they were waiting, Larsen and the others realized they were going to have another problem refueling. They had ordered two barrels of benzol, but the contents turned out to be gasoline. Fortunately, the local taxi company used benzol in their cabs, so the fliers were able to secure a supply. Larsen arranged for the taxi company to send a tank truck to Swope Field to wait with them for Acosta.

In the meantime, Acosta landed in a wheat field about ten miles away and caught a ride to Swope Field. Everyone was surprised when he showed up without the airplane. Once Acosta explained where he had left the airplane (and Buehl), they all joined a tiny convoy to guide the tank truck.

Unfortunately, the wheat field was not big enough to allow them to take off with all passengers aboard, so Acosta had to find another, larger field, and then signal to them from the air by "pointing" with his plane to the location where he would be. Eventually, they were able to reassemble, and they took off at 11:15 AM.

The flight was very pleasant, for a change. Acosta flew with abandon, having fun, playfully zig-zagging, dipping, and "jazzing" (Allyne's word) through the clouds. At 1:40 PM, as they passed over Ft. Madison, Iowa, where he had once owned a factory, Larsen dropped a message from the airplane.

Near Oswego, Illinois, they found themselves low on oil and were forced to land. People from the area came out to visit with them, taking a lively interest in the airplane. They took off again about 30 minutes later, landing in Chicago at 4:30 PM. Allyne notes, "We have no more than landed, when we see a Junkers Plane coming from the east on its maiden mail carrying flight."

Return Trip: Cleveland

Rickenbacker remained in Chicago to conduct some business but planned to join them again in Cleveland. The rest of the party took off at dawn on August 18, flying directly into the sun, which was fiercely bright.

Over Lake Erie by 9:20 AM, they encountered what Allyne described as a "fairyland" of gigantic, beautiful clouds. Acosta decided to take aim at one of them "charges it, zooms up into it and bores through it." Allyne commented appreciatively that his face got wet as they flew through the cloud. (There were operable windows in the passenger cabin).

Traveling at 135 miles per hour (a very good speed for that time) at an altitude of only about 3,500 feet, they could see many details on the ground, so it was entertaining to watch the airplane's shadow racing over the landscape.

By 10:15 AM, they reached Cleveland, Allyne noting the locations of his foundry and his residence. As they arrived over Martin Field, he could see his car. Nearby, his family waved to them. Acosta performed some maneuvers for the benefit of those on the ground, including flying the plane "on edge." As they came in, they were flying just under a cover of heavy black clouds that extended as far as they could see.

They landed in Cleveland at 10:25 AM and went to rest at the Allyne home until the next morning.

Return Trip: Cleveland to Bellefonte

After breakfast with the Allyne family, and all spruced up with fresh flowers in their lapels, the crew and passengers took-off at 10:10 AM. They planned to be in New York by early afternoon.

However, the cloud ceiling was again very low, as it had been when they landed in Cleveland. At 3,800 feet, they were flying through clouds and into a strong head wind. By 11:40 AM, the ceiling had descended to only 2,500 feet, and visibility was poor. Acosta determined that they would have to land, but it was raining, and the country below was hilly. He needed to choose a favorable place before they were forced to land in less appropriate circumstances. At 2,000 feet it seemed as though they were skimming over the hills. Acosta's search proved fruitless, and he was forced down by bad weather at 12:30 PM, landing the plane on the side of a hill. The ground was soft, and they stopped abruptly as the soft ground grabbed the wheels and tail skid.

Unexpectedly, another Junkers mail plane from the east had also put down nearby. They walked over to visit with the pilot, Stevens, who would die in a flaming crash only about a week later.

Larsen and the others decided that the passengers would leave Buehl and Acosta to bring the plane off the hillside as soon as the weather permitted, while the rest went on to Bellefonte, which had a mail field. They stayed in Bellefonte and had dinner at the local Country Club with a judge, several attorneys, some offspring of ex-state governors, and others. Also present was Slim Lewis, an airmail pilot who, as Allyne said, "can fly a washboard."

Return Trip: Arrive in Long Island

The next day, they spent the morning at the Mail Field waiting for Acosta. At 11:55 AM, they heard a JL-6 directly overhead, but it did not stop. Larsen was furious. Nearly spitting, he declared that it was Acosta going right on to New York. Allyne and Rickenbacker each bet Larsen $100 that Acosta would come back for them, but by 3:00 PM they received a telephone call from the manager of Larsen's field at Long Island saying that Acosta had landed there. Acosta claimed that he flew past them because he could not find the field at Bellefonte.

Larsen ordered him to come back immediately and pick them up, but Acosta decided to wait until the next day. While Larsen, Allyne, and Rickenbacker spent another evening at Bellefonte, Slim Lewis was dispatched to New York with instructions to bring the plane back.

The passengers went out to the airfield in the morning on 22 August, but the weather was so bad it became evident that Lewis would not be able to get back before 1:30 PM. They left the field and went to lunch. Lewis arrived at 1:45 PM.

At 3:55 PM, the plane was refueled and readied for takeoff. This particular corridor between Bellefonte and New York was known for its difficult flying because of the mountains, the tricky winds, and the reliably murky weather. In fact, in 1919, it was reported that this route was the most difficult in the entire airmail service.

According to Allyne, the weather on 22 August was worse than it had been when they were forced down on the 19th. The mountains were covered with fog, and visibility was poor. Everyone agreed that it would be unwise to try to make it to New York, but they were impatient to get back. Lewis was very experienced on this route, though, having flown it regularly since December 1919. When the mountains were closed in as they were, the peaks and ridge tops remained visible. Lewis felt sufficiently familiar with the landscape that he thought he could try it.

Flying low, Lewis practically skimmed the tops of the trees and hunted his way from one gap to the next. They slid over ridges. It was raining hard, and at times the view ahead looked like a curtain of blackness. Dodging severe weather as much as they could, by the time they reached New York City they were unable to see the Statue of Liberty due to the fog. They could barely make out any landmarks but could see just enough to keep their bearings.

They reached Larsen Field at 7:05. Allyne commented: "A splendid record for machine and pilots." The flight "has been a contribution to the progress of aviation." He concluded: "The trip was a most pleasant adventure and the party was loath to break up at the end of the journey."

‏

Messrs. Allyne, Larsen and Rickenbacker being greeted on their return to New York by Mr. C. B.   Kirkham, manager for Mr. Larsen.

This photo appears on the back cover of Allyne's log. It shows Larsen's engineer, Charles B. Kirkham, greeting Allyne, Larsen, and Rickenbacker upon their return. PHOTO/EBC, PUBLIC DOMAIN

Selected Sources

Allyne, Edmund E. *First Round Trip Transcontinental Passenger Flight: July 29th to August 22nd 1920.* self-published, 1921.

Andersson, Lennart, Gunter G. Endres, Rob J. M. Mulder, and Gunther Ott. *Junkers F13: The World's First All-Metal Airliner.* EAM Books EEIG, 2012.

Birdseye, Claude H. "Stereoscopic Phototopographic Mapping." *Annals of the Association of American Geographers* 30, no. 1 (March 1940): 1–24.

Bisbee Daily Review. "All-Metal Plane Breaks Propeller." August 14, 1920.

Boyer, Diane, and Robert Webb. "Damming Grand Canyon: The 1923 USGS Colorado River Expedition." All USU Press Publications, January 1, 2007.

"Cheyenne Airfield, Fountain: Photographs, Written Historical and Descriptive Data, Field Records." Historic American Engineering Record Intermountain Regional Office, National Park Service, U.S. Department of the Interior, 12795 West Alameda Parkway, Denver, CO 80228., n.d.

Cleveland Plain Dealer. "Woman, Children Fall In Airplane Mrs. E. E. Allyne and Family Then Go Up With Rickenbacker." July 31, 1920.

Davie, John L. *His Honor, the Buckaroo: The Autobiography of John L. Davie.* Reno, NV: Jack Herzberg, 1988.

Ernie Buehl Talks to the Experimental Aircraft Association, Pennsylvania Chapter 76. Videotape, 1986.

Eytinge, Bruce. *Field Guide and Pilot's Log Book*. Eytinge & Uden, NYC, 1920.

Grand Forks Daily Herald. "John M. Larsen Made Defendant in Damage Suit at Omaha, Neb." November 8, 1921.

Hugo Junkers—Ein Leben für die Technik. "18 Februar 1921: Junkerspilot Emil Monz tödlich verunglückt," Website. https://hugo.junkers.de/blog/junkerspilot-emil-monz-toedlich-verunglueckt/. Accessed March 18, 2014. lang. German

Greater Southwestern Exploration Company. "1926 Airway Beacon Concrete Arrow." April 6, 2017. Photo. https://www.flickr.com/photos/gsec/34414282051. Accessed July 16, 2023

Lent, Leon B. "United States Air Mail Survey Flight New York - San Francisco." U.S. Postal Service, n.d. RG 18 Stack area 190, row 39, compartment 16, shelf 1. National Archives.

Lind, Harold B. "Checkerboard Air Field." Franzosenbusch Heritage Project (blog), 2006. http://www.fhproject.org/Histories/Checkerboard%20Field/Checkerboard%20Air%20Field_expanded%20version.htm. Accessed July 16, 2023

Maurer, Maurer. "Aviation in the U.S. Army, 1919-1939." General histories. Office of Air Force History, United States Air Force, 1987.

Montana.gov Official State Website. "Airway Beacons," https://www.mdt.mt.gov/aviation/beacons.aspx. Accessed January 7, 2021.

National Aviation Hall of Fame. "Acosta, Bertrand 'Bert' B."

Nevada State Journal. "Mail Airplanes Leave Today on Flight to Coast. Local Field Too Small." August 7, 1920.

New York Times. "Air Mail to Span Continent." March 14, 1920.

New York Times. "Phone to Pacific from the Atlantic." January 26, 1915.

Omaha Daily News. "Lost over Lake Erie with Dwindling Gas Supply Has No Appeal to Gould Dietz," August 2, 1920.

Omaha World Herald. "From Pony Express to Swift Air Mail," October 31, 1920.

Omaha World Herald. "Larsen Ill, Halt Trip of All Metal Planes." August 2, 1920.

Rickenbacker, Edward V. Rickenbacker: An Autobiography. First. Englewood Cliffs, NJ: Prentice-Hall, 1967.

Salt Lake City Tribune. "Pioneer Airplane Carrying U.S. Mail Arrives in City from Cheyenne in Four and One-Half Hours." August 5, 1920.

Smithsonian National Postal Museum. "Pilot Stories: Lewis, Harold T. 'Slim,'" 2004.

APPENDIX 6

Oil Rush

The Discovery Well

When the "Discovery Well" was established in Canada in the middle of the Northwest Territory, Imperial Oil Company personnel anticipated a rush of people who would attempt to stake claims on oil in the area. In response, Charles Taylor, the Edmonton-based manager for Imperial Oil, ordered two JL-6 aircraft so that the company could explore and make the claims before anybody else could reach these new fields.

Worry that people would soon be rushing into these remote regions was justified. Private air service operators quickly announced that they would take passengers to Fort Norman. A display ad in the 17 January 1921 *Edmonton Journal* offered to take anyone who wanted to go "absolute safety and comfort for what it costs to hire guides and buy outfit. Flying time about eight hours each way."

Taylor observed that their greatest need was simply to explore the area. Imperial Oil did not have enough land under lease to justify the expense of developing their fields at Fort Norman or their other location at Windy Point, on Slave Lake. No matter what else, they needed to go ahead with geological exploration so that they could understand these fields.

To illuminate Taylor's point a little more, it is useful to recall the events of the 1897 "gold rush" into the Klondike region of northwestern

Canada. Gold was discovered and soon the region was full of uncounted numbers of independent, hard-scrabble prospectors who went up there with hopes to strike it rich. This hope led to prospectors scouring large regions of the far north, looking for gold.

There were important differences, though, between prospecting for metals versus prospecting for oil. For one thing, it was a lot easier to reach the gold fields of the Klondike than the oil fields in the Mackenzie territory. More importantly, a lone prospector working in an area with the right geology, equipped with just a hammer, a shovel, and not much else, had some chance of finding a worthwhile deposit of precious metals. However, it requires a well-financed, highly skilled team just to confirm the presence of a commercially viable deposit of oil.

Even so, there was a strategy available to an individual prospector. It was possible to stake a claim near a known oil field and then force a company like Imperial Oil to buy it. In early 1921, Imperial had about 25,000 acres under lease around Fort Norman and about the same area leased at Windy Point. (This is an area that could be bounded by a square having a fraction more than six miles on a side). Given the difficulty of developing this resource, they needed more land under lease to begin commercial development. Individuals going up there to stake random claims could easily tie up land that would become important to the company's success.

Something similar happened in the early days of the Internet and World Wide Web. Before the commercial value of the Web was widely understood, a number of modern day claim-jumpers had the insight that they could reserve potentially valuable domain names, such as "pepsi.com", and then force large companies to buy them.

The Well Itself

By 1919, Imperial Oil was engaged in serious exploration in the far north, and in the summer of that year they began preparations to drill exploratory wells. That first year they could only work for three months during the summer (of course, there are as many as 20 hours of daylight in the summer in those latitudes). They were able to build some shelter for themselves and construct a derrick before winter set in.

Link and his team were able to begin drilling that summer. On 23 August, the drill hit a depth of 700 feet. The team informed Link they could see oil standing in the casing pipe just a few feet below the surface. Link responded, "Don't bother me again until it overflows." When the drillers hit a depth of 783 feet, oil began to gush from the well to the top of the mast, and Link came running. Pressure from the well was substantial but intermittent. The well gushed oil two or three times over a span of 40 minutes, and when it next subsided the drillers rushed in to cap the well.

Ottawa's Response

The concern about people traveling into these remote regions was shared by many. Ottawa was so worried there would be a rush of people to stake claims that the government announced a temporary suspension of oil leasing in the area. It was announced "there will be no more claims permitted in the Great Slave Lake or Fort Norman fields, or anywhere else in the Mackenzie territory." Still, given the lag time between the government announcement and the arrival of news from the area, 40 claims arrived at Edmonton from Fort Simpson "by the overland dog-train mail service from the far north" by 1 April 1921.

There was some immediate speculation that Imperial Oil had requested this suspension, but Charles Taylor flatly denied it. In fact, he said that the ruling "came like a bolt from the blue" and they were themselves trying to absorb the implications.

In the end, Ottawa's concern was for public safety. In my personal experience of working in similar regions, even in the early 21st century anyone traveling to bush villages in the far north has to do so with the knowledge that there are no accommodations for travelers, there is no place to buy food, there is limited availability of water for drinking or sanitation. Even if one is only flying in for the day, in many villages a visitor can become an unwelcome guest if he has not brought his own food to eat and water to drink. In 1921, the burden on locals in the far north would be even greater.

The locals not only would be exposed to the burden of hosting prospectors, but these visitors could also be carrying diseases. Not even the most basic medical services were available in the Mackenzie territory; there was not anywhere one could purchase something as basic as antiseptic and bandages. Outsiders could bring in alcohol and any number of disruptive activities. This would be impossible to control because there was no law enforcement in the region other than the occasional patrols of the Royal Canadian Mounted Police.

From their experience with the Klondike, Ottawa knew that many, many people who had no idea what they were in for would attempt to travel to the far north. Given the excitement surrounding the discovery of "black gold" in the Mackenzie territory, the government had little option but to shut down travel to the region. By 28 January 1921, Ottawa realized they would need to clamp down a little more, ordering that anyone traveling by any means – by land, water, or air - into that region had to have a permit from the RCMP.

Extreme Cold

When working in extremely cold temperatures, frostbite is a serious risk. When wind chill reaches -50°F, exposed flesh will turn to ice in five minutes. This degree of wind chill is reached at an air temperature of -20°F with a 24-mile-per-hour wind. At -52°F, the air temperature Buehl mentioned when interviewed, a wind of only two miles per hour produces conditions that Environment Canada says are so dangerous that even people who are accustomed to severe conditions should not go outside at all.

It is said that if one spits when it is that cold out, the saliva will freeze before it hits the ground. The problem with testing that hypothesis is obvious to anyone who has ever had the opportunity to try it: it is too dangerous even to try to spit when the temperature is so low.

It is hard to think of a safe way that a person can experience the kind of cold Buehl had to work in. More people have the experience of being scalded by hot coffee than of being frostbitten. A difference is that one recovers from scalds. Half a century later, one can forget having had a minor burn, but frostbite is never forgotten. Areas of one's feet that were frostbitten 50 years earlier will still turn purple and ache every winter for the rest of one's life.

Standing in a food freezer is not even close to cold enough. Most food freezers are set to 0°F, which can be painfully cold, but a person can defend himself against that cold by dressing warmly. Holding normal ice in one's hand is too warm. Dry ice is too cold to hold safely. At about -109°F, dry ice immediately begins to turn warm skin into ice crystals and the damage will be permanent. Buehl was experiencing wind chill equivalents lower than -109°F.

Beyond the personal risk of frostbite, there are other problems with working in very cold temperatures. Machinery breaks down. Even today, Texas oil field workers who come to North Dakota or Montana often arrive assuming that the difference between +32°F and -32°F is not meaningful to machines. They know, of course, water freezes below +32°F, but imagine nothing else changes after that, no matter how much colder it gets. The fact that at -32°F oil itself freezes, that rubber shock absorbers become solid and brittle and no longer serve their function, that machinery becomes sluggish, and that even steel snaps is very surprising to them when they come to the northern oil fields.

It is hard to keep engines operating. In many places that are affected in winter by arctic cold, leaving an automobile outdoors for just a couple of hours with the engine turned off can render the vehicle unusable until either the weather warms up or the vehicle can be towed to a heated garage to thaw out. In these places, automobile engines are equipped with block heaters that keep the oil from freezing. In communities in Alberta, it is common for parking places on the streets downtown to be equipped with electrical outlets so that shoppers can plug in.

Over time, pilots to the far north worked out methods that allowed them to keep the machines operable in the conditions they faced. They had to land the airplane with power on, so that the engine would not cool too quickly. After landing, they would shut off the fuel system and allow the carburetor to run dry before switching the engine off. The crew would then move quickly to jack up the airplane so that the skis were not touching the ground, to prevent them from freezing to the snow overnight. It was necessary to cover the engine, at least with a tarp. Eventually, someone figured out how to use a small "nose hangar" that would cover the engine while the rest of the airplane sat exposed, but this innovation came years after Buehl was in Canada. They would drain the oil into a large container. When starting up again, the mechanic would place a gasoline-fueled fire pot under the engine cover. He would warm the oil over another fire pot. Once both the engine and oil were warm, the oil was poured back into the engine and the engine started. If the engine did not start, the oil had to be drained again and both engine and oil had to be warmed some more. Commonly, it would take an hour and a half to start the engine.

Modifications for Use in Canada

Some sources say that the JL-6s sent to Canada all used the Mercedes engine rather than the BMW-IIIa. However, import records show that at least one of the airplanes was shipped from Germany with a BMW engine.[*] Also, Charles B. Kirkham, Larsen's chief engineer, later

---

[*] The René arrived with BMW engine number 1780.

stated that the engines were modified BMW-IIIa, having the high compression pistons replaced with low compression pistons, reducing the fire danger and making them capable of running on ordinary gasoline.

There were other modifications made to the JL-6 aircraft delivered to Canada, to make them better able to deal with the cold weather conditions they would face. Key modifications were:

+ insulated oil lines
+ more efficient radiator shutters
+ carburetor intake heaters.

Route to Canada

K.M. Molson, Canadian aviation historian, corresponded with Buehl in the 1970s. He asked about the route to deliver the airplanes to Canada. In a handwritten response to Molson, Buehl gave the following:

+ Long Island, New York
+ Bellefonte, Pennsylvania
+ Cleveland, Ohio
+ Chicago, Illinois
+ Minneapolis, Minnesota
+ Virden, Manitoba
+ Regina, Saskatchewan
+ Saskatoon, Saskatchewan
+ Edmonton, Alberta
+ Peace River, Alberta

From Long Island to Peace River. MAP/R. BUEHL, MAP DATA FROM OPENSTREETMAP

Selected Sources

Andersson, Lennart, Gunter G. Endres, Rob J. M. Mulder, and Gunther Ott. *Junkers F13: The World's First All-Metal Airliner.* EAM Books EEIG, 2012.

Edmonton Bulletin. "Forty Claims from Norman Are on File." April 1, 1921.

Edmonton Bulletin. "Larson [sic] Plane Zoomed down Thursday 3 P.M. Flying Time from New York Was Twenty-Eight Hours and Twenty Minutes." April 1, 1921.

Edmonton Bulletin. "Story of the Fort Norman Oil Well." March 5, 1921.

Edmonton Journal. "No Clearance for North by Any Route but through Police." January 28, 1921.

Edmonton Journal. "Staking of Oil Claims in North Will Cease in One Month." January 24, 1921.

Gayner, W.R. "Fly to Fort Norman. (Advertisement)." *Edmonton Journal.* January 17, 1921.

Hofmann, Angelica. "Werknummernverzeichnis der Junkers F 13." Die Junkers F-13, February 6, 2013. http://wayback. archive.org/web/20110721154641/ http://www.ju-f13.de/F13/werknr. htm#Werk-Nr.%20610 Accessed

Molson, K. M. Pioneering in Canadian Air Transport. Winnipeg, Ont: J. Richardson, 1974.

Morning Bulletin. "News of Oil Fields in North and Other Parts of Continent." April 23, 1921.

The Globe and Rutgers Fire Insurance Company against John M. Larsen. Vol. 5929. Supreme Court of New York, Appellate Division-First Department, 1924.

C. Alfred Anderson

First Black Pilot to Get an ATL

There is controversy on the question of whether or not Anderson was the first black pilot to earn the Air Transport License (ATL). Anderson's license was #7638. However, the honor of being first may go to E.C. Malick. Malick indisputably held the ATL. His was number #1716, which predates Buehl's by nearly a year. Malick received his license on 30 April 1927.

The controversy is over whether or not Malick was black. One of his family members, Mary Groce, maintains he was black, but this racial designation is not universally accepted. It is beyond the scope of this book to discuss this question.

Malick lost his license following injuries he received on 20 March 1928. On that date, he suffered a severe crash, injuring his eyes. After that he could no longer pass the physical requirements to be a pilot.

ॐ

Allowing black pilots into the fraternity of aviators was not popular and a number of well-respected fliers opposed it. Lindbergh openly opposed it, making public statements to the effect that blacks would never be able to learn to fly well enough. Even years later, in 1961, Chuck Yeager opposed allowing black candidates into the space program.

It is the case that there were other trainers willing to work with black candidates, but they were few. One in Massachusetts was working with John W. Greene at about the same time Buehl was working with Anderson. The uncommonness of the kind of courage it took to train a black pilot is implied by the fact that in the decade following the granting of the ATL to Anderson, in spite of interest and talent, only six more black pilots in the entire United States were able to earn the top rating. Buehl did not train any of these six pilots, but he did employ one of them, Charles M. Ashe, as a trainer at Somerton. The door was still mostly closed. However, the living example of Anderson told everyone it was possible.

In the following list, license numbers do not reflect the order in which the Transport licenses were granted. Of the pilots on this list, Renfro was the third to earn the ATL, and Coffey was the fourth. Allen held a "Limited commercial" license until about 1940, then upgraded to Commercial. Terry held a Private license, and Ashe held a Student license until about 1940. The CAA did not issue the Transport License after 1 November 1937. After that, the top license was Commercial.[†] The list gives the license number, name, community of residence, and year the license was earned when known.

- 7638 C. Alfred Anderson, Bryn Mawr, PA (1932)
- 15897 John W. Greene, Jr. Boston, MA (1932)
- 29452 Robert Terry, Besking Ridge, NJ
- 32546 Earl W. Renfro, Chicago, IL (1936)
- 32630 George Allen, Latrobe, PA
- 36609 Cornelius R. Coffey, Oaklawn, Chicago, IL (1936)
- 54573 Charles M. Ashe, Philadelphia, PA

By 1940, in addition to the pilots listed above, two pilots held the limited commercial license.

- 43814 Willa B. Brown, Chicago, IL

---

† This list appears in at least three sources and is the same in all of them.

    • 30217 Grover C. Nash, Chicago, IL

When this list was compiled and published by the Bureau of the Census, the Bureau explained that they relied on information provided by the CAA and they admitted that there may have been omissions.

It is not known how many omissions there may be to the list, but one omission that is known is Lewis Albert Jackson, license number 38719. He learned to fly in 1932, and the first license examination he sat for was for the transport license. He never obtained a private or limited commercial license, and this may be the reason he was overlooked in the Census Bureau list. Lewis believed he may have been the fourth or fifth black pilot to obtain the transport license. In 1942, Jackson, now holding the commercial license, obtained an instrument rating. He believed he might have been the first black pilot to have been so rated.

The Tuskegee Experiment

The "Tuskegee Experiment" was set up to see if it was possible to train black pilots for military service. Incredible now, the Army's official policy stated that blacks were too physically slow and mentally incapable to learn to fly airplanes. It was for these reasons that training blacks to be military pilots was considered to be an "experiment." The fact was, though, that it was not much of an experiment. Many young black men had taken advantage of the Civilian Pilot Training Program (CPTP) in 1939 and had clearly proven their competence.

The formation of a segregated, all-black flying unit was dramatized in the 1996 Hollywood movie, The Tuskegee Airmen, with Lawrence Fishburne. Anderson's training was said to have "touched many thousands of the nation's military and civilian pilots, such as General Benjamin O. Davis, Jr., General Daniel (Chappie) James, Colonel Herbert Carter, and other Tuskegee Airmen during the Tuskegee Experiment."

A more recent movie by George Lucas, Red Tails (2012), presents a fictionalized account of the Tuskegee Airmen. Red Tails focuses almost entirely on their experiences in combat rather than on their training. Another movie, *Double Victory: The Tuskegee Airmen at War* (2012), is a documentary that provides a factual account and includes interviews with actual Tuskegee Airmen. In another short, informal documentary available online, Anderson recalls the training of the Airmen.

On 29 March 2007, the Tuskegee Airmen were awarded the Congressional Gold Medal, the highest civilian award presented by the US Congress, for their "unique military record that inspired revolutionary reform in the Armed Forces." Clarification is necessary to understand Anderson's role in the Tuskegee program. He did not establish the program, and he was not the administrator in charge of the program. He was the chief trainer.

Key individuals at Tuskegee who pursued the vision of pilot training for black students were Director of Mechanical Industries G.L. Washington, and President of the Institute Frederick D. Patterson. For a couple of years before the US entered World War II, they actively sought a formal relationship with civilian and military aviation authorities for training black pilots.

As a result of the efforts of Washington and Patterson, and because of the location of the Institute, Tuskegee was better positioned to take the program than any other of the historically black colleges and universities in the country. Also, it was clear that the Army Air Force preferred segregated training for black pilots, noting the resistance they would face if they tried to integrate black pilots, who would all be officers, into existing (white) units. Tuskegee had always been willing to accommodate segregation as long as it was possible to expand opportunities for blacks.

In the summer of 1940, the CAA (Civil Aeronautics Authority) approved Tuskegee to provide secondary pilot training. The program was to be staffed as much as possible with black pilots. Anderson was the first black trainer recruited. At the time, he was teaching the elementary CPT (Civilian Pilot Training) courses at Howard University. Tuskegee offered him the opportunity to teach advanced CPT courses, and he quickly accepted.

As of June 1946, Tuskegee Army Air Field graduated its last student and the program at Tuskegee closed. Nearly everyone else involved with the program left. Anderson, though, stayed and continued to train pilots at Moton Field.

Perhaps surprisingly, after the War, Anderson's contribution was greatest; it was largely for his activities then that Anderson became known as "the Father of Black Aviation." For nearly the remainder of his life after the War, Anderson trained uncounted numbers of individuals how to fly, many of whom went on to careers in military and commercial aviation. He helped to found the Negro Airmen International (NAI) and constantly promoted aviation and aeronautical education among African Americans. Over time, because of the connections he made as a result of training so many individuals, Anderson could look up influential people throughout the worlds of commerce and military and get them to listen to him. He used these connections throughout his career on behalf of black aviation.

The question Buehl asked was "Who has the right to use airplanes?" In 1930, when he took Anderson as a student, Buehl's answer was "Everyone." The same question faced Anderson. His answer, too, was to say that everyone had the right to join the aviation industry or serve as pilots in the military, including blacks. It was, more than anything, his untiring advocacy on behalf of black aviators that led to his being dubbed the "Father of Black Aviation."[‡]

---

‡ My thanks to Bennie J. McRae, who was a close personal friend of Anderson's, for guiding me to this understanding.

Buehl's grandson, Carlos, enjoying a biplane ride in 2013 with Anderson's granddaughter, Christina. PHOTO/AUTHOR

(above) Buehl's granddaughter, Rosanna, and Anderson's granddaughter, Christina, being interviewed by Bryan Williams for a documentary about Anderson. PHOTO/AUTHOR

(below) Buehl saved this brochure from the NBCFAE *1982 Awards Banquet honoring Anderson.* PHOTO/EBC

NBCFAE SPRING CONFERENCE
'82
First Annual Awards Banquet

honoring
THE MOST
FAMOUS BLACK AVIATOR
IN AMERICA

C. Alfred Anderson
March 12, 1982
Atlanta, Georgia

Honors to Anderson

Throughout his life, C. Alfred Anderson received a number of major awards. In 1985, he received the National Aeronautics Association's Frank G. Brewer Trophy for his "significant contributions of enduring value in the fields of aviation and aerospace education." In 1992, he received the NAA's Elder Statesman of Aviation Award. In 2013, he was inducted into the National Aviation Hall of Fame, an honor that has been compared to an actor being awarded an Oscar. In 2014, he was honored with a US postal stamp for his role as "a pioneer in aviation who played a crucial role during World War II in training the nation's first black military pilots, the Tuskegee Airmen."

We know that Anderson and Buehl remained friends long after World War II. Both the Anderson and Buehl families have materials these two men kept that express their mutual respect.

In 1973, both Anderson and Buehl were honored together at an event held at Buehl Field in

Langhorne, Pennsylvania. The event was sponsored by the Philadelphia Chapter of the Negro Airmen International (NAI).[§]

Buehl saved the brochure from a 1982 National Black Coalition of Federal Aviation Employees (NBCFAE) awards banquet. Although he was unable to attend, he was connected to the event telephonically, and the audience listened in as Anderson received Buehl's warm congratulations. The Anderson family saved a 1982 letter from Buehl from this same event in which Buehl expresses his pleasure in the accomplishments of his student.

Anderson died at his home on 13 April 1996.

Not a One-Off

When I first learned that there was an association of Buehl with Anderson, and because I knew Buehl trained military pilots during World War II, I checked his materials to see if he had anything to do with the Tuskegee program itself. The answer is no. I was able to check this when I visited with Roscoe Draper in April 2012. Buehl did not travel to Tuskegee to work with any trainees there.

However, Buehl not only trained black students, among the many instructors he hired at Somerton was Charles M. Ashe, a multiracial pilot.[☾]

Ashe became known for being an excellent instructor. It was not long before he was recruited away to teach at Lincoln University,

Roscoe Draper was the second in charge of primary training for the Tuskegee Airmen. While Anderson was known as "Chief," Draper was known as "Coach." He is shown here in 2014 with Buehl's granddaughter, Rosanna, at the unveiling of the USPS postage stamp honoring "Chief" Anderson in Bryn Mawr, Pennsylvania.
PHOTO/R. BUEHL

§ *The Philadelphia Tribune* story covering this event contains an error: it says Anderson was "the first black man to receive a private pilot's license," rather than Transport pilot's license. Anderson never claimed to be first to hold the private pilot's license.

☾ Ashe earned ATL #54573, being one of only seven black pilots to hold it before 1941.

(above) Toby Tolbert showing Buehl's grand-daughter his early log books. Looking on is Mrs. Tolbert. PHOTO/AUTHOR

(below) Colonel Charles McGee (ret.) visits with the great-grandson of Chief Anderson while the boy's grandfather, Charles Anderson, and family friend, Jerry McRae, look on. As a Tuskegee Airman during World War II, Korea, and Vietnam, McGee flew a total of 409 combat missions. McGee is an inductee of the National Aviation Hall of Fame, and as of 2018 he is honored with his own US postage stamp. Taken at Moton Field, Tuskegee, Alabama, on February 15, 2014. PHOTO/AUTHOR

in Jefferson City, Missouri. Ashe was recruited from Lincoln University to join Cornelius Coffey, Willa Brown, and others at the Coffey School of Aeronautics, in Chicago.

The Tuskegee Airmen, Inc. (TAI) today is an organization whose membership is open to anyone who believes in the importance of guiding the next generation. Its mission includes mentoring children and youth. Tuskegee Airmen, Inc., has a particular interest in guiding black youth toward careers in science, technology, and aviation. According to their website: "TAI's chapters use the life lessons learned from the engineering legacy of the original Tuskegee Airmen—determination, courage, refusal to accept limits, the ability to seize opportunity—to teach career and leadership lessons in a variety of aviation-themed educational programs on a local level. TAI itself also supports nationally an active, well-endowed Scholarship Foundation."

The influence of the Tuskegee

Airmen continues to be significant. Toby Tolbert, an African-American pilot whom Buehl trained after World War II, noted the importance of the Airmen as positive role models. Reminiscing in 2012, Tolbert said that when he was growing up there were few well-known black men he could idolize. There was the boxer, Joe Lewis, but "all he could do was fight." Anderson and the Airmen, on the other hand, gave him a pattern to emulate for a successful life.[**]

[**]   Tolbert gave these remarks informally following a presentation about E.C. Malick, given by Mary Groce at a meeting of the Bensalem Historical Society on 5 April 2012

The Tuskegee Institute

The main program for training black pilots for the Army Air Force ended up in Alabama. The Tuskegee Institute provided the early stages of training, and then their graduates were picked up by the Army's own program for training in military aircraft. This arrangement was not inevitable, as there were several programs around the country interested in hosting training. The training could have been located in Chicago, where two strong programs were training black pilots.

The Chicago School of Aeronautics, originally the Curtiss-Wright school, located at Glenview, trained one class of black pilots in the 1930s. Because of rampant prejudice against people of color, the classes were scheduled only at night and were segregated. Even so, when white students learned that the school was training black students, they threatened to boycott the school. After that, black students had to go elsewhere. The Coffey School of Aeronautics emerged as the school that served primarily black pilots.

The Challenger Aero Club, organized at the Harlem Airport on Chicago's Southside, was owned and operated by Cornelius Coffey and his partner, Willa Brown. The club provided mutual support for students at the school and made it possible for a number of students to overcome barriers to getting lessons.

Continued on the next page.

Continued from the previous page.

Barriers black students faced included the difficulty of finding anyone who would train them, finding airplanes they would be allowed to fly, and being able to find lessons that would be affordable. The Coffey School provided help in all of these respects.

Chicago was a city having a large black population that was able to demonstrate enough political power to be taken seriously.

The Chicago Defender, one of the more influential black-owned newspapers in the nation, strongly supported the push for training black pilots. (It was the *Defender's* owner, Robert S. Abbott, who sponsored Bessie Coleman to go to France for pilot training). *The Defender's* editor, Enoch P. Waters, became a key voice for black aviation.

Enoch Waters, Cornelius Coffey, Willa Brown, Chauncey Spencer, and others worked to form a lobbying organization to promote laws authorizing training for black aviators, the National Airmen's Association of America. Working with Edgar Brown, their lobbyist in Washington, DC, the NAAA organized a demonstration flight in which two fliers from Chicago, Chauncey Spencer and Dale White, went to meet with Illinois' Senator Dirksen and others in Congress. On this trip, they recruited another strong advocate in the Senate, Harry S. Truman.

A deciding factor to locate the Army training program in Tuskegee rather than in Chicago was a preference within the Army for a segregated program. Tuskegee had a strong tradition of accepting segregation, while it seemed likely that the program would get bogged down in racial bickering if it were located in the North.

Selected Sources

Atlanta Daily World. "Pioneer Negro Ace Teaching at Lincoln," October 3, 1940.

Chicago Defender. "Seven Pilots Get License in Illinois Area," April 5, 1941.

Department of Commerce and Bureau of the Census. "Negro Statistical Bulletin, Issues 1-17." Bureau of Foreign and Domestic Commerce. Negro Affairs Division, 1940.

Encyclopedia of Alabama. "Tuskegee Flight Training Program." https://encyclopediaofalabama.org/article/tuskegee-flight-training-program

Informal Interview with Chief Anderson. HBCU Tours Black College Tours. Moton Field, Tuskegee, Alabama, 1994. (YouTube)

Jakeman, Robert J. *The Divided Skies: Establishing Segregated Flight Training at Tuskegee, Alabama, 1934-1942.* Tuscaloosa, Alabama: University of Alabama Press, 1992.

Maksel, R. "The Unrecognized First." *Smithsonian Air & Space,* March 2011.

NASA Spaceflight.com. "Challenger STS-8—In the Dark of the Night," May 23, 2015. https://forum.nasaspaceflight.com/index.php?topic=37640.20

National Air and Space Museum. "Congressional Gold Medal, Tuskegee Airmen," March 16, 2016.

Philadelphia Tribune. "First Black Private Pilot To Be Honored," September 29, 1973.

Robie, William and National Aeronautic Association (U.S.). *For the Greatest Achievement: A History of the Aero Club of America and the National Aeronautic Association.* First Edition edition. Washington: Smithsonian, 1993.

Spencer, Chauncey. *Who Is Chauncey Spencer?* Detroit: Broadside Press, 1975.

Warbirds News. "Today Airman Charles Anderson, Sr. Is Honored With a United States Postal Stamp," March 13, 2014.

APPENDIX 8

Langhorne Fire

B uehl's attention was pulled in more than one direction during the time he was working to get approval for his airport.

On 7 January 1963, while Buehl was anticipating his Grand Opening and was busy preparing to resubmit his proposal for a change in zoning so that his airport could legally operate, a home he owned burned down. Buehl had it underinsured, so he lost a lot of money in this fire.

It was located on the land Buehl had purchased for the airport and had been the residence of the previous owner of the land. It was a beautiful three-story fieldstone building designed in traditional Colonial style. *The Levittown Times* described the home as a "mansion" valued at $75,000.[*] No one was able to say exactly how old it was. Buehl had been planning to use it for the airport's administrative office.

An investigation was held but reached no conclusion. The home had been occupied by renters whom Buehl evicted. Buehl required them to remove their litter before vacating. According to what the Buehl family could see, the renters tossed all of their trash into the fireplace, lit it at about 10:00 PM, and then left. The resulting blaze spread from the fireplace into the unoccupied house.

Although the main house burned, there was another smaller fieldstone house not far away that did not burn. It had been built for the family of the hired help. Buehl's son ended up occupying this house during the years the family operated the airport.

---

[*] "$75,000 Fire Hits Mansion in Langhorne," *Levittown Times*, January 8, 1963.

Karl Bühl

Many people thought Buehl had been a combat pilot for Germany in World War I. He was not. However, his older brother, Karl, was a German test pilot during the war. Karl also spent time in ground combat, fighting in the trenches.

I include a summary of Karl's experience in World War I for three reasons. *First,* Karl started the war on horseback, in the cavalry, but by the end of the War, airplanes replaced the role held by horses in 1914. This forms a little example of how aviation began to find its early role in our lives. *Second,* this material provides a valuable glimpse of the wartime experience from the point of view of a German soldier. Karl kept a chronicle of his activity during the war. I do not have this sort of perspective directly from Buehl, but I think that Karl's experience is likely to have been comparable. *Third,* Karl's participation throughout the entire length of the war gives us a way to summarize the history of the war itself.

Karl Bühl on horseback, 1915, in Auby, France. At the time this was taken, he was so ill from a urinary tract infection that he could barely keep himself in the saddle. He is dressed here in the field uniform of the dragoons. As airplanes replaced horse-mounted cavalry, Karl later flew for the military as a test pilot. PHOTO/EBC

Highlights of Karl's Combat Experience

Karl began the war in the cavalry, in the 1st squadron, 3rd Baden Regiment "Prince Karl" #22, garrisoned at Mulhouse (now Muhlhausen). Cavalry generally was assigned to perform tactical reconnaissance, backup patrols, and to relay messages.

Karl's war chronicle begins on 31 July 1914 at 4:00 PM. By 7:30, he, along with six dragoons, was ordered to occupy the train station at Dammerkirch (now Dannemarie), in the area called by Germans *Elsaß Lothringen*, but by the French as *Alsace-Lorraine*. By 5 August, he was engaged in destroying critical communications infrastructure, including telephone and railway. These actions soon developed into the Battle of the Frontiers, fought from 7 August to 13 September 1914. Karl was involved mainly in conducting patrols.

By the 11th of May, the horses sick and exhausted, Karl found himself assigned to a trench. Soon he was engaged in what became known among the Allies as the Second Battle of Artois. This ferocious engagement involved one of the strongest artillery attacks ever mounted by the French up to that point. He wrote:

"The Frenchman opened fire on our reserve position with grenades and shrapnel like we seldom experienced before. Hit on hit into and close to our position so that after 8 hours of the bombardment we had the loss of seven wounded comrades. Out of necessity, we survive more like moles than like humans. As soon as we took position, every one of us dug with the spades. We became more and more fond of concealing ourselves in a hole (I wrote these lines while in such a hole). Indeed, none of us would be alive if we had not done this.

So the evening came and we got some silence. When the darkness set in, an order came: we should take part in an assault with the infantry this night. The assault failed. So the night passed quite silently. Only the moaning of the returning wounded, hastening to the casualty *station behind us, broke the silence of the night."**

By 19 May, Karl was in Neuville-Saint-Vaast, a village that was already pounded to ruins in the fighting. His unit was ordered to establish a new position 30 meters (about 98 feet) in front of the French lines. Under nearly continuous bombardment, at 11:00 PM he and his fellow soldiers crawled one by one over an open field until they were in position and then began to bury themselves in order to get shelter from the fire. They had a deep trench by 3:00 AM. They dug their way into some of the cellars of nearby houses and sheltered there during the day. On the 21st, though, German artillery fire began to land on his position, causing some casualties. The next day, his division was going to attack, but again their own artillery batteries were landing one in four shells into their own lines. Some landed quite close to Karl. This horrifying error prevented the attack from going forward. His unit was finally extracted from the battle on 24 May 1915. Once they were out of danger, one of his regiment, a shell-shocked Corporal, committed suicide.

It was estimated that a single day of fighting on the Western Front cost as much as the entire cost of the Franco-Prussian War of 1870–71. In a related comparison, it can be noted that by the end of the battle, more soldiers had been killed in the six weeks between 3 May and 18 June 1915 than had been killed in the entire nine months of the Franco-Prussian War. However, like many other battles of World War I, this one ended inconclusively. Nothing of strategic value was gained by either side.

One of the events that Karl's military experience illustrates is the replacement of horse-mounted cavalry with airplanes. Airplanes replaced cavalry for observation and reconnaissance and for attacking fragile infrastructure such as telegraph lines and railroads.

---

* Translation provided by Michael Bauer, grandson of Karl.

German Pilot Training

By summer of 1916, he received orders to transfer to Gotha to be trained as an airplane pilot. He reported there on 29 July 1916 and had his first training flight on 30 July.

Buehl did not fly for the military during WWI, but his brother, Karl, did. He was transferred from the cavalry to an airplane repair facility, where he served as a test pilot.
PHOTO/EBC

Karl received almost daily in-air flight training for over a month before he flew solo on 1 September. He continued to practice and took his first examination on 10 September. He had another 75 days of almost daily flying, including more overland flights, before his second examination on 24 November 1916. It was not until 16 February 1917 that his training was complete. In all, he received 201 days of intensive training.

It is curious to compare Karl's training in World War I with the training received by Eddie Rickenbacker in 1917. Rickenbacker became a "pilot" after only 17 days of flight school, and with another 25 hours of flight time he was commissioned a first lieutenant. Rickenbacker received some additional instruction at gunnery school and had his first opportunity to get shot at on the first day of spring 1918.

At the end of his basic flight training, Karl received advanced training in flying "G" aircraft. According to the Idflieg classification system used in Germany from 1916 on, "G" aircraft were large, two or three-engine biplane bombers. After his training, he was assigned to the aircraft maintenance depot at Adlershof as a test pilot.

Within one month of beginning his job, he was testing a Rumpler GII 123/15 when it crashed, on 11 April. He was injured and placed on leave for nearly three weeks, until 30 April, for recuperation. Almost as soon as he returned to duty, on 3 May, the Albatross C VI 1812/16 he was flying crashed. There is no mention of the need for time for rehabilitation following this crash. On 1 October, he had another bad landing, when the chassis on the Rumpler GII 121/15 broke when he touched down.

Karl had another serious crash on 15 November 1917. This time his Albatross CIII 4020/17 was completely destroyed in the crash. Karl himself suffered a significant injury. He was hospitalized until 15 December, then put on leave for rehabilitation. He was not able to return to duty until 22 January 1918. After his return from rehabilitation, he had no more than ten months of duty before the war ended on 11 November 1918.

Selected Sources

Bühl, Karl. _Kriegs Chronicle_ (War Diary). 1914-1918. manuscript. lang. German.

Groom, Winston. _The Aviators: Eddie Rickenbacker, Jimmy Doolittle, Charles Lindbergh, and the Epic Age of Flight._ Washington, D.C: National Geographic, 2013.

Rickenbacker, Edward V. _Rickenbacker: An Autobiography._ First. Englewood Cliffs, NJ: Prentice-Hall, 1967.

APPENDIX 10

What Happened to the Challenger?

B uehl kept the Challenger for his entire career. It was used for years at his first airport (Somerton) as one of the trainers, then retired from routine service and hung from the ceiling of a hangar. When Buehl Field was transferred to his second airport (Eddington), Buehl flew the Challenger to the new location, and then he flew it to his final airport (Langhorne) when the business moved there. It was

The Challenger could always draw a crowd. In this 1957 photo, the Challenger has landed and is taxiing to its position on the tarmac at an air show at McGuire Air Force Base. Although the military aircraft on either side dwarfs it, people are flocking to it for a closer look. McGuire's base newspaper, Airtides, described Buehl's arrival as "the outstanding action event of the day." The Challenger is about halfway up in this picture and a bit to the right. PHOTO/EBC, USAF OFFICIAL PHOTO

taken out from time to time and flown for special events, so it was constantly maintained in good flying condition.

After taking it to Langhorne, Buehl stripped the linen off of the plane, down to its ribs, recovered it entirely, and then repainted it to its original colors. Before he restored it, it had been painted all red. Within the Buehl family, the Challenger often was referred to as "the ox-5," and there was little recognition in conversations that the aircraft was actually a Fairchild. Perhaps this casual identification of the aircraft with its engine rather than its airframe led to some confusion among a wider audience.

Many people remember Buehl's Challenger, and many thought it was a World War I trainer, a Curtiss JN-4 "Jenny." It did have the same Curtiss engine that powered the JN-4, a model of engine that was notoriously unreliable. In fairness, when the ox-5 was introduced it was considered to be reliable by comparison with other engines of the time. However, thirty years later it was considered to be unreliable. The valve train was fragile, and the magnetos available did not hold up well. Cold weather starting was difficult, and ox-5 engines leaked coolant.

Buehl stands in front of his beloved Challenger with Al Maye and Jack Anderson from the Fairchild Corp. PHOTO/EBC

This being the engine in his own airplane, Buehl was among the few mechanics who could keep an ox-5 running well in all seasons. It was for this reason that one of his customers, General Abby Wolf, kept his planes at Buehl Field. (Wolf's ox-5 was equipped with the notorious Berling magneto, and even the mechanics at Pitcairn could not make it work. They recommended Wolf take it to Buehl. This was remarkable because Pitcairn was one of the more well-known aircraft manufacturers in the country, while Buehl just operated a small airport).

Fairchild purchased the Challenger in 1982 and put it on display at their headquarters. By 1988, as the company was struggling to maintain any involvement in aviation, Fairchild decided not to keep the Challenger. By that time, they had drained the oil and allowed the crankcase to dry out, so the engine would no longer run without extensive overhaul. Al Maye, a Fairchild representative who helped arrange the purchase by Fairchild in 1982, wrote a letter to his boss at Fairchild describing its condition: the wings had warped, the fabric had decayed, and the control rigging was "beyond repair."

Even so, Fairchild immediately got two firm offers from interested purchasers, the highest bid for $20,000. Maye's assumption was that someone buying it at that price would resell it "for a sizable profit because of its antique value." In a letter to Buehl, Maye conveys Fairchild's offer to deliver the Challenger back to Buehl for $21,500. The price would include the $11,500 chrome-plated stand on which it was displayed at Fairchild. He also let Buehl know that the condition of the Challenger was not as bad as he had indicated to Fairchild executives.

As of this writing, the Challenger is back in individual hands and is being restored to flying condition. The current owner has commented in correspondence that he found quite a few places where the linen had been patched with chewing gum, a fact that surprised no one among Buehl's descendants. Buehl often used chewing gum to plug holes in a variety of applications.

Selected Sources

Airtides. "Armed Forces Day." May 24, 1957. EBC.

Pattillo, Donald M. *A History in the Making: 80 Turbulent Years in the American* *General Aviation Industry.* New York: McGraw-Hill, 1998.

APPENDIX 11

Timeline

Buehl lived in an era characterized by astonishing changes. Those of us who are the children and great grandchildren of men like Buehl and who have not experienced the events themselves may find having a timeline that shows him and his accomplishments against the background of other important events that shaped aviation.

1783	First balloon ascent
1855	First photograph taken from a balloon
1862	Coxwell and Glaisher enter the stratosphere in a balloon
1897	*Ernest H. Buehl is born*
1903	Wright brothers achieve heavier-than-air flight at Kitty Hawk
1904	Wilbur Wright achieves a controlled turn
1906	Santos Dumont achieves the first heavier-than-air flight certified by the FAI
1906	Fokker sees an airplane for his first time
1908	Wrights publicly demonstrate their Flier in France
1909	Wilbur Wright takes the first photo from an airplane
1909	Duralumin alloy becomes commercially available
1909	Bleriot crosses the English Channel
1910	Fokker builds his first airplane
1910	*Buehl sees airplanes for his first time*

1911   *Buehl begins appren-*
       ticeship at Graf

1913   Rapp Motors is founded

1913   First photo taken from
       an airplane for the
       purpose of mapping

1914   *Buehl completes his*
       apprenticeship at Graf

1914   *Buehl begins to learn to fly*

1914   German army crosses
       into France, World
       War I begins

1915   First coast-to-coast
       telephone call is
       placed in the US

1915   Airplanes replace cavalry
       for reconnaissance.

1915   Junkers produces the
       J-1, the first produc-
       tion airplane to use
       cantilevered wings

1916   Rapp Motors be-
       comes BMW

1916   First use of aluminum
       in aircraft by Junkers

1916   *Buehl is enlisted in the*
       Bavarian Army and
       stationed on Germa-
       ny's eastern front

1917   *Buehl is ordered back to*
       Munich, to BMW, after
       being wounded in battle

1917   The BMW-IIIa engine
       goes into production

1918   World War I ends

1918   Emil Monz sets an
       altitude record for a
       passenger-carrying
       airplane—16,400 feet

1919   First nonstop crossing
       of the Atlantic, 15 June

1919   Franz Zeno Deimer
       flies so high his air-
       plane leaves a va-
       por trail, 7 June

1919   Test flight of the first
       Junkers F-13, 18 July

1919   ELTA in Amsterdam, 1
       August to 12 September

1919   *BMW sends Buehl to Hol-*
       land to work with Fokker

1920   *Larsen recruits Bue-*
       hl to come to the US

1920   *Buehl takes part in*
       the first transcontinen-
       tal airmail and round
       trip passenger flight

1920   Post Office JL-6 aircraft
       are catching fire in mid-
       air. The problem is fixed

1921   JL-6 aircraft deliv-
        ered to Canada.

1921   *First report in a news-*
        paper that Buehl had
        been a German "ace"

1921   The Larsen Race takes
        place in Omaha

1921   Stinson and Bertaud
        establish an endur-
        ance record in a JL-6

1922   Fire at Larsen's air-
        field on Long Island

1922   Amundsen prepares to
        fly over the North Pole

1922   *Buehl confesses to setting*
        the fire at Larsen Field,
        at Larsen's direction

1923   *Buehl is invited to work*
        for Brock & Weymouth,
        in Philadelphia

1924   *Buehl marries*
        Anna Manso

1926   *Buehl obtains his*
        first pilot's license, is-
        sued by the FAI

1927   Lindbergh wins
        the Ortieg Prize

1928   *Buehl obtains his CAA*
        Transport License,
        #1918, 15 March

1928   *Thomas Trivigno and*
        Buehl establish Flying
        Dutchman Air Ser-
        vice (within the first
        week of January)

1928   *Buehl purchases his*
        Challenger and takes
        over the business, 7 July

1928   *Buehl opens his air-*
        port at Somerton

1928   *Buehl becomes a natu-*
        ralized citizen of the US

1930   *C. Alfred Anderson begins*
        training with Buehl

1932   *Anderson completes*
        his training and, with
        Buehl's advocacy, obtains
        his Transport License

1942   *Somerton closed for World*
        War II, Buehl trains Navy
        pilots at Franklin & Mar-
        shall College, in Lancaster

1945   Victory in Europe

1947   Yeager breaks the
        sound barrier

1949   *Buehl opens his air-*
        port at Eddington

1951   The Piper Tri-Pacer is
        introduced. Its land-
        ing gear strongly pre-
        fers a paved runway

1954   Bensalem High School is built directly under the approach to the runway in Eddington

1960   *Buehl sells his Eddington airport to a real estate developer*

1960   *Buehl begins work at Langhorne*

1961   First man in outer space, Yuri Gagarin

1969   First men land on the Moon

1982   *Buehl sells the Challenger to Fairchild*

1985   I meet Buehl at his 88th birthday celebration

1989   Anna Buehl dies

1990   *Ernest Buehl dies*

The home of Ernest and Anna Buehl in Langhorne, Pennsylvania PHOTO/EBC

Index

The author on a mountain top at 10,000 feet.
PHOTO/R. BUEHL

About the Author

Mark Taylor grew up in Billings, Montana. He earned a B.A. degree from Rocky Mountain College, with majors in art and English. Attending graduate school at Cal Poly Humboldt in California, Mark obtained his master's degree in psychology. In his 35-year career serving rural eastern Montana, Mark worked in residential child care, operated a mental health center satellite office, and he worked as a specialist in more schools than he can remember. In 1997, his peers selected him as Montana's School Psychologist of the Year.

Now retired from school psychology, Mark helped to found an independent bookstore in Billings, and he has written a biography of Ernest H. Buehl, Sr., a pioneer aviator.

mpliance